2.

not even bicycles. The people are
well fed but cowed. One sees whole
families - all their belong[ings] [in a]
carriage or other such vehicle - walking
along the roads - to a home they left during
the war. One sees innumerable German
soldiers - in uniform and with packs but
without arms trudging back home.

grand [hotel] [which] [was] the
am in [the] [hotel] [w]here he
housed h[is] [guests] [w]hen the Nazi party
congress was held. the main part of the
hotel is not habitable. My room is quite
comfortable. the walls are all ripped out
- bullett holes in them - no glass in the
windows - the ceiling is half gone -

EARLY PRAISE FOR *Letters from Nuremberg*

"Tom Dodd was not only a most competent pretrial interrogator and court-room prosecutor, but was admired and liked by me and all others who worked with him. *Letters from Nuremberg* shows how much that famous trial still affects us today. Tom Dodd's letters have the immediacy and emotional power of a novel. This book is a terrific addition to the Nuremberg legacy."

—**Richard W. Sonnenfeldt,** chief interpreter for
the American prosecution at the Nuremberg
trials and author of *Witness to Nuremberg*

"In researching my book on Nuremberg, the trial sprang to life when I encountered the role of prosecutor Thomas Dodd. Fortunately, in hundreds of letters home, Dodd recorded an unvarnished insider view of the tribunal. Today the outcome of Nuremberg may seem foregone. But Dodd's vivid account reveals how feuds among allies, prosecutors, and judges nearly sank the world's first trial in which the rule of law triumphed over a reign of barbarism."

—**Joseph E. Persico,** author of
Nuremberg: Infamy on Trial

Grace Murphy Dodd and Thomas J. Dodd
reunited briefly during a Christmas break in the trial.

LETTERS *from* NUREMBERG

My Father's Narrative of a Quest for Justice

SENATOR CHRISTOPHER J. DODD
with Lary Bloom

Published in the United States by Crown Publishers, an imprint of the
Crown Publishing Group, a division of Random House, Inc., New York.

www.crownpublishing.com

Crown is a trademark and the Crown colophon is a
registered trademark of Random House, Inc.

Page ii and photo insert, pages 1–4, page 5 (top left and second
from left, and center left and right), and page 8 (center):
Thomas J. Dodd Research Center
Photo insert, page 5 (top, third from left): Truman Library
Photo insert, page 5 (top right and bottom left): U.S. Government
Photo insert, pages 6–7 and page 8 (top and bottom): Dodd family photos

Library of Congress Cataloging-in-Publication Data

Dodd, Christopher J. (Christopher John), 1944–
Letters from Nuremberg / Christopher Dodd with Lary Bloom.
Includes index.
1. World War, 1939–1945 — Atrocities — Germany.
2. Dodd, Thomas J. (Thomas Joseph), 1907–1971 — Correspondence.
3. Nuremberg Trial of Major German War Criminals, Nuremberg, Germany,
1945–1946.   4. War crime trials — Germany — Nuremberg.
5. Senators — United States — Correspondence.
6. Lawyers — United States — Correspondence. I. Bloom, Lary. II. Title.
D804.G3D64 2007
341.6'90268 — dc22   2007013380

ISBN 978-0-307-38116-3

Printed in the United States of America

DESIGN BY LEONARD HENDERSON

10 9 8 7 6 5 4 3 2 1

First Edition

To Mary Grace Murphy Dodd, the great love of my father's life;

and Tom and Grace Dodd's grandchildren and great-grandchildren,

that you find time in your lives to be a part of

something larger than yourselves

CONTENTS

LETTERS *from* NUREMBERG

Prologue

My FATHER WAS THIRTY-EIGHT YEARS OLD when he went off to confront many of the Nazis responsible for the most devastating crimes in history. He returned from the International Military Tribunal in Nuremberg fifteen months later, in October 1946, profoundly changed — a transformation I didn't fully comprehend for a half a century, until well after his death.

Back in the postwar years, my parents Thomas J. and Grace Murphy Dodd and their six children — Tom Jr., Carolyn, Jeremy, Martha, Nicholas, and I — lived at 63 Concord Street in West Hartford, Connecticut. It was certainly the only house in that serene neighborhood in which relics of the Third Reich could be found — a flag bearing a swastika, German helmets, and medals that Nazis awarded to mothers who bore a sufficient supply of Aryan children. It makes me uncomfortable to think of it, but back then these souvenirs were seen as reminders that America and its Allies had triumphed over a juggernaut of evil.

Our house was also, I may reasonably presume, the only one thereabouts that held evidence from the darkest period in human history in its attic — evidence so ominous that the Dodd children were forbidden to see it. Worried about the impression these artifacts would leave, our parents instructed us never to venture up to the third-floor storage room — a restriction, my parents should have known, we would ignore.

In various forays, the six of us rooted through the boxes and were horrified by what we saw. There were photographs from concentration camps — piles of emaciated bodies and evidence of medical experiments. We discovered old German comic books that we couldn't translate; nevertheless, we could determine their purpose — to characterize Jews as less than human and to blame them for most of Germany's ills. There were pictures, too, of key moments in the trial and one that is burned in all of our memories — my father holding for news photographers a prosecution exhibit he had introduced: the shrunken head of a Polish prisoner.

We, of course, could not discuss these with our parents because we could not admit having seen them. This was an era before the terms *genocide* and *Holocaust* came into widespread use — well before, too, the proliferation of powerful films on the Nazi era. At that time the attention of those many citizens who cared about world affairs had been diverted toward Korea and the Soviet Union, and the proliferation of the atomic bomb.

Even so, my father always used such circumstances to bring the subject back to the lessons of Nuremberg, where he became the second-ranking U.S. prosecutor under Supreme Court Justice Robert H. Jackson. During family dinners, he sometimes recalled his days there. He described the defendants to us, and though he never soft-peddled their crimes, he avoided gruesome details. As my siblings attest, my parents wanted us to be aware of international realities but at the same time provide a safe haven at home. As a result, there were elements of the trial that remained mysterious.

As the years passed, and as my own curiosity about the world grew, there were things I wanted to ask my father about Nuremberg. Who else had a father, after all, who had known Hermann Göring, Alfred Rosenberg, Albert Speer, Joachim von Ribbentrop, and other "Nazi big boys," as he called them?

When I became a student of the law, I was fascinated by the idea of Nuremberg and by its principles. There had never been a trial like it before, and its very existence proved enormously controversial.

I thought of my father's service in a tribunal that sought not only to punish war criminals but also to demonstrate the capacity of the Allies to follow and uphold the rule of law even when a cry for vengeance was heard from all quarters; civilized countries would produce a fair trial even for mass murderers who didn't seem to deserve one. Winston Churchill was against the very idea — and favored summary execution. The Soviet Union, never known for extended efforts on behalf of its accused, had similar ideas. There were well-known American critics as well, including the chief justice of the Supreme Court, Harlan Fiske Stone, who called the idea "Jackson's lynching expedition." Others argued that indictments would be ex post facto, in that the Nazis would be tried for international crimes that hadn't been explicitly on the books.

The argument that eventually prevailed was based on two powerful ideas. By trying those who carried out a criminal war, a complete record of their actions could be shown to the world, therefore announcing once and for all that such behavior would not be tolerated by the community of civilized nations. And, in giving the defendants a chance to hear the evidence against them and to defend themselves, the Allies would take the moral and legal high ground.

As Jackson said in his opening statement: "That four great nations, flushed with victory and stung with injury, stay the hand of vengeance and voluntarily submit their captive enemies to the judgment of the law is one of the most significant tributes that power has ever paid to reason."

People like my father set a clear and binding standard, saying, in effect, that here precisely is what happened as a result of tyranny and that any attempt to repeat such behavior would be seen for what it is. We were naïve, of course, in this view. Since Nuremberg, the world has demonstrated time and again its capacity to stun us with outrage and inhumanity — Cambodia, Rwanda, Bosnia, Darfur. Yet there is no doubt that Nuremberg remains more than an event of historical significance — it has become a word in the language that reminds us of ultimate collective responsibility for aggression, racism, and crimes against humanity.

All this I understood. But what was the inside story of Nuremberg? How had my father risen from a relatively low-ranking member of Jackson's enormous staff to be the man who often was in charge of the proceedings? The whole thing seemed odd and ironic to me. In a way, the Nuremberg defendants had known my father during that time in a way my siblings and

I never could. Albert Speer had written, in *Inside the Third Reich*, that my father was "sharp and aggressive." Franz von Papen, the former vice-chancellor of Germany, wrote in his *Memoirs* that my father was "polite, correct, even kind" and that after the trial—he was one of the three defendants acquitted—my father gave him a box of Havana cigars. My father's courtroom achievements were recalled on the sixtieth anniversary of the trials by *Der Spiegel*, the German magazine. "The star of the courtroom was Thomas Dodd . . . [He] had the gift, in lawyer's jargon, of being able to make the 'evidence sing.' He provided the macabre high point of the trial . . . the shrunken head of a Pole who had been hanged. It had been found on the desk of the camp commander Karl Koch, who had used it as a paperweight."

The chances to ask about these things were rare. Much of what I knew about my father's Nuremberg tenure came from others. Walter Cronkite, for example, told me that Baldur von Schirach, head of the Hitler Youth, tried to bring similarities into play. Von Schirach pointed out that he and the man prosecuting him had a lot in common—both were Catholic and had led large organizations of young people. (My father served for three years as head of the Connecticut program in the National Youth Administration.) But my father would have none of it. "We're nothing alike," he told von Schirach.

I was very interested in such stories but circumstances and other priorities intervened. After several years of practicing law in Connecticut, my father won a seat in the U.S. House of Representatives and then in the Senate. I was off on my own adventure—to the Peace Corps, serving in a rural village in the Dominican Republic, and then to law school. By the time I had a chance to focus on Nuremberg, my father, at the age of sixty-four, was gone—suffering a fatal heart attack. My mother, the other obvious source of information, died a year and a half later of a stroke.

In the years that followed, I had to be content with what I knew. I was aware, somehow, that my father had written letters to my mother during the time he served in Nuremberg—I had vague recollections of family discussions about them. But I never thought of these—nor did my siblings—as anything other than routine, if they existed at all.

In due course, I followed my father's path to Washington — elected to the House and then to the Senate. And like my father, I became involved in foreign affairs. He had been known for his fervent anti-Communist stance and for his participation in cold war strategies. In just his fourth year in the Senate, his collected speeches on foreign policy were published. The preface said that Thomas J. Dodd "is generally recognized, both in this country and abroad, as the principal Congressional spokesman for those nations which have fallen captive to Communist rule." He often used his Nuremberg experience to warn Congress of the Communist threat and to argue against a policy of appeasement, which had been disastrous in trying to deal with Hitler. And, in a speech delivered to the Senate in March 1960 titled "Anti-Semitism, the Swastika Epidemic, and Communism," he said, "Between the brutality of Soviet anti-Semitism and the brutality of Nazi anti-Semitism, there is little to choose. About all that is lacking so far in the U.S.S.R. is the gas chamber."

My father's legacy had, of course, influenced my own work in the Senate and on its Committee on Foreign Relations, though much of my focus was in a different geographical direction — Latin America. By November 1989, the Berlin Wall had crumbled and the Soviet Union was about to disband.

Even so, my father's sense of humanity — his argument that oppression and freedom would be a continuing struggle — was always on my mind. I knew the lessons well that he had delivered to us long before at the dinner table. What I didn't know, and thought I might never know, was the detail of his struggles at Nuremberg.

There had been so many excellent books on the subject that heightened my curiosity. Many were written by participants in the trial; others were written by historians and journalists. And, of course, the Holocaust became a literary category all its own. That my father — a literate man — never wrote his own book seemed strange.

And then I discovered his letters. Or, to be precise, my siblings discovered his letters. This was a revelation. For one thing, many of my parents' personal possessions were lost in a fire in Rhode Island, where they had been stored in a warehouse. For all I knew, any letters they had written to each other went up in flames, too.

But the letters, it turned out, were never in the warehouse. They were in the basement of my sister Martha's house.

In the summer of 1990, I began the process of putting them in chronological order. I decided not to read any of them until I could finish the process, so that I could fully appreciate my father's emotional and intellectual journey. This took some time. I also discovered souvenirs buried in the letters — including a drawing made by Hitler's chauffeur of the headquarters bunker in Berlin where the führer and Eva Braun committed suicide. The drawing showed where the bodies were.

Finally, in my Washington, D.C., apartment, I sat down to read the collection. The first letter was dated July 28, 1945. I looked at the calendar on the wall — it was July 28, 1990, precisely forty-five years to the day that my father wrote the first words with his fountain pen on thin air mail stationery: "My Dearest, If my letters seem lengthy and detailed, you will understand that first of all I am trying to string out my time with you — for while you are in my mind at all times during the day, at letter writing time I have you alone, with no interruptions. Thursday morning, standing in the main portal of the Union Station in Washington, you made a memorable picture for me as I gazed out the taxi cab window until the dimness of the dawn light blotted your loveliness out." As I finished that first letter, and I thought about the way he described my mother, I wept.

The power and eloquence of my father's words overwhelmed me. I had known my parents as children do. I had not seen them in this intimate way — as characters in a love story. And if I had yearned for an inside view of the Nuremberg experience, I certainly found it.

In that first letter, he wrote from London about survivors of Germany's rocket attacks — that they looked at him "with eyes that I could not meet." It occurred to me then that he had produced a kind of instant and intimate history of the seminal years and events of his lifetime. As I continued reading, I saw in the letters things I had never read about the trials. Most significantly, I saw in my father's own words how the great events of the twentieth century impacted the lives of those who were sent to make perpetrators of unspeakable crimes account for their actions.

For here, in this collection, is the first insider view of the infighting that occurred in Robert Jackson's colonel-laden staff. My father was initially impressed by the brass, but that sense of awe didn't last long. He soon witnessed the bureaucratic bungling and wrote that the whole prosecutorial effort was at risk. He called it "a maelstrom of incompetence." This was much later confirmed by Cronkite, who covered the trials for United Press. He told me that if it weren't for my father, the Nuremberg trials might have descended into chaos and might have failed to prove the human consequences of Nazi oppression.

Justice Jackson appreciated my father's firm and steady hand. He also noted his interrogation skills. Desperate for honest and expert help, Jackson eventually elevated my father from being staff attorney to his right-hand man and reduced the role of military participants. My father's letters detail this often frustrating period — he had been clearly discouraged by the initial scope of responsibilities and considered asking Justice Jackson to relieve him of his duties.

I also saw in these letters an intimate portrait of Justice Jackson himself; my father's affection and admiration for the chief prosecutor grew as the trial proceeded. These men spent not only day after day in court but evening after evening arranging dinner parties for dignitaries and visitors: royalty, heads of state, members of the international press corps. He also provided a rare glimpse of Jackson in the wake of the chief prosecutor's troublesome cross-examination of Göring — and the toll that it took on the justice. He held nothing back in his commentary. He revealed his own concerns about the number of Jewish prosecutors who wanted to participate in the trial. I understand this perspective for what it was — a frank concern that Jews needed protection, after all that had happened, from charges of vengeance. Even as I read such difficult passages I knew that if my siblings and I ever made the decision to publish these letters, such material would have to remain. This would be necessary to protect the authority and historical significance of the collection.

Other opinions that my father expressed were not so much controversial as prescient — such as his views on the Soviet threat. Though he seemed to like a few of the Soviet staff members personally, he loathed what they stood for and considered their participation to be the Achilles' heel of the trial. Nuremberg was intended to punish inhumane behavior, and the Soviets had committed dreadful deeds on an enormous scale.

There were many other surprises in the letters, including the relationships my father developed with the defendants Wilhelm Keitel and Franz von Papen. In the letters, he indicated that every morning before court began he would acknowledge the presence of each of them. I understood this, because even as my father held strong resentments for their actions, in daily conversations with these men he came to know them.

My father's letters, as I discovered, formed an attempt to record history as it happened. They were written as events unfolded in front of him, and as he struggled with finding his place at Nuremberg even as he yearned to go home, a circumstance that often colored his tone. In writing to my mother, my father clearly felt the freedom that comes with the intimacy that the two of them shared, and, as a result, what he wrote was often raw and unprocessed — his frustrations of the moment. This is a first draft of history, unlike later volumes that appeared about Nuremberg since those writers, including eyewitnesses or participants in the trial, knew the endings. My father's in-the-moment account reveals inconsistent views, or ones that he later altered. For example, some letters relate unduly critical opinions of people he admired. But that is one of the characteristics of such a collection of letters — unvarnished, honest, and emotional.

Even so, a decade and a half passed after our discovery of them before my siblings and I decided to make this collection public. During that time, our family worked to secure Thomas J. Dodd's legacy. We were all heartbroken by what happened to him in his last years in the Senate — it has been the family opinion that his censure was unjustified. This led to a bitter ending of his public life and contributed to his early death.

But we knew that he had left a proud record as a public servant. He had been ahead of his time as a crusader for civil rights — before Nuremberg, prosecuting the Ku Klux Klan in the South and, afterward, addressing outrages in distant lands that reminded him in any way of what the Nazis had done. To honor this work, we established the Thomas J. Dodd Research Center at the University of Connecticut in 1995, where, among many other programs, awards are presented to champions of human rights. President Bill Clinton and Nobel Peace Prize winner Elie Wiesel spoke at its opening. Wiesel, a survivor of Auschwitz and Buchenwald, said that after the liberation he lived in a children's home in France, "desperately trying to find a reason for hope. I read in the Yiddish newspapers of the [Nuremberg] trial. There was something metaphysical about it. At long last murderers were accused of murder. The solemnity of the court, the awesome words of Robert Jackson and Thomas Dodd, the arrogance of Göring, the expressionless face of Rudolf Hess . . ." All of this, Wiesel said, was part of the most compelling courtroom confrontation in history.

Even as the Dodd Center flourished, we did not make my father's letters public. It was only when I began to wonder how he would react to what is happening in the world — and in the United States itself — that we made our decision to release the letters. The rule of law that my father addressed in Nuremberg and the standards so eloquently expressed at the trial can seem lost in an array of abuses, some of them committed by our own country.

Among the leaders of the Nuremberg generation there was a shared understanding, particularly among Americans, that they were uniquely placed in history to do things for other people in the world: to minimize the future risk of war, to provide assistance, to guarantee basic liberties and to ensure that the postwar world would be rooted in shared goals and shared values. They understood that the ability of the United States to help bring about a world of peace and justice was rooted not in our military might alone but our moral authority. This depended not only on our tanks and planes but also on our ability to convince others that our values and our ideals were right. Our ability to succeed in spreading values of freedom and democracy and human rights would only be as effective as our own willingness to uphold them.

Martin Luther King Jr. once said that the moral arc of the universe is long, but it bends toward justice. All of us want to believe that ideal, but the disheartening course of recent events call it into question.

For six decades, we learned the lessons of the Nuremberg men and women well. We continued to stand for the right things. We didn't start wars — we ended them. We didn't commit torture — we condemned it. We didn't turn away from the world — we embraced it.

But that has changed in the past few years. There's a sense that "the world is beginning to doubt the moral basis of our fight against terrorism." Those are not my words; they belong to former secretary of state and former chairman of the Joint Chiefs of Staff, General Colin Powell.

If, for sixty years, a single word, *Nuremberg*, has best captured America's moral authority and commitment to justice, unfortunately, another word now captures the loss of such authority and commitment: *Guantánamo*.

We may also trace the loss to a single speech of an American president, standing in the Rose Garden of the White House, trying to convince members of his own party that America should reinterpret the Geneva conventions that have defined human rights in this world for half a century. In a mockery of justice, we lock away terrorism suspects for years and give them no real day in court. We deny the lessons of Nuremberg, of universal rights to justice.

Now, as in the era of Nuremberg, this nation should never tailor its eternal principles to the conflict of the moment, for if we do, we will be shadowing those we seek to overcome. In the end, what we lose could be much more than we gain.

Our enemies today will never be influenced by international sensibilities or appeals to do what is right. They mock our laws, as Hermann Göring once mocked our treaties and international alliances as "just so much toilet paper."

My father wrote in his letters that he felt bad about leaving my mother alone with the children for so long, but that "I'm doing the right thing and I feel sure we will not regret it. Some day it will be a great landmark in the struggle of mankind for peace. I will never do anything as worthwhile . . . Someday, the boys will point to it, I hope, and be proud and inspired by it. Perhaps they will be at the bar themselves and perhaps they will invoke this precedent and call upon the law we make here."

There are other reasons to bring out my father's letters. As hard as it may be to believe, there is a world of ignorance out there about

Nuremberg and its meaning. And there is Holocaust denial. Even though the Nazis themselves left tons of documents proving their crimes, even though defendant Hans Fritzsche said, "No power in heaven or earth will erase this shame from my country — not in generations — not in centuries," there are many in high positions who remain belligerent on the subject.

The president of Iran, the head of a state of seventy million people, denies that the Holocaust ever happened and in 2006 hosted an international conference of "scholars" that belittled all of the documentation and other evidence of the biggest crime in history.

The century-old literary hoax, *The Protocols of the Elders of Zion*, remains influential in many countries (like Syria, Iran, and even Saudi Arabia) where the governments still employ it for propaganda purposes a century after it was discovered to be a fraud. *Mein Kampf* remains in wide circulation. As I write this, it ranks in books sold on Amazon.com well above William L. Shirer's masterwork, *The Rise and Fall of the Third Reich*, and just a hair below the most intimate book on the Holocaust, Anne Frank's *Diary of a Young Girl*. It is sometimes possible to believe that nothing was learned at Nuremberg.

At the dedication of the Dodd Center, Elie Wiesel said that the goal of the Nazis "was not just to kill the Jews but to eradicate their memory. Memory is the key."

In the release of Thomas J. Dodd's letters from Nuremberg, my brothers and sisters and I will feel as if we have contributed one more piece of persuasive and human evidence of the best and worst that humans can do.

PART ONE

The Legacy

That Dodd is smarter than he looks.

> —Hermann Göring to Karl Doenitz,
> overheard in the defendants' dock,
> April 17, 1946

CHAPTER 1

Nuremberg, Undermined

IN EARLY SEPTEMBER 2006, a tense crew of Senate Democrats gathered in S-211 — the Lyndon Baines Johnson Room — at the U.S. Capitol. In all, there were fifteen of us, senior members of various committees, addressing difficult and timely issues during our monthly lunch meeting. In a few weeks, Americans would go to the polls and our party seemed to have a reasonable chance of regaining Congress for the first time in a dozen years. But no one seemed overconfident, and for good reason.

Room S-211 has a sense of seriousness and timelessness. It features marbleized walls, period window cornices, a chandelier installed during the Grant Administration, and the elaborate ceiling fresco of caryotid figures that it took the Italian artist Constantino Brumidi a decade (from 1857 to 1867) to complete. In that place of serious appointments, many heavy decisions have been made.

It is where LBJ, as Senate majority leader, twisted arms of fellow Democrats until they came around to his viewpoint. It is the venue where in 1959 Johnson promised my father, newly elected to the Senate, a seat on the Foreign Relations Committee. Forty-seven years later, in that historic room, I would try a little arm twisting of my own.

When Carl Levin's turn to speak came, we prepared for the inevitable. Carl, one of the most respected members of the Senate and the highest-

ranking Democrat on the Armed Services Committee, addressed our political bind. But there were certain facts he didn't need to review — we knew
them too well.

President George W. Bush was looking for a way around his legal road-
block. Before the Supreme Court ruling that summer in *Hamdan v. Rumsfeld*, he had seized unprecedented war powers, deciding that the
Administration alone had the authority to determine how to treat prisoners
in the war on terror.

He rejected domestic law and international treaties on methods of
interrogation — a policy that led to allegations internationally that Americans endorse torture.

The president has maintained that the United States is in a state of war
against terrorism, and therefore he has the authority to hold enemy combatants indefinitely without trial, formal charges, or revealment of evidence against them. For those detainees that he decided to try, he
established military commissions. Appeals could not be made through the
court system. There was no significant challenge to them until the case of
Hamdan v. Rumsfeld reached the Supreme Court.

Salim Ahmed Hamdan, a native of Yemen, had been captured in
Afghanistan in 2001 and then shipped to Guantánamo Bay, where he was
held along with several hundred others. Hamdan was suspected of deliver-
ing weapons to Al Qaeda and charged with conspiracy to commit terrorism. Hamdan brought suit, arguing that the military commission formed
to try him was illegal and that, as a defendant, he lacked the protections
specified by the Uniform Code of Military Justice and the Geneva conventions. The argument persuaded the lower court but not the federal court
of appeals.

In its ruling, which by a 5–3 vote overturned the appeals court, the
Supreme Court said among other things that the president needed the
approval of Congress to pursue measures other than those expressly dic-
tated by existing U.S. laws and treaties. The president's quick response was
to propose legislation that would have Congress rubber-stamp his initial
practices — reinstating the commissions as originally structured and
redefining the Geneva conventions by weakening its protections. He

demanded a free hand in interrogations — a circumstance, we knew from the examples of Abu Ghraib, Guantánamo, and secret prisons around the globe, that was deeply troubling.

As the fifth anniversary of September 11 approached, the country was once again reminded of the treachery that can come from any direction at any time. Since that dreadful day in 2001, many Republicans have tried to paint Democrats as weak on defense. Any objections to the Iraq policy were portrayed as cowardly or even treasonous.

In a speech to the Republican National Committee in January 2006, Karl Rove offered advice similar to what he delivered four years earlier in advance of the 2002 midterm elections: proclaim the Democrats weak on protecting America. Indeed, when Democrats pointed out, correctly, that National Security Agency warrentless wiretapping was illegal, Rove and his crowd twisted this fact for political advantage. The president was soon saying that Democrats were "opposed to listening in on terrorists."

Sloganeering against the "cut-and-run" Democrats became a more reliable policy than any actual foreign policy. Starting the war in Iraq, as time proved, was a mistake, but the president stuck by his guns. I had been among those who voted to give him authorization, because at the time I believed the Administration's characterization of the intelligence that raised the specter that Saddam Hussein already possessed or was actively pursuing a deadly stockpile for imminent use. I hoped that with my vote, the Administration would be able to present a strong case to the UN to aggressively support the UN inspections of Iraq in order to fully determine whether Saddam Hussein was stockpiling weapons of mass destruction. The Administration chose not to do so but instead went to war in Iraq. It soon became clear that the intelligence — hence, the primary reason to go to war — was wrong. And as the war became a heavy burden on America — drawing us, as it did, from a more sensible and effective strategy against worldwide terror — I and others worked to find ways to end it.

The president, however, tried to turn the Supreme Court defeat in *Hamdan v. Rumsfeld* into an offensive maneuver. As he saw it, it was a chance to solidify the Republican stance on terror. Carl Levin and others concluded that the best we as Democrats could do — with the elections so imminent—was to support a new compromise measure. The senatorial trio of John McCain, John Warner, and Lindsey Graham, all of them experienced in military matters, seemed to favor a reasonable plan for treatment of prisoners and retain elements of habeas corpus—a basic right that our justice system, and the international community of civilized countries, have held dear.

None of us thought the compromise suggested by the three senators was perfect, but the group as a whole seemed content to let the issue rest. This is the nature of politics: You push until you can push no further, and at the close of the Senate day, you are at least satisfied that you have helped steer the body from a ruinous course.

I had not, after all, parachuted into this fray. I had been involved in the fight for human rights ever since, as a freshman senator, I became a member of the Foreign Relations Committee in 1981. This was a natural extension of my father's legacy at Nuremberg and of his priorities in the U.S. Senate. It was a result, too, of my Peace Corps service in the 1960s, when, in the Dominican Republic, I saw firsthand the results of oppression and became committed to addressing such issues.

The big human rights debates of the early 1980s centered on Latin America, where I focused much of my work. I developed relationships with key figures in hot-spot countries—Guatemala, Honduras, El Salvador, Costa Rica, and Nicaragua. The U.S. political landscape at the time was charged in a way similar to what would happen years later in relation to Iraq.

President Reagan reduced the many volatile political situations in Central America to what he saw as a worldwide Communist plot, making the region a major focus of his foreign policy. The Soviet Union funneled arms and other resources to certain parties, and in President Reagan's view, it was necessary to back those who stood against Communism, no matter their own records on human rights.

President Reagan, for example, wanted to send support to the government of El Salvador, led at the time by a civilian/military junta, which was fighting leftist guerillas. The government's notorious death squads also targeted those who opposed its power. The archbishop Óscar Arnulfo

Romero, three American nuns, and a lay worker — all of whom supported economic and political reform — were gunned down. This was in an era of high political crimes throughout the region, from Argentina, where in the "Dirty War" thousands of dissidents disappeared, to Chile and to small villages of Central America.

I had seen all of this from a quite different perspective from President Reagan. To him, Communism was the issue. In American politics, such broad stances continued to play well with a significant segment of the public. Phil Gramm, the senator from Texas, weighed in during the debate on Nicaragua and whether to aid the contras in their rebellion against the leftist Sandinista government. To paraphrase my former colleague, he would often say that Nicaragua is only ten days by tank from Texas.

My own investigations made it clear to me that the excesses of power transcend political labels. The rule of law, on which my father's stance was always firm, is the ultimate standard. Murder, in short, is still murder. The idea of simply sending unrestricted funding to anyone fighting Communism was, as Senator Edward M. Kennedy said, "giving a blank check to death squads and despotism."

My view on Communist influence differed from that of my father's — he had firmly believed in the domino theory, so prevalent in regard to Vietnam. But I recalled that in his later years he understood that there were ominous forces quite apart from anything supported by the Soviets.

In the case of El Salvador in the early 1980s, it was clear to me that the wisest stance for the United States was to send aid to that country's government only if certain conditions were met. And so, as a freshman senator, I introduced an amendment to a foreign appropriations bill that tied such support to measures of human rights.

Political opponents called this effort naïve, particularly in that it was the idea of a Senate newcomer. But my experiences in Latin America had taught me otherwise, and I pressed on. A report in the New York Times on February 28, 1982, revealed the results: "In approving aid last fall, Congress, under Mr. Dodd's prodding, made support for El Salvador conditional on a Presidential certification that the junta was making progress on human rights."

This policy was not only correct for us but, moreover, proved useful to some of those in power in Central America. I remember my conversations with El Salvador's leader, José Napoleón Duarte, who had come to Washington to lobby for support. In the years before his ascension to high office, he too had been victimized, imprisoned by a military dictatorship. Once in power, he had initiated land reforms and other progressive policies. Even so, death squads were still prevalent. He told me that my efforts to tie aid to human rights measures had actually helped him against his political opponents. There was now a standard that had to be met if the political power structure in the capital of San Salvador hoped to survive.

I thought of all this as the 2006 debates on President Bush's tactics intensified. I recalled that although Democrats did not hold the White House or the Senate during the debates on Central America, they had still made a significant difference in foreign policy. I was determined to make that happen again.

During our lunch in the LBJ Room, I argued that if we were to go along with the compromise plan, and therefore lend our support to a policy that undermined the rule of law, we would one day regret our actions.

We were, in effect, rolling back the Magna Carta and undermining the Geneva conventions, the dramatic and humane precedent of Nuremberg.

We could regret such a move even more than we regretted our original support for the war in Iraq. I was concerned about the welfare of our own soldiers — what it would mean to those fighting this war and future wars — if we abandoned humane treatment. I was concerned, too, that information gained from unlawfully cruel treatment is not reliable. Even John McCain, whose patriotism has never been in question, admits that when things got bad enough during his more than five years as a prisoner of the North Vietnamese he would tell his captors anything they wanted to hear.

My colleagues around the table did not dispute my points. They nodded approvingly. Patrick Leahy argued eloquently in support of them, saying that the Administration's policy was "flagrantly unconstitutional." But we were in a box. The election was coming up, and the Republicans would no doubt transform any reasonable defense of human rights into thirty-second spots that played to the fears of voters. We all knew this from painful experience.

I thought of my friend Max Cleland. In 2002, the senator from Georgia was ambushed by the lowest kind of political attack. Max was a Vietnam hero — a triple amputee in the war. He served with distinction in Congress, but just before the 2002 election he expressed opposition to labor restrictions in the president's Homeland Security bill that unduly restrained the rights of U.S. citizens.

Though Max voted in favor of the bill, Republicans painted Max as a man who lacked the courage to be a leader in a time of crisis. In one television spot, images of Max and Osama bin Laden were presented in the same grainy way. The Republicans did this even though Cleland had certainly demonstrated his courage on the battlefield. That such a tactic worked disheartened us. I remember the reaction of Robert Byrd to the disgraceful campaign. The very senior senator from West Virginia had an incredulous look on his face and said, "Have they no shame? Have they no shame?"

I had no doubt that if we, as a group, had the audacity to take a firm stance against the commander in chief on the interrogation issue we'd get the same treatment.

But we also knew there was another side to this that transcended politics as usual. The stakes had become very high. What looked like a mere compromise was something else — an abandonment of principle.

In all of my time in Congress, I have been influenced by the lessons of what my father did in Nuremberg — and by his defense of principle. The trial that consumed him in 1945 and 1946 was the most important work of his life; he knew this even at the time, as he expressed in his letters.

He was among those who stood firmly on the side of the rule of law — of giving even the world's most notorious criminals the right to examine fully the evidence against them and to defend themselves with every possible legal tool.

It would be harder to imagine more horrible crimes than the ones those Nuremberg defendants committed. The war of aggression they undertook and waged so ruthlessly led eventually to fifty-five million deaths worldwide — about a fifth of those by murder. But in 1945 the rule of law triumphed. And my father, in a dignified if difficult setting, interrogated and cross-examined Nazi thugs in the same manner that, in the years previous, he had gone about his work in the U.S. Department of Justice, prosecuting members of the Ku Klux Klan.

It may be argued that at Nuremberg the stakes were different from those at Guantánamo. That war, after all, was over. The top Nazis had been reduced to a group of vulnerable and disoriented men who came to understand that they would finally be held accountable for what they had done. But even then there were fears that politically the trial could be dangerous. Many worried that Hermann Göring and others would use the proceedings as an opportunity to spark a new Nazi fire from the ashes. In fact, Göring, on the witness stand for several days, tried to do just that.

In the end, though, the rule of law became the clear winner in Nuremberg. As Hanson W. Baldwin of the *New York Times* reported the day after the sentencing, the Nuremberg trials "have greatly increased the prestige of Anglo-American and Allied justice. Here, clearly, was no mock trial, no foregone verdict; the justice was military and severe, but it was justice." The sentences meted out reflected a thoughtful and deliberate process. Twelve of the twenty-one defendants who sat in the dock received the death penalty, a statistic that defied the pretrial odds. Others received prison time, and three of the defendants were acquitted. This was, for the nations of France, Britain, the United States, and even the Soviet Union a bold and meaningful precedent that could be respected and built upon.

Over the next forty years, the precedent that even the strongest nations must respect the rule of law would prove to be an important weapon in our country's next life-or-death struggle, the one that my father so clearly predicted: the cold war against Soviet Communism. While there are many reasons why Soviet Communism crumbled, one of them was that the people of the Warsaw Bloc lost faith in their own governments that repeatedly demonstrated they had no interest in following the rule of law. The collapse of Communism showed that even the mightiest empires and most powerful governments ultimately need the support of their people, and one of the easiest ways to lose that support is for a ruling elite to demonstrate that it places itself above the law. Crucially, throughout the cold war, the United States and its allies demonstrated that countries could survive and prosper — even in the face of external threats — all the while agreeing to be bound by the rule of law. In the end, the principle that citizens do not have to live in fear of an oppressive government may have been more important in defeating Communism than tanks and missiles. I'd like to think in some small way my father was at least partially responsible for this.

But now — Guantánamo and Abu Ghraib and secret prisons. I thought of how my father would react. I felt I had to press the fight further. All I had to do was review my father's presentation of evidence at Nuremberg to be reminded that eras change but human nature doesn't.

On the morning of December 13, 1945, my father presented to the court an argument that has an eerie connection to the present. He charged the Nazis, among many other heinous crimes, with "the apprehension of victims and their confinement without trial, often without charges, generally with no indication of the length of their detention."

I thought of this, certainly, when in the days after our lunch in the LBJ Room I learned that we had been played. The compromise that we as a group had acceded to became much changed after Senators McCain, Warner, and Graham negotiated with the White House.

The legislation, in its final form, allows the president to define our commitments under the Geneva conventions through regulation rather than legislation. It allows the president's interpretation to be authoritative as a matter of U.S. law, in the same manner as other administrative regulations. It essentially gives the president authority to define what specific techniques do not constitute "grave breaches" of the Geneva conventions and are therefore allowable. The definition in the bill of "unlawful enemy combatant" is broad and can result in summary imprisonment for legal immigrants. It strips the federal courts of its powers. The law also allows coerced and secret evidence. And it provides a basis for defense to those who may have committed war crimes before the act was passed.

In agreeing to all this, Congress has shirked its oversight responsibilities. We had already undermined the separation of powers, a guiding doctrine of our Constitution, in allowing the executive branch to decree unilaterally which interrogation techniques are permissible without legislative review.

The Administration and Republican leadership would have the American people believe that the war on terror requires a choice — the U.S. government can either protect America or uphold the basic tenets upon which our country was founded, but not both.

I reject that reasoning. We have the capacity to balance our responsibilities to bring terrorists to justice while at the same time protecting what it means to be American. To choose the rule of law over violent revenge is to uphold the same values of equal justice and due process that were codified in our Constitution.

The Bush Administration's creation of secret military tribunals was a blatant disregard of what Justice Sandra Day O'Connor said in *Hamdan v. Rumsfeld*, a case decided in 2004: "A state of war is not a blank check for the President."

Our founding fathers established the legal framework of our country on the premise that those in government are not infallible. And it is for that reason that even when the president acts with the best of intentions to protect our citizens from harm, he can make errors in judgment.

We shouldn't forget the historic implications of Japanese American internment during World War II. More than one hundred thousand Japanese Americans were relocated from the west coast to camps in remote areas of the country. While the last of these camps closed in 1945, it was not until 1988 that Congress enacted legislation issuing a formal apology on behalf of the U.S. government, noting that these actions were based on "race prejudice, war hysteria, and a failure of political leadership." This stain on our nation's history cannot be erased, but we do almost as grave an injustice if we fail to learn a lesson from such mistakes. While we may reasonably fear the attacks our enemies may try to carry out, we must not let such fear undermine our judgment.

At Nuremberg, defendants were given the right to face their accuser, the right to confront evidence against them, and the right to a fair trial. Underlying that decision was the conviction that this nation must not tailor its most fundamental principles to the conflict of the moment—and the recognition that if we did, we would be walking in the very footsteps of the enemies we despised. As our nation turned away from violence in the name of the law, we set a shining and lasting example for the international community as a society grounded in the principles of peace and justice.

How can we expect developing nations around the world to give credence to the rule of law when our own leaders choose to ignore it? On what moral authority can we tell other countries not to detain unlawfully and torture American citizens when we fail to abide by the same rules?

What I found particularly compelling was that the Senate Armed Services Committee received testimony from six current and former leaders of each of the military services' judge advocate general. Believing that the Administration's attempts to deviate from the Uniform Code of Military Justice were so contrary to our nation's interests, they publicly advocated for an adherence to Common Article III of the Geneva conventions, which among other measures prohibits, "outrages upon personal dignity, in particular humiliating and degrading treatment." These were not politicians in business suits decrying the Administration's conduct of the war on terrorism. These were generals and admirals standing up for their belief that the rule of law should be preserved and that detainees should be tried within the Uniform Code of Military Justice under slightly modified conditions, in the interest of national security.

A group of retired federal judges wrote, "For two hundred years, the federal judiciary has maintained Chief Justice Marshall's solemn admonition that ours is a government of laws, and not of men. The proposed legislation imperils this proud history by abandoning the Great Writ to the siren call of military necessity."

These powerful arguments had been, in the end, ignored.

I thought again of my father. Among the tens of thousands of papers stored at the Thomas J. Dodd Research Center at the University of Connecticut, there is the text of a speech he delivered in Hartford, Connecticut, when he returned home from Nuremberg. He talked in that address about the moral victory the Allies had achieved in the courtroom.

He said, "Those of us who were privileged to serve at the Nuremberg

Trial are proud of the entire proceeding. Whatever else may be said about the case, no man can charge that the case was tried unfairly. Every right of the defendants was scrupulously observed. They were given every possible opportunity to make every possible explanation and every possible defense. Witnesses were obtained for them merely at their request. Documents were made available, library facilities were at their disposal, and throughout every hour of the trial they were afforded every opportunity to answer every charge . . . This [was a] demonstration of judicial process honestly at work. I saw it take place — this moral victory — from day to day, slowly but surely in the dock and at the defense tables."

Not so today. Increasingly, our country is abandoning the moral high ground and the putting aside of weapons that inspire people in global struggles and that proved so crucial in bringing the cold war to a largely peaceful and triumphant conclusion. Thus I fear that each step we take from presenting ourselves as unambiguously dedicated to preserving the rule of law is a step in the direction of a less secure United States. What good is the information gained from torturing one Iraqi insurgent if doing so causes us to be despised by a million Iraqi children?

This deep concern for our security and moral authority is what drove me in the days after the revised compromise was turned into something I couldn't recognize or support. I spoke with my colleague Byron Dorgan, of North Dakota, who also felt we had been outmaneuvered. We decided to press fellow Democrats on behalf of an extreme measure.

Senator Dorgan and I knocked on the door of Harry Reid, then the Senate minority leader. We explained our objections to the rewritten bill and argued on behalf of a filibuster. By succeeding with this tactic, we could effectively delay any action on the bill at least until the new Congress was seated in January 2007 — and that new Congress could contain a Democratic majority.

Reid was sympathetic to the idea but pointed out the practical and political reality. He said Democrats shouldn't vote for filibuster unless we had enough support to prevail. And, of course, we would risk giving the Republicans more ammunition. Some of them were already arguing that a vote for a Democrat was a vote for a more vulnerable America.

In light of this, Senator Dorgan and I decided to back off the filibuster plan. We knew we would find other ways, in time, to right a terrible wrong. In the meantime, it was important to speak out against the bill on the Senate floor. I did so standing at the very Senate desk that my father used for twelve years.

I concluded my remarks with these words, "I will vote <u>no</u> on final passage when that occurs later today. I would hope that our colleagues would give serious consideration to doing so as well. As Justice Jackson said at Nuremberg, 'We must never forget that the record on which we judge these defendants today is the record on which history will judge us tomorrow. To pass these defendants a poisoned chalice is to put it to our lips as well.' To rubber-stamp the Administration's bill would poison one of the most fundamental principles of American democracy. I urge my colleagues not to allow that to happen."

But in the end, the president got his way. The vote on the Military Commissions Act of 2006 (some referred to it as the torture bill) was closer than I had expected, 65–34. The filibuster might have worked. Dropping it, I decided, would be my last compromise on the issue.

In January 2007, I declared my candidacy for the presidency and my vision for America. I had my first public rally at the Old State House in Hartford, a building of great historic significance built on the site where our country's first written constitution, known as the Fundamental Orders, was adopted in 1639. It was more than a symbolic move in that sense. It was, in part, out of respect for what the rule of law has meant to all of us.

Standing near the spot where George Washington and French general Rochambeau met to plan strategy in the American Revolution, where statesmen of courage and vision assembled to do the work of the people, where in 1838 abolitionists stood up for human rights and succeeded in having murder and mutiny charges dropped against Africans bound for slavery on the ship *Amistad*, I knew that one of the first things I would do if elected president would be to take steps to overturn the onerous Military Commissions Act of 2006. And then to build on the legal legacy that my father, Justice Robert Jackson, and their colleagues had worked so hard to establish at Nuremberg.

CHAPTER 2

"Frightful Retribution"

Five days after his ninetieth birthday, Walter Cronkite arrived at his CBS office in New York City a few minutes behind schedule. As customary, he was in the company of Marlene Adler, his staff director, who on that November afternoon juggled several requests to see or talk to the television icon called "the most trusted man in America."

A film producer wanted his thoughts on a new project. There were pleas from television stations for on-camera interviews about the morning's big news at CBS: the death of reporter Ed Bradley, who had succumbed to leukemia. There were those, too, who wanted to know what Mr. Cronkite thought of the 2006 midterm elections — what President Bush called a "thumpin'" for the Republicans, as Democrats gained control of both houses of Congress.

But Walter Cronkite had his own work to attend to: lectures; a documentary, *Legacy of War*; and, a priority for that day, recalling the Nuremberg trials.

He sat at his large wooden desk and reminisced about my father at the trial and what happened back when Walter Cronkite's name was known only to those newspaper subscribers who read his United Press dispatches from the war and its aftermath.

He seemed surprised when he learned that my father had included him and his late wife, Betsy, in his letters — though actually in only one reference, to a dinner party that my father gave for correspondents.

"A long time ago," Mr. Cronkite agreed in that steady voice still familiar and resonant.

He settled back in his chair and closed his eyes for a moment, as if this was the key to memory. He had taken off his suit jacket but remained a picture of authority. His white shirt was crisp, his gray and blue tie muted but distinctive, his white hair still in abundance. The bookcase behind him held histories, biographies, sailing magazines, a tall-ship model, two of his Emmys, and other relics of a long public and personal life.

Mr. Cronkite's eyes lit up when he recalled his lodgings at Nuremberg — in the large Faber castle, which is mentioned in my father's letters as a place where tribunal staff members attended shows. Mr. Cronkite recalled, too, the singing frauleins and in particular the nightly piano performance of classical pieces by a Polish reporter. "We wanted him to play jazz, too," Mr. Cronkite said, "but he wouldn't, or couldn't."

On many of those nights my father hung around with him and his reporter colleagues. "We spent a lot of time at the bar — and by that I'm not referring to the legal establishment. I liked Tom immensely. And I was charmed by his ability in the courtroom. I thought he was the major strength in the large cast of lawyers." The two became so close that my father, knowing that they would not be reported, confided his trial frustrations.

In recalling that relationship, Mr. Cronkite turned his head for a moment and paused, as if he wasn't certain that he should say what he was thinking. "I doubt very much that Tom Dodd would tell you this if he was around today, but I think he was at some points disappointed with the presentation of [Robert H.] Jackson.

"Jackson had a certain failing. He was not great at cross-examination. This was idle talk around the courthouse. And Jackson's difficulty had consequences — most importantly when Göring took the stand."

The New York Times reported in March 1946 that Göring "seemed to enjoy his day in court. He beamed, smiled, shook his head and nodded." When it came time for Jackson to cross-examine, he continued in this vein.

Walter Cronkite's memoir, *A Reporter's Life*, offers more detail on this point: "Although Jackson's table was piled high with the documents that conclusively established Goering's [note that Cronkite used the English spelling of Göring] guilt, the defendant had only his astounding memory and a few notes in the lavender notebook his jailers had provided . . . Thus armed, Goering parried many of Jackson's thrusts, frequently correcting dates and figures that Jackson misquoted from the documents in front of him. Jackson was totally unnerved by Goering's almost jovial impudence. To Goering's insouciance he could respond only with bluster and a posture reminiscent of the country lawyer he once had been."

In his CBS office, Mr. Cronkite recalled that "Jackson was sometimes blue in the face," so frustrated he didn't quite know how to proceed. "Once he approached the witness stand as if, out of desperation, he was going to physically confront Göring. He did not have the razor sharpness, the kind of sharpness one would expect in a trial that the world watched. We expected more talented counsel. In that regard, Tom was far superior to his boss. Even Tom's British colleagues believed the Americans should put somebody else in the prosecutor's chair during cross-examination. His cohorts were urging him to talk to Jackson. They egged him on. It was a very touchy situation, of course — to go to the boss and ask him to step aside. I suppose he said that he could take some of the load off of Jackson."

In any case, as the trial proceeded, my father was given more of that responsibility. And as he worked, he reminded Mr. Cronkite of the "kind of lawyers I had seen in the movies — superb at trapping the witness, pushing the witness to an admission the witness didn't want to divulge."

It seems odd and almost unbelievable, even to Walter Cronkite, that there would have been any challenge in trying twenty-two key Nazis in a court of law — their crimes had been so enormous. But the trial itself, as historians have recorded, provided opportunity for failure and chaos. Both the enormity and great stakes in the proceedings were captured in the first words of Jackson's opening statement on November 20, 1945. Whatever his shortcomings at confronting witnesses, Robert Jackson left nothing to be desired as an orator: "The privilege of opening the first trial in history for crimes against the peace of the world imposes a grave responsibility. The wrongs which we seek to condemn and punish have been so calculated, so malignant, and so devastating, that civilization cannot tolerate their being ignored, because it cannot survive their being repeated."

Even so, the legal basis for Justice Jackson and his fellow prosecutors was shaky. There was considerable dispute over whether such a trial was even legal. No precedent had been set for prosecuting war crimes by an international tribunal, and there was no universally recognized right to try war criminals. Standards recognized by the community of nations covered only a few aspects of "acceptable" behavior in the conduct of war. As a result, as grotesque as the Nazis' actions were, most of them didn't fit conveniently into legal categories. Opponents of an international tribune argued that such proceedings would be ex post facto — a practice abhorrent to all Western legal traditions.

As Mr. Cronkite put it in a National Public Radio documentary on Nuremberg in February 2006, "The law had not kept up with the realities of 20th Century conflict. Mechanized war and systematic genocide had invented systems of violence no legal system had ever imagined. But I wrote at the time that Nuremberg had to serve as a judicial precedent for world order." Mr. Cronkite argued this was necessary not only because of the implications of the chambers of death perfected by the Nazis but also because of the emergence of the nuclear age.

Legal scholars who favored trying the Nazis cobbled together an array of documentation to address the ex post facto objection. They pointed to ratification of a series of Geneva conventions, starting in 1864 and leading to a 1925 international ban on poison gas and bacteriological warfare, as well as one four years later on proper treatment of wounded prisoners of war.

The Hague conventions of 1899 and 1907 outlined so-called rules of war and limited the weapons that could be used. In 1914, there was agreement internationally on certain definitions of war crimes, though there was never any consensus on the matter of prosecuting them.

In any case, there was clear momentum for the idea of bringing Nazi leaders to justice. As early as 1941 President Roosevelt warned that "[o]ne day a frightful retribution" would occur. And, as time passed, evidence of Nazi atrocities was clearly known at the highest level of Allied governments.

In 1942, British foreign secretary Anthony Eden told the House of Commons, "The German authorities are now carrying into effect Hitler's oft repeated intention to exterminate the Jewish people of Europe." Soon after, Churchill said, "The atrocities committed in Poland, Yugoslavia, Norway, Holland, Belgium and particularly behind the German front in Russia, exceed anything that has been known since the darkest and most bestial ages of humanity."

In 1943, the United Nations War Crimes Commission (though the United Nations wasn't officially formed until 1945, the term was used at the time), made up of representatives of seventeen nations, met in London to begin collecting material and accounts it needed to lay the groundwork to prosecute such offenses.

Nevertheless, British support in this effort had limits. Churchill's view of what should be done was similar to Stalin's. The Soviet dictator proposed a toast at the Tehran summit in 1943: "To the quickest possible justice for all the German war criminals . . . I drink to the justice of the firing squad."

Such sentiment was not limited to foreign shores. Henry Morganthau, Roosevelt's secretary of the treasury, agreed with Churchill and Stalin. The opposite view was held, most significantly, by Henry L. Stimson, the secretary of war, who argued that a trial would have at least two benefits: It would produce a framework that would set a standard of universal legality and it would become a basis for international cooperation. He also warned against the kind of vengeance that led to the onerous Treaty of Versailles following World War I — the conditions of which led to economic ruin and to dictatorship in Germany only a few years later.

In support of his views, Stimson cited the Kellogg-Briand Pact of 1928. Sixty-three nations had signed it, including Germany. The treaty renounced war as an instrument of aggression, or as a national policy for solving disputes.

The British, however, continued to object to a trial. Lord Simon, the lord chancellor, argued that "a trial would be exceedingly long and elaborate." It would be seen as "a put-up job to justify a punishment they have already resolved on."

However, FDR's longtime confidant and speechwriter, Judge Sam Rosenman, continued to push hard on the issue, and after FDR died on April 12, 1945, Rosenman found an even more sympathetic ear in Harry Truman. The new president's appointment of Supreme Court Justice Robert H. Jackson to head the U.S. prosecution was a clear sign of his high priority of trying the Nazis for their grave offenses.

Nevertheless, there were several risks. Nazi defendants could use any trial as a platform to further their demented ideas and create a rebirth of their movement. There was also concern about possible trial outcomes — that the defendants would escape justice. As Jackson said in a speech to the American Society of International Law on April 13, 1945, "The ultimate principle is that you should put no man on trial under the form of judicial proceedings if you are not willing to see him freed if not proved guilty. If you are determined to execute a man in any case, there is no occasion for a trial. The world yields no respect to courts that are merely organized to convict."

There was another significant legal question, one of nexus. As *Der Speigel* pointed out in its sixtieth-anniversary series, "Tom Dodd could make as much evidence 'sing' as he wanted — but how was the prosecution going to prove that the 'gangster' Göring and other Nazi bigwigs were responsible for such inhumity? The central problem of the historical experiment of Nuremberg remained unresolved: how could the International Court prove that the ruling class in faraway Berlin actually bore the legal responsibility for what had happened in Buchenwald and elsewhere?"

The prosecutorial effort that emerged demonstrated a seriousness of purpose and effort, and creative thinking — this would be no lynching.

The Allies pressed aggressive legal theories. One of them was the charge of conspiracy. This idea came from Lieutenant Colonel Murray C. Bernays. He proposed a plan that included trying not only individual Nazis but also, at the same time, Nazi institutions. In this way, evidence could be held against the individual and his organization. The Nazis could be seen as con-spiratorially plotting acts from the beginning of their movement that had criminal intention. Then, at later trials of lesser-known defendants, it would be legally clear that the accused were members of criminal organizations.

The charge of conspiracy had been used in American courts in trials of organized crime figures. But it can seem vague — particularly in the context of the enormous number of very real deaths caused by the Nazis. A conspiracy charge was also legally risky. In Europe it was traditionally viewed with suspicion.

Even so, the prosecution developed that strategy, and as time passed, opposition to it and to the tribunal itself dissipated. British objections ended after the suicides of Hitler and Joseph Goebbels and with Mussolini's capture and execution. Nevertheless, there were many issues to be resolved, including where such a trial would take place.

The British held out for Munich, the Bavarian city where the Nazi movement was born. But it had been leveled by bombers to the extent that no large trial could be held there. The Soviets pressed for Berlin — this was the heart of its new occupied territory. That fact made it unattractive to the Americans, British, and French, not only for its isolation but because the Soviets were not known for providing the comforts necessary for such an undertaking.

When Jackson visited Nuremberg, a city that once had also been flattened by Allied bombs, he was astounded to discover that its main courthouse, the Palace of Justice, was still standing, though in need of repair. There was other infrastructure — including the contiguous prison to house the defendants and available lodging for staff members in the Grand Hotel and in nearby towns.

Jackson also liked the idea of Nuremberg for its symbolic significance. This was where the annual Nazi rallies had been held and where the laws against the Jews were written and announced. Even so, the Soviets objected until a compromise could be worked out — the actual trial would take place in Nuremberg if Berlin became the official headquarters of the tribunal.

As for the rules of the court, another compromise was reached — a melding of Continental and U.S. practices. The accused had a right to counsel and to hear the charges specified against them in their own language. They had the right to testify in their own defense, though they would also be sub-ject to cross-examination, a practice that was uncommon in much of Europe. They could also make a final statement that wouldn't be subject to challenge.

The makeup of the court itself became a diplomatic exercise. Each of the four nations would have two judges — one primary, one alternate. It had been assumed, as the United States was the key force behind the trial and had provided most of the funding for it, that one of its judges, Francis Biddle, would preside.

Jackson, however, argued that "in the division of the case, the major part of the trial work has been assigned to us because we are the people best prepared to carry it through. If we were also to provide the presiding officer, there would be the danger that these trials would look like a purely American enterprise. If anything should go wrong, all the animosities and blame will be centered upon the United States."

Biddle stepped aside, and the British jurist, Lord Geoffrey Lawrence, took the gavel. Even with all this decided, there was much to do in prepa-ration for the trial, and that's where my father began to play a role that, in time, would increase measurably.

When he arrived in Nuremberg in September 1945, he was one of four lawyers, and the only civilian, who interrogated the defendants. The British didn't participate because they felt these sessions would give away too much — they would indicate to defendants how the prosecution would present its case. The French and Soviets weren't staffed for interrogations.

Historian Richard Overy, in his book *Interrogations: The Nazi Elite in Allied Hands, 1945*, describes what took place:

Each interrogation was conducted on standard lines. Most took place in a small room with large windows on the third floor of the court building. The room contained a table and a dozen chairs. There would usually be present the interrogator, an interpreter and a court reporter/stenographer. When they were assembled a small button was pushed, alerting a waiting military policeman outside to usher in the prisoner. The formal proceedings opened with the administration of an oath by the interrogator to the interpreter: "Do you solemnly swear to translate from English into German the questions I am about to ask the witness, and his responses from German into English, to the best of your ability, so help you God?" Only then did the interrogator turn to the prisoner and administer the standard legal oath requiring "the truth, the whole truth and nothing but the truth."

My father also had a seat on the body that reshaped the indictments. In his letters, he referred to the mess made of the indictments in London, and the heavy work that had to be done pre-trial to make them into a document that would accurately and specifically outline the scope of the proceedings.

A month before the trial began, the key defendants were informed that they faced these four primary charges:

Formulation of a common plan or conspiracy to commit Crimes Against Peace. Namely, planning, preparation, initiating or waging a war of aggression, or a war in violation of international treaties; War Crimes: Namely violation of the law or customs of war [including] murder, ill treatment, deportation, the forced labor of civilian populations, the murder and maltreatment of prisoners of war or hostages, the plunder of private and public property, and the wanton destruction of towns or villages; Crimes Against Humanity: Namely, murder, extermination, enslavement, deportation, and other inhumane acts committed against any civilian population, before or during the war, or persecutions on political, racial or religious grounds . . . whether or not in violation of the domestic law of the country where perpetrated.

The wording of the indictment expressed in a brief space the general havoc the Nazis had perpetrated. The world's press embraced it. The London *Evening Standard* was representative: "In its concise, factual phrases it catalogues crimes so vast, so nightmarish, that it would seem at first impossible to convey the sense of them to the imagination."

Even so, it left out the word *Jews*, as in the murder of six million. That

it did remains something of a mystery, and to my friend Elie Wiesel, a survivor of Auschwitz and Buchenwald, it is a glaring omission. "I was shocked
when I read it," he says, referring to the indictment and the trial transcript.
"I am not sure why the Jewish tragedy did not play the major role it should
have." In the millions of words in the transcript, a relatively small percentage is devoted to Hitler's grotesque measures against the Jews.

Wiesel, who as author of nearly forty books, professor, and peace activist
has devoured everything written about Nuremberg, says, "The more I read
about it the less I understand. Hitler, after all, was more obsessed with
killing Jews than winning the war." Wiesel pointed out that the trains that
carried Jews to their deaths had priority over military transports.

In her book, *The War Against the Jews, 1933–1945*, historian Lucy S.
Dawidowicz writes, "Hitler's ideas about the Jews were at the center of his
mental world. They shaped his world view and his political ambitions,
forming the matrix of his ideology and the ineradicable core of National
Socialist doctrine."

My guess is that my father might not have agreed on the point of the
Jewish tragedy being underplayed. This is because so much of his work at
the trial dealt directly with slave labor and concentration camps and with
trying to get Nazi defendants to take responsibility for murdering Jews. But
if Wiesel is right and the Jewish aspect didn't emerge to the extent that it
should have, it clearly did so in the years following. Today Nuremberg sym-
bolizes the effort to bring to justice men who attempted to obliterate an
entire culture and its people. And for that fact alone, the word Nuremberg
stands for the trial not only of the twentieth century but one that would set
a standard for all time.

My father certainly sensed that — he refers to the importance of the trials often in the letters. And when, on the morning of November 20, 1945,
he took his seat at the table in the middle of the prosecutorial section
reserved for the U.S. contingent, he was clearly in awe of what was happening in the courtroom.

To his left were Soviet and French prosecutors, and to his right the
British and the International Military Tribunal secretariat. The eight
judges were perched on the right, the defense counsel for each of the

accused were in the center, and on the left sat twenty-one of the world's most notorious men.

They were dressed neatly. Every night during the proceedings they turned in their suits or uniforms for pressing and donned prison garb until the next morning. Göring took his spot as the first among equals, sitting in the first seat in the first row on the left—from where he would try, with measured success, to intimidate and control his fellow defendants.

Göring was the highest-ranking defendant, having been second only to Hitler in authority (though in the last days of the war, the führer denounced Göring as a traitor and stripped him of all offices and honors. Hitler's last will expelled him from the Nazi party).

Göring had been Hitler's heir apparent. He had lived in a luxurious style that none of his peers approached. His servants wore antique costumes, and he enjoyed an extensive art collection, most of it seized from the rightful owners. He ran a manufacturing firm, the Hermann Göring Works, that profited greatly from German rearmament, particularly after he became minister of the economy. Already head of the Luftwaffe, he then became a field marshal, and the next year became chairman of the Reich Council for National Defense. In 1940, Hitler gave Göring the unprecedented rank of Reichsmarschall. In the succeeding years, Hitler grew less enamored of his right-hand man as the Luftwaffe couldn't live up to Göring's boast that he would remove the British Royal Air Force from the skies and as the Allies began to bomb German cities.

Despite Göring's decline at the war's end, he remained the key defendant. Others who would have been tried at Nuremberg—Hitler, Himmler, Goebbels—had committed suicide. Even in captivity, Göring retained influence over the others, who still looked to him as the Nazi standard-bearer, or at least as the man whose bluster and indignity could still reduce them to quaking underlings.

As the *New Yorker* reported at the time, Göring's colleagues "seem dominated by him in the prisoners' dock, just as when they were all free. By his superior supply of theatrical energy, fancy clothes, and interest in the proceedings, and by his air of participation, Göring maintains his position as Prisoner No. 1."

The other defendants:

Martin Bormann (tried in absentia) won the total confidence of Hitler partly though his mastery of the führer's personal finances. In 1941, Bormann was named head of the Party Chancellery, where he wielded great power, controlling access to Hitler and helping to set in motion deadly measures against Jews, Slavs, and Christians. After Berlin fell, he was thought to have been killed by a Soviet antitank shell. His body wasn't found until 1972.

Karl Doenitz was a grand admiral and supreme commander of the German navy. Hitler's last will made him Reich president and supreme commander of the German armed forces. His U-boats destroyed an estimated 21.5 million tons of Allied shipping, and he was held accountable, among other things, for refusing to rescue enemy combatants at sea — a practice endorsed, as Doenitz pointed out, by U.S. admiral Chester Nimitz.

Hans Frank became head of the Nazi legal office in 1929 and in 1933 Bavarian minister of justice. After Poland was conquered, he became governor-general there, ruling from Kraków. Known as the "Butcher of Kraków," he set out to kill Jews, intellectuals, and professionals and to make the rest of Poland a source of slave labor. Frank kept voluminous diaries that became a valuable source of early Nazi history.

Wilhelm Frick's membership in Hitler's inner circle dated back to the early Nazi years. As minister of the interior, he drafted the *Gleichschaltung* laws, which removed the rights of German individual states. He closed down churches that did not cooperate with Nazi policies and had other oppressive influence over cultural matters. Frick was the only one of the tribunal defendants who refused to testify on his own behalf.

Hans Fritzsche joined the Nazi Party in 1933, when Goebbels appointed him head of the German radio service. In that capacity, he briefed editors, "guided" what they printed, and issued releases for the foreign press. In 1940, he became head of the Home Press Division in the Propaganda Ministry.

Walther Funk served as a propagandist, and later became Reichsminister of economics, succeeding Hjalmar Schacht. He then became president of the Reichsbank. In this capacity, he was responsible for the wealth of the Third Reich and of the loot stashed by the SS. At the time of the trial he was in poor health, suffering from diabetes and bladder pain.

Rudolf Hess had been Hitler's private secretary and in that capacity took the dictation of *Mein Kampf.* During the 1930s, he had great influence on the party and was appointed to the Council for Reich Defense. Hitler named him as second in line of succession (behind Göring), though he complained that Hess was "totally inartistic." Hess flew over Britain in 1941, bailed out, and asked to see the Duke of Hamilton, whom he knew, in order to persuade the British of Hitler's friendly intentions. He was instead held prisoner. When he was sent to Nuremberg, he seemed to have no memory of events — a circumstance that changed somewhat over the time of the trial.

Alfred Jodl was chief of Wehrmacht operations from 1939 to the end of the war, working under only Hitler and Wilhelm Keitel. In May 1945, he signed the unconditional surrender on behalf of Germany. Jodl had personal reservations about Nazism and had an argumentative relationship with Hitler, but as a professional soldier he carried out whatever orders were issued to him.

Ernst Kaltenbrunner was appointed Austrian minister for state security and then, in 1941, was made lieutenant-general of police. In 1943, he became head of the Reich Main Security office (which included the Gestapo; Criminal Police; and the SD, the security service of the SS). He administered the concentration camp system and the program for the extermination of the Jews. He hoped to improve the technology of mass murder.

Wilhelm Keitel, the top military commander of the Third Reich, was nevertheless known as "Lakeitel," a term meaning "lackey Keitel." The primary reason that he was included in the defendant's dock was because, at Hitler's insistence, he issued the Nacht und Nebel decree in 1941. This measure made it possible to rid the Third Reich of people thought to be its opponent without the benefit of trial — they would vanish "into night and fog."

Constantin Freiherr von Neurath was foreign minister before being named president of the Secret Cabinet Council, and a member of the

Council for Reich Defense. Von Neurath instituted laws that abolished press freedom, political parties, and trade unions. However, he played a peripheral role once Hitler soured on him for being too lenient in his actions.

Franz von Papen served as chancellor of Germany briefly, before Hitler's rise to power, and then became the führer's vice-chancellor in 1933 and resigned in 1934. He had been instrumental (as the trial and my father's interrogation showed) in Hitler's ascension, though he was not a great supporter. He later became minister to Vienna and then ambassador to Turkey.

Erich Raeder commanded the German navy from 1933 to 1943 and ended with Hitler's fury over Raeder's failure to stop Allied convoys. (He was replaced by Doenitz.) He was included among the top Nuremberg defendants as a key planner of the war and because he had issued orders to kill POWs.

Joachim von Ribbentrop had spent much of his life as a businessman (including a few years in Canada). After he joined the Nazi Party he became Hitler's adviser on foreign affairs, then became ambassador to London and finally foreign minister, replacing von Neurath. He was a key figure in the bullying of Czechoslovakia and Poland, and negotiated the Nazi-Soviet Pact.

Alfred Rosenberg was named minister for occupied territories in 1941, after heading a task force to loot countries of their art treasures. He had been well known to the public as a best-selling author (*The Myth of the Twentieth Century*) and as a vocal anti-Semite, though he claimed to be shocked by the Final Solution.

Fritz Sauckel was Reich director of labor who moved five million people from occupied Europe to work as slaves in Germany. In this capacity, he worked directly for Albert Speer. According to Goebbels, Sauckel was "one of the dullest of the dull." Like many other defendants, he proclaimed no knowledge of the concentration camps.

Hjalmar Schacht had been president of the Reichsbank, minister of economics, and plenipotentiary general for the war economy. He devised financial devices to conceal the inflation resulting from rearmament. After the bomb plot against Hitler, he was replaced by Walther Funk and spent the remainder of the war in various concentration camps.

Baldur von Schirach was the son of an American mother and the grandson of a soldier who lost a leg at the Battle of Bull Run. He became head of the six million member Hitler Youth (membership was made compulsory after 1939). Later, as governor (*Gauleiter*) of Vienna, von Schirach deported 185,000 Jews to concentration camps in Poland as his "contribution to European culture." Near the end of the war, he hid in the Austrian Tyrol and posed as an author writing about the life of actress Myrna Loy.

Arthur Seyss-Inquart, who had been minister of the interior and who played key roles in the Austrian Anschluss, became Reich commissioner in the Netherlands in 1940. He reigned over a brutal regime that at first banned Dutch Jews from holding key positions in the economy or media and then took more extreme measures: sending most of the 140,000 registered Jews to Auschwitz and other camps.

Albert Speer had been Hitler's chief architect and the minister of war armaments. In the latter capacity he ruled over a slave labor program that included the importation of five million foreign workers to Germany. Speer's reputation was different from many who sat in the dock — he appeared to be more reasonable, and accepted some responsibility, though like others he still denied knowledge of the Final Solution.

Julius Streicher was one of Nazi Germany's most influential anti-Semites, attacking Jews in speeches and newspaper articles and urging that they be banned from public transport, places of entertainment, and many schools. Hitler named him director of the Central Committee for the Defense against Jewish Atrocity and Boycott Propaganda. In this capacity, he prospered through the sale of property confiscated from Jews.

As a group, these defendants, or as Walter Cronkite referred to them, "these degenerates in the dock," and their individual histories made for a composite study in the rise of Nazism and its policies of oppression and brutality. The challenge for my father and his colleagues was to apply those actions into a body of law that, in effect, didn't really exist but, they fervently hoped, would endure.

CHAPTER 3

The Evidence of Genocide

I'VE TRIED TO IMAGINE what my father was thinking on the morning of December 13, 1945, as he prepared for his day in court. He must have been focused on the trial's difficulties — particularly the way the Allied prosecutors had turned the case of dramatic crimes into a crashing bore.

Robert H. Jackson had relied too heavily on the valuable gift of self-incriminating evidence that the Nazis had left behind. His motive appears reasonable enough. As he later observes, "The Teutonic passion for making every last detail a matter of written record provides us with our greatest trial weapon. From their own written orders, directives, diaries, journals, memoranda and correspondence, the overwhelming proof of the guilt of the Nazi defendants was made crystal clear." But even this voluminous evidence had its limits in terms of keeping courtroom occupants awake. Just the day before, one of the exasperated judges asked prosecutors if they intended to go on much longer quoting from documents.

Janet Flanner, writing under the pen name Genet in the *New Yorker*, reported in the January 5, 1946, issue, "Ever since our own Chief Prosecutor Jackson's precise, idealistic, impressive opening, we weakened our case, already difficult because the charge lacks precedence, by our irrelevancies and redundancies [we] have succeeded in making the world's most completely planned and horribly melodramatic war seem dull and incoherent."

I suspect my father was thinking, "I told you so." For weeks, he had been pressing Justice Jackson and others to rely less on tedious recitations from stacks of paper and more on evidence that viscerally demonstrated how the Nazis dehumanized their victims.

Perhaps he had reminded Jackson of what he learned about courtroom work before coming to Nuremberg. He talked of his forays, for example, into courts in the American South, where he prosecuted members of the Ku Klux Klan in civil rights cases. In those courtrooms, the crimes of the Klan became much more graphic when witnesses were presented. The jury could see on the faces of men and women affected by hate crimes the horrific consequences of such acts. At Nuremberg, humanity seemed lost amid a barrage of paperwork.

The trial is but one of the things, however, that has given him restless nights. He is also hopeful that a small miracle will occur — that he will be able to temporarily escape what he calls "the dead city of Nuremberg" to fly home to Connecticut for Christmas. He misses my mother terribly. It never occurred to either of them they would be separated so long. When he left for Germany in late July, it seemed he would be gone a few weeks at most. Now, it appears he will be away for many more months.

As he completes his preparations that December morning in 1945, he must have thought about how much his life had changed over the past six months. He looks much older than his thirty-eight years. The full head of black hair has turned almost completely white. I'm sure he was wondering about his children — whom he sometimes refers to as his "bairns" — will they recognize him when he returns? I know he was thinking about Grace Murphy Dodd and worrying about her capacity to take care of everyone, including herself, in his absence.

He thinks of the girl from Rhode Island he met at the Yale/Harvard boat race in New London, Connecticut, a dozen years earlier. She was a Latin scholar, a graduate of Trinity College in Washington, D.C., who loved to ride horses and to paint landscapes. She was taken with the young man she met, the recent grad of Yale Law School who plied her with stories of growing up in the small city of Norwich, Connecticut. He told her how his father, a contractor, quoted Shakespeare and could recite from inaugural addresses of many presidents. And that his mother, a school-teacher, used to stand her little son up on the kitchen table and tutor him in the art of advocacy. She somehow knew even then that Tom Dodd would become a public man.

In the years after my parents were married, Grace Murphy Dodd also became an advocate. My father was proud of this and of the way she led the movement in the town of Lebanon to start the public school's first kindergarten class. She convinced skeptical poor families in the remote rural parts of the community to enroll their children. Grace Murphy Dodd could be very persuasive.

When she had applied for a secretarial job at an insurance company during the Depression, she was asked by the manager of the office what she saw herself doing for the firm. She boldly replied, "I'd like to be manager of the office."

So on one level during his tenure at Nuremberg, my father knows that his wife can manage affairs at home. He knows, too, that she is an excellent mother — dressing us up for church, taking the older children to concerts and the theater, and reading to all of us from wonderful books every night. But I think that as a man who lost his own mother while he was still a teenager, my father clearly maintained a heightened sense of vulnerability. This certainly comes through in his letters home.

The letters also refer to another stress: the unexpected professional struggle that he must address in absentia. In his effort to become licensed to practice law in Connecticut, he had been blindsided.

My father had been a federal prosecutor for many years and had gained a reputation as a gangbuster. While he and my mother lived in St. Paul, Minnesota, he was part of the effort to find John Dillinger, the most wanted criminal of the era. And he tracked down "Doc" May, the gangland medic who treated Dillinger for his wounds. After his Minnesota tenure, he came to Washington to help organize the Justice Department's Civil Rights Division. It was here that he prosecuted Klansmen. He also worked to defend the rights of union workers, and later prosecuted cases of industrial sabotage and subversion.

Afterward, my father applied for a license to practice in Connecticut.

He had taken the state bar exam right after finishing Yale Law School but hadn't passed. He assumed he would be given credit on his return home for his considerable federal legal experience — an alternative way to enter the bar. After he was granted a license, a lawyer in New London brought suit, arguing the federal experience was not enough. Oddly, the court agreed, and my father had to fight this (a battle he eventually won).

The letters from early December 1945 also re-create the increasing tensions of the trial. Though my father wrote almost every day during this period, he didn't record his thoughts about the proceedings on the critical dates of December 12 and 13 when he was so heavily involved in the courtroom drama. At the end of the trial proceedings on December 13, Justice Jackson told him that he could be spared for two weeks. He flew home to Connecticut the next day.

So it is left to my imagination what he might have written had he not been granted this respite. He might have told my mother of the only bit of damning evidence to date that registered on the faces of the accused Nazis. A few days earlier, my father had introduced a documentary film on concentration camps. It showed emaciated survivors in the midst of corpses. It also included German photographs that had been captured by the Soviets — graphic evidence of mutilated prisoners, of executions of Slovenian partisans, and of Auschwitz. The film also included French photographs of tortured prisoners, bodies, and the appalling conditions in the concentration camps.

When the film ended, the courtroom was silent. It was clear that almost everyone was deeply affected by it, even the defendants. Jackson saw three of them wiping away tears. Concluding that further proceedings would be impossible, Sir Geoffrey Lawrence, the chief judge, adjourned court for the day.

My father was gratified that at last the emotional consequences of the Nazis' horrific acts were clearly evident. But since the screening of the film, the prosecution had gone backward — pulling out one document after another.

On December 12, my father had been obliged to present several long and tedious exhibits and to read them all: Document 1526-PS, Exhibit

USA-178, written by the chairman of the Ukrainian Main Committee at Kraków in February 1943; Document R-124, Exhibit USA-179, excerpts from minutes of the meetings of Hitler's Central Planning Board; and Document 019-PS, exhibit number USA-181, a letter from Defendant Sauckel to Defendant Rosenberg.

In all, in one day, my father introduced and quoted from about three dozen documents in his effort to argue his part of the case at that time — the economic factors, including the use of slave labor by the Nazis.

All of them were damning in their content. All difficult to read and digest. It is one thing, for example, to cite the fifteen points addressed in Document EC-68, Exhibit USA-205, the "Directives on the Treatment of Foreign Farm Workers of Polish Nationality," which include restrictions in travel, prohibitions against attending theaters, motion pictures, restaurants, sexual intercourse, gatherings, and so on. It is quite another thing to present the human consequences of such restrictions. That could only be done with specific personal testimony, in ways that resonate, from the point of view of the victims.

No doubt my father told his colleagues of his plans for the afternoon of December 13. Plans that would, in the words of the *Stars and Stripes* report, bring gasps to the courtroom and change the tenor of the proceedings.

Indeed, on that afternoon, Thomas J. Dodd set up his surprises for the court going through familiar and routine procedures — reading more documents. But all the while, courtroom occupants must have wondered what was under the white sheets that covered two tables near the witness stand. Then my father zeroed in on the documents that suggested what was to come.

He told the court:

Himmler in 1943 indicated that the use of the concentration camp against the Jews had been motivated not simply by Nazi racialism. Himmler indicated that this policy had been motivated by a fear that the Jews might have been an obstacle to aggression. There is no necessity to consider whether this fear was justified. The important consideration is that the fear existed; and with reference to it we refer to Document 1919-PS, which bears Exhibit Number USA-170. The document is a speech delivered by Himmler at the meeting of SS major generals at Posen on 4 October 1943, in the course of which he sought to justify the Nazi anti-Jewish policy. We refer to a portion of the document or this speech, which is found on Page 4, Paragraph 4, of the English translation, starting with the words, "I mean the clearing out of the Jews."

I mean the clearing out of the Jews, the extermination of the Jewish race. It's one of those things it is easy to talk about. The Jewish race is being exterminated, says one party member. That's quite clear. It's in our program; elimination of the Jews, and we're doing it, exterminating them.

My father went on to say that the concentration camp had been "one of the principle weapons by which the conspirators achieved the social cohesion which was needed for the execution of their plans for aggression. And, after they launched their aggression and their armies swept over Europe, they brought the concentration camp to occupied countries and they also brought the citizens of the occupied countries to Germany and subjected them to the whole apparatus of Nazi brutality."

An hour later, my father sprung his surprises.

We have had turned over to us two exhibits which we are prepared to show to this Tribunal only because they illustrate the depths to which the administration of these camps had sunk shortly before, at least, the time they were liberated by the Allied Army. The Tribunal will recall that in the showing of the moving picture, with respect to one of the camps, there was a showing of sections of human skin taken from the human bodies in the Buchenwald concentration camp and preserved as ornaments. They were selected, these particular hapless victims, because of the tattooing which appeared on the skin. This exhibit, which we have here, is Exhibit Number USA-252. Attached to the exhibit is an extract of an official United States Army report describing the circumstances under which this exhibit was obtained, and that extract is set forth in Document 3420-PS, which I refer to in part. It is entitled:

"Mobile Field Interrogation Unit Number 2; PW Intelligence Bulletin: 13. Concentration Camp, Buchenwald. Preamble. The author of this account is PW Andra Pfaffenberger, ... 43 years old and of limited education. He is a butcher by trade . . ."

"(He Said) . . . All prisoners with tattooing on them were ordered to report to the dispensary. No one knew what the purpose was, but after the tattooed prisoners had been examined, the ones with the best and most artistic specimens were kept at the dispensary and then killed by injections administered by . . . a criminal prisoner. The corpses were then turned over to the pathological department where the desired pieces of tattooed skin were detached from the bodies and treated. The finished products were turned over to SS Standarten-fuhrer Koch's wife, who had them fashioned into lamp shades and other ornamental household articles. I myself saw such tattooed skins with various designs on them, such as 'Hansel and Gretel' . . . This work was done by a prisoner named Wernerbach."

The relics of obscenity were uncovered for all to see. Lampshades of all shapes and sizes defined inhumanity in a way that formal charges and readings could not. Then my father brought before the court the most compelling (and nauseating) exhibit to date in the trial. As he talked, eyes turned to a table in the front of the courtroom, on which a white sheet covered another piece of evidence.

"We do not wish to dwell on this pathological phase of the Nazi culture; but we do feel compelled to offer one additional exhibit, which is offered as Exhibit Number USA-254 . . ."

At this point, my father instructed a courtroom guard to remove the white sheet. There was a stunned silence. After a dramatic pause, my father continued: "[A] human head with the skull bone removed, shrunken, stuffed, and preserved. The Nazis had one of their many victims decapitated, after having had him hanged, apparently for fraternizing with a German woman, and fashioned this terrible ornament from his head."

This macabre evidence, obviously, caused a great stir in the courtroom. And soon thereafter, hundreds of newspapers around the world showed a photograph of my father holding the shrunken head. It is a gruesome sight, and the idea of using it as a model must have given him pause. But at that point in the trial, he wanted to show that beyond the numbers, beyond the stacks and stacks of documents, hidden in the vaults of memory was evidence for the ages of inhumanity.

In many ways, the tattooed skin and the shrunken head had the same effect on the courtroom as the atrocity film, but the court did not adjourn at that point. My father continued on — returning to the use of documents, but doing it in a way that would resonate with him for many years — by reducing an unfathomable crime to a comprehensible and grotesque mind picture. In speeches he gave after returning from Nuremberg, he often referred to Document 493-PS, Exhibit USA-251.

We have no accurate estimate of how many persons died in these concentration camps and perhaps none will ever be made [later in the trial, Rudolf Höss, the commandant of Auschwitz, admitted to between 2.5 million and 3 million murders there alone], but as the evidence already introduced before this Tribunal indicates, the Nazi conspirators were generally meticulous record keepers. But the records which they kept about concentration camps appear to have been quite incomplete. Perhaps [this] resulted from the indifference which the Nazis felt for the lives of their victims. But occasionally we find a date book or a set of index cards. For the most part, nevertheless, the victims apparently faded into an unrecorded death. Reference to a set of death books suggest at once the scale of concentration camp operations, and we refer now to Document Number 493-PS, as Exhibit Number USA-251. This exhibit is a set of seven books, the death ledger for the Mauthausen concentration camp. Each book has on its cover the word: "Totenbuch [Death Book] Mauthausen."

In these books were recorded the names of some of the inmates who died or were murdered in this camp, and the books cover the period from January of 1939 to April of 1945. They give the name, the place of birth, the assigned cause of death, and the time of death of each individual recorded. In addition each corpse is assigned a serial number, and adding up the total serial numbers for the five year period one arrives at the figure of 35,318.

An examination of the books is very revealing insofar as the camp's routine of death is concerned, and I invite the attention of the Tribunal to Volume 5 from Pages 568 to 582, a photostatic copy of which has been passed to the Tribunal. These pages cover death entries made for the 19th day of March 1945 between 15 minutes past 1 in the morning until 2 o'clock in the afternoon. In this space of 12 and three-quarter hours on these records, 203 persons are reported as having died. They were assigned serial numbers running from 8390 to 8593. The names of the dead are listed. And interestingly enough the victims are all recorded as having died of the same ailment — heart trouble. They died at brief intervals. They died in alphabetical order. The first who died was a man named Ackerman, who died at 1:15 a.m., and the last was a man named Zynger, who died at 2 o'clock in the afternoon.

I can only imagine my father that evening in conversation with his Nuremberg housemates. He must have felt complex emotions — satisfaction as a lawyer for a job well done, revulsion as a human being.

My older siblings remember that he was much changed when he came home for Christmas — and not simply the color of his hair. People would come up to him in restaurants and congratulate him on his work, which they had read about in the local newspapers. He seemed, however, uncharacteristically subdued, as if he didn't want to talk much about Nuremberg. I suspect my father had conflicting feelings, like a man taking an R&R from a war, knowing he was still in the thick of battle and not knowing when he would return for good or what scars he would bring home with him.

When he went back to Nuremberg, my father was promoted to executive trial counsel and in time ran the day-to-day trial for the U.S.

prosecution, particularly when Justice Jackson was away. My father's letters show his growing impatience for the trial to proceed and to be able to do as much of the cross-examinations of the defendants as possible. Jackson intended to spread that responsibility around, so my father had only a few, but they were memorable.

I am struck, for example, by exchanges he had in the courtroom during the testimony of Alfred Rosenberg, during the session that examined his offenses as Reichsminister of the Eastern Occupied Territories.

From Sidney Gruson's report in the *New York Times*: "Admission after admission fell from the lips of Alfred Rosenberg, the Nazi philosopher, today as the American prosecutor, Thomas Dodd, destroyed his self-portrait as a kindly benefactor and forced him to admit responsibility for the Nazi regime . . . Rosenberg squirmed under Dodd's cross-examination."

A small sample follows from the April 17, 1946, official transcript, as my father attempted to get Rosenberg to accept responsibility for his actions — a struggle that was typical at the trial. My father was good at setting a trap, a key element of cross-examination.

MR. DODD: With respect to your attitude towards the Jewish people, in your Frankfurt speech you suggested that they all had to leave Europe and Germany, did you not?

ROSENBERG: This phrase —

MR. DODD: All you need to say is yes or no. Did you make that suggestion or not in your speech in Frankfurt in 1938 —

ROSENBERG: Yes, but I certainly can't answer yes or no on an incorrect quotation.

MR. DODD: I do not think you need to explain anything at all. I merely asked you whether you said that in Frankfurt in your Party Day speech.

ROSENBERG: Yes, essentially that is correct.

MR. DODD: Now, in your Party Day speech to which you made reference yesterday, you said you used harsh language about the Jews. In those days you were objecting to the fact that they were in certain professions, I suppose, and things of that character. Is that a fair statement?

ROSENBERG: I said yesterday that in two speeches I demanded a chivalrous solution and equal treatment, and I said then the foreign nations would not accuse us of discriminating against the Jewish people.

MR. DODD: Yes, very well. Did you ever talk about the extermination of the Jews?

ROSENBERG: I have not in general spoken about the extermination of the Jews in the sense of this term. One has to consider the words. The term "extermination" has been used by the British Prime Minister —

MR. DODD: You will refer to the words. You just tell me now whether you ever said it or not? You said that did you not?

ROSENBERG: Not in a single speech in that sense.

MR. DODD: I understand the sense. Did you ever talk about it with anybody as a matter of State Police or Party policy, about the extermination of the Jews?

ROSENBERG: In a conference with the führer there was once an open discussion on this question apropos of an intended speech which was not delivered. The sense of it was that now a war was going on and that the threat which had been mentioned should not be discussed again. That speech was not delivered.

MR. DODD: When was it you were going to deliver that speech? Approximately what was the date?

ROSENBERG: In December, 1941.

MR. DODD: Then you had written into your speech remarks about the extermination of Jews, hadn't you? Answer that yes or no.

ROSENBERG: I have said already that that word does not have the sense which you attribute to it.

MR. DODD: I will come to the word and the meaning of it. I am asking you, did you not use the word or the term extermination of the Jews in the speech which you were prepared to make in the Sportpalast in December of 1941? Now, you can answer that pretty simply.

ROSENBERG: That may be, but I do not remember. I myself did not prepare the phrasing of the draft. In which form it was expressed I can no longer say.

MR. DODD: Well then, perhaps we can help you on that. I will ask you be shown Document 1517-PS. It becomes Exhibit USA-824.

(Witness handed document.)

Now, this is also a memorandum of yours written by you about a discussion you had with Hitler on 14 December 1941, and it is quite clear from the first paragraph that you and Hitler were discussing a speech which you were to deliver in the Sportpalast in Berlin and if you will look at the second paragraph, you will find these words:

"I remarked on the Jewish question that the comments about the New York Jews must perhaps be changed somewhat after the conclusion (of matters in the East). I took the standpoint not to speak of the extermination *(Ausrottung)* of the Jews. The führer affirmed this and said that they had thrust the war upon us and that they had brought the destruction; it is no wonder if the results would strike them first."

From there, it became very difficult for Rosenberg. First, he tried to argue that the word *Ausrottung* has no connection with extermination. My father asked Rosenberg: "Are you very serious in pressing this apparent inability of yours to agree with me about this word or are you trying to kill time? Don't you know that there are plenty of people in this courtroom who speak German and who agree that that word does mean to wipe out, to extirpate?"

And so it went, as my father presented documents about Eastern European exterminations that were clearly initialed by Rosenberg, though the defendant in pitiful fashion tried to argue that the top of the capital *R* looked different from the way he usually wrote the letter.

Rosenberg tried this tack: Yes, his subordinate might have known about such exterminations, but he did not. When he had dug this hole for himself, my father got Rosenberg to admit that five people who directly reported to him had full knowledge of the exterminations because they had helped to carry them out. Finally, Rosenberg said, "Yes. They knew about a certain number of liquidations of Jews. That I admit, and they have told me so, and if they didn't, I have heard it from other sources."

A month later at Nuremberg, my father's cross-examination pounded away similarly at Walther Funk, who headed the Reichsbank and played other key roles in the Nazi regime.

Over the course of an intense day of testimony on May 7, 1946, Funk, known as a bon vivant who smoked cigars and drank expensive scotch, was reduced to a coughing, helpless soul after being persistently pounded and trapped.

My father got Funk to admit that he was the one who named what later became known as Kristallnacht, "the night of broken glass," and much more.

The impetus for Kristallnacht came from an incident in Paris. Seventeen-year-old Zindel Grynszpan, then living with an uncle, was outraged that his family members had been expelled from Germany, their possessions confiscated, and that they were forced to go to Poland. He went to the German embassy in Paris with the intent of shooting the ambassador. When he learned the ambassador was not there, young Grynszpan shot Third Secretary Ernst von Rath instead. Von Rath died two days later, on November 9. The Nazis used this opportunity, the murder of a low-ranking official, to intensify their campaign of terror against Jews by urging citizens to seek revenge any way they could. The intent was to cast this uprising as a product of spontaneous public outrage — though the government had been behind it from the start.

On the nights of November 9 and 10, 1938, mobs throughout Germany and the territories it had acquired through force and intimidation attacked Jews in their homes and on the street, in their places of work and at worship. More than one thousand synagogues were burned and ninety-six people killed. About seventy-five hundred Jewish businesses were destroyed, cemeteries and schools were vandalized, and more than thirty thousand Jews were arrested and sent to concentration camps.

Funk took part in the framing of Kristallnacht as a natural outcry in response to the murder in Paris. My father's job that day in Nuremberg was to set the record straight on the issue. The transcript from May 7 contains the following:

MR. DODD: . . . When did you first learn that the uprisings of November 1938 were not spontaneous?

FUNK: On the morning of 9 November, on my way from my home to the

Ministry, I saw for the first time what had taken place during the night. Before that I had not had the slightest hint that such excesses and terror measures had been planned.

MR. DODD: I think you misunderstand me. I did not ask you when you first came to know about the uprisings: I asked you when you first learned that they were not spontaneous; when you first learned that they were instigated and planned by somebody else.

FUNK: I only found out about that later.

MR. DODD: Well, how much later?

FUNK: I believe very much later. Later on there was much discussion about this matter and it was never clear just who had been the instigator of these measures of terror and violence and where the order had originated. We knew that it came from Munich. We had learned that in the meantime on 9 November; but, whether it was Goebbels or Himmler, and to what extent the führer himself participated in this measure, I was never able to find out clearly. From my telephone conversation with Goebbels, which I mentioned today, one thing was clear: The führer must have known about this matter, for he told me that the führer had decreed, and Göring also said this, that the Jews were completely to be eliminated from economic life. From this I had to conclude that the führer himself knew about this matter.

MR. DODD: Now from that telephone conversation we can also see one other thing. You knew that Goebbels had started this business, did you not, and that was the day after it happened? You knew it was not spontaneous and that is why you called up Goebbels and got after him; is that not so?

FUNK: Yes.

MR. DODD: How many days later did you make that inflammatory speech about what should be done to the Jews? About six days afterwards, did you not? I am referring to the one that was published in the *Frankfurter Zeitung.*

FUNK: Yes, to begin with . . .

MR. DODD: And in that speech you tried to make it appear to the public that that was a spontaneous uprising, did you not?

FUNK: Yes.

MR. DODD: That was not true, was it?

FUNK: I did not know that at the time. At that time I still believed that it was really something favored by large elements of the population. Very much later I found out that routine machinery had been put in motion.

MR. DODD: Are you telling this Tribunal now that on the morning of your telephone call to Goebbels, when you in effect blamed him for these uprisings, you were not well aware then that he had started it? Is that your position?

FUNK: At that time I did not know who had started this regime of terror and how it had been carried through; that was entirely new to me.

MR. DODD: If you did not know who started it, you knew that somebody started it and that it was not spontaneous?

FUNK: Yes.

MR. DODD: And still in your speech of 15 November you tried to make it appear to the public that it was just an uprising on the part of the German people, did you not?

FUNK: I based that on the attempted assassination of — I do not know who he was; some attaché in Paris — and actually the attempt caused much agitation. There is no doubt of it.

MR. DODD: Now I think you understand my question, Witness. You said on that occasion, you used these words: "The fact that the last violent explosion of the indignation of the German people because of a criminal Jewish attack against the German people took place," and so on, and you went on. You were trying to make it appear there that this was a spontaneous reaction of the German people, and I insist that you knew better and had known it for some days, had you not?

FUNK: But I did not know that that is what took place. I admit that I knew that an impulse had come from some office or other.

MR. DODD: Well, all right. When did you coin the expression "crystal week"?

FUNK: Crystal week?

MR. DODD: Yes.

FUNK: Yes, I did use these words once in connection with this action.

MR. DODD: You coined the phrase.

FUNK: Because much was shattered.

MR. DODD: You are the fellow who started that expression. You are the man, are you not? That was your expression?

FUNK: Yes, I used it.

MR. DODD: And you were using it — because you made this *Frankfurter Zeitung* speech?

FUNK: I once characterized that action with that term, it is true, because much had been shattered.

Indeed. The shattering of European Jewry could be traced to Kristall-nacht if not for the fact that anti-Semitism in Germany was by then an unstoppable phenomenon leading to its ultimate and tragic end.

My father was not finished with Funk. After the defendant denied knowing anything about the "human" deposits in his institution, my father pounded away at him.

MR. DODD: When did you start doing business with the SS, Mr. Funk?

FUNK: Business with the SS? I have never done that.

MR. DODD: Yes, sir. Business with the SS. Are you sure about that? I ask you again, sir. When did you start business with the SS?

Funk admitted that he learned of SS deposits but assumed they were routine. He said he was aware that the SS had taken gold watches off con-centration camp prisoners and that all Germans were ordered to turn in their gold coins. This, he argued, would have been the essence of what was brought into the vaults.

My father, having sprung his trap, then produced an affidavit from Funk's deputy, Emil Puhl, which indicated Funk was entirely aware of all of the contents of the SS deposits: the diamonds, the pearls, and the most intimate items stripped from the doomed Jews of Europe. With Funk still desperately clinging to his hopeless defense, my father asked another ques-tion: "Just a minute. Were you in the habit of depositing gold teeth in the Reichsbank?"

As the testimony proceeded, as my father produced for the court documentary evidence of Reichsbank deposits, Funk crumbled under the duress. As my father said in one of his last questions, "The trouble is, there was blood on this gold, was there not, and you knew it since 1942?" Funk left the stand a broken man.

I could turn to many other examples from the transcripts of my father's work at Nuremberg. Suffice it to say that when he looked back on it, he considered his tenure there as the single most important body of work he produced in his lifetime. He pointed with pride to the trial's outcome — that in trying nearly two dozen defendants for such horrible crimes, distinctions were made between them, and they received a variety of sentences. This was a testimony to the trial's fairness and thoroughness.

The experience of Nuremberg certainly shaped and fueled his subsequent pursuits. This was particularly so when he was elected to the House and then the Senate, where he built a reputation as a crusader for human rights. Often this manifested in his strong anti-Communist stance, a position that grew out of his work at the tribunal.

He told a reporter in 1963, "I learned of the desperation and terror of hundreds of thousands of Russian war prisoners and slave laborers held by the Nazis whom, through ignorance, were returned against their will to the Soviet authorities. I am still tormented by accounts of mass suicides in which men slashed their wrists with tin cans and women jumped with their children from upper-story windows, rather than face return to Russia."

When Soviet premier Nikita Khrushchev was invited to tour the United States in 1959 — the first time a Soviet head of state received such an invitation — my father objected. He stood on the Senate floor to remind his colleagues, "Khrushchev rose as a hangman of the Ukraine. In a single year 400,000 men, women and children were murdered under his direction. I have documentation here, if anyone wants to see it." He also reminded fellow senators of the premier's role in subduing the Hungarian rebellion in 1956 when he earned the title of the "Butcher of Budapest."

My father's career in Congress was rich in purpose and achievement. He further pressed his strong anti-Communist views and was a champion of universal human rights. He fought on behalf of the poor — for minimum wage hikes, for higher Social Security benefits, and for Medicare. After his death, the *Hartford Courant* editorialized, in part:

> Many of the crusades upon which Mr. Dodd embarked first focused nation-wide attention upon conditions and issues that were to become our priorities. Juvenile delinquency, drug-abuse, civil rights crime and gun controls were among these . . . Thus he lived, a man committed to public life, proud of his patriotism and proud to serve his country, selecting what he thought was right, no matter what the party affiliation of its other proponents, and giving no quarter until he had seen the cause through to the end.

Unfortunately, the *Courant* was also obliged to refer to the darkest days — days that my brothers and sisters and I still struggle with. Days that we are convinced were the reason for our father's untimely death and, a year later, our mother's as well.

In 1967, Thomas J. Dodd was censured by his fellow senators for alleged misuse of campaign funds. He was charged with no crime and broke no law. But a frenzy stirred by muckraking columnists Drew Pearson and Jack Anderson focused on what they saw as inappropriate use of donations. Senate colleagues abandoned my father. He always argued that he had done nothing wrong. But the job that he adored was gone. Early in 1970, my father abandoned any hope of receiving the Democratic nomination for his third term. He announced his intention to run as an independent. Connecticut Democrats chose their candidate; my father's independent bid failed. He came home to Old Lyme hurt in many ways and died six months later.

After the election, he put on a brave front. I remember Sue Nicholls, a reporter from the *New Haven Register,* coming to interview him at home. She asked him whether he would it do all over again — this public life — if he knew that the end would be so painful? Yes, he answered, he would. He explained that doctors have only so many patients, lawyers only a certain number of clients they can help, but a person who holds public office can change for the better a great many lives.

All of this is grist, certainly, for the full biography that may one day be written. I know that at the end of his life, he still had dreams, and still had lessons to teach us.

My father died on May, 24, 1971, in what might be called a stately and dignified fashion. He sat at the dining room table in Old Lyme telling my mother an engaging story. And, in the middle of the story, his heart gave out.

My siblings and I think of the many blessings of his life and work— evidence of them remain everywhere in our respective homes. There is no doubt that a certain heartbreak about our father will always be with us, but there remains so much to celebrate in the way of his achievements.

On April 24, 1946, a few months before the trial ended, Justice Jackson wrote a letter to President Harry Truman in which he had this to say about his thirty-eight-year-old executive trial counsel at Nuremberg:

> I would like to mention a young man . . . who has done extremely creditable work here. He is Tom Dodd, assistant United States attorney in Connecticut, who, I am told, is being looked upon favorably by the Democratic leaders of his state. He has done such excellent work that I should have put him in charge in my absence had I been returning to the States, and I think you are apt to hear of him in the future. In any place for which you are ever in need of a first-class legal mind, enriched by industry and backed by sound character, his name is worth bearing in mind.

Subsequent to this, my father was awarded a Presidential Certificate and the Medal of Freedom, the nation's highest civilian honor. The citation of the latter:

> Thomas J. Dodd, American Civilian, for exceptionally meritorious achievement which aided the United States in the prosecution of the

war against the enemy in Continental Europe, as Vice Chairman, Board of Review, and later as Executive Trial Counsel, Office of the United States Chief of Counsel for the Prosecution of Axis Criminality at Nürnberg, Germany . . . He displayed outstanding professional skill in directing the courtroom strategy through the vital and important defense phase of the trial of major Axis war criminals before the International Military Tribunal and in conducting brilliant cross-examinations of the majority of the defendants for whom the United States assumed responsibility. His experienced judgment in trial technique, his sound grasp of legal issues, and his tact and diplomacy contributed in large measure to the harmonious and successful cooperation of the staffs of the different prosecuting powers and to the successful operation of the International Military Tribunal.

Even so, in some ways there is an achievement that stands out above all others that he left for his six children — the love story that he wrote, on the pages that follow, to the woman he adored.

PART TWO

The Letters

Grace, my dearest one, Here I am in the dead city of Nürnberg . . .

—Thomas J. Dodd, August 14, 1945

Eyes That I Could Not Meet

THOMAS J. DODD, A FEDERAL PROSECUTOR of espionage and civil rights cases, is assigned to the support staff in the trial of twenty-two men charged with the gravest crimes in history. In the first of more than three hundred letters he'll send to his wife, Grace, Dodd describes London, where the case is being prepared by the Allies. Eager to learn all he can, he tours a devastated city — "the East End is a desolate ruin." The prosecution's plans, he soon decides, are also in ruin. Dodd is also introduced to a "colonels' clique" that has managed so far to make a mess of the indictments. He also gets his first glimpse of Soviet legal participation and fears the Soviets will "put on a farce." Planning continues in Paris, which he tells Grace is "trying hard to be gay." So is Dodd. He is discouraged by his low standing and by the simple tasks he is given by the brass. His mood is further darkened by the separation from his wife, though it appears it will only be for a few weeks. He can go home, he assumes, when his assigned interrogations are done and begin practicing law or starting a life in public service. He attends the trial of Marshal Philippe Pétain, head of the Fascist-controlled Vichy government, a sad affair that foreshadows what he will experience at Nuremberg. What follows are key excerpts from Dodd's letters home.

July 28, 1945
London, England

My Dearest,

If my letters seem lengthy and detailed, you will understand that first of all I am trying to string out my time with you. I consider it such — for while you are in my mind at all times during the day, at letter writing time I have you alone, with no interruptions.

Thursday morning, standing in the main portal of the Union Station in Washington, you made a memorable picture for me as I gazed out the taxicab window until the dimness of the dawn light blotted your loveliness out.

When I arrived at the Air Transport Command, we were briefed for about one half hour — on the use of life rafts. At 7:45 a.m., after some delay caused by a defective automatic pilot, we left on a cargo plane, heavily loaded with pounds of mail and freight, two former German professors, two Air Transport Command officials, a soldier, and the crew. The trip to Newfoundland was rough at times, particularly over eastern Connecticut and Rhode Island. We had box lunches — two sandwiches, soggy doughnuts, hot coffee and a candy bar. We arrived at 1:45 EST, and after a good meal at the officers' mess, refueling and checking of the plane and with a new crew, we left Newfoundland at 2:30 p.m. for Prestwick, Scotland. The trip was smooth, the day clear. We saw the sun set and the moon rise almost together. Then darkness fell and the North Atlantic rolled and pitched some seven thousand feet beneath us under a brilliant moon. The captain of the crew — Trimble — advised us that we would be twelve hours en route and it developed into just about that. Around midnight all the passengers excepting [one named] Houston and I fell asleep on stretchers. We sat up and talked. Sometimes the flight clerk joined in, sometimes the radio officer, for a few words. The flight clerk was a sober youngster from Harlan, Kentucky. Has been flying back and forth for a long time. I looked upon him as living proof of the safety of air travel to Europe until he told me in sour tones that he wanted to get a new job. I said,

"This one looks interesting." He looked at me and said, "Yes, if the plane stays up." I said, "Well, nothing can happen and if it does we can bet on the rafts and we are to be picked up—the officers in Washington told me that." He answered, "Oh, yeah!—did they tell you about the litter ship that went down off Iceland and they didn't even find a trace of it, or about any of the others?" For the next hour he regaled me with stories of lost planes and the improbability of survival.

The sun came up beautifully about 4:30 a.m., London time, and the radio officer came back to tell me of Churchill's defeat[1] (no connection between the two in my mind).

At 5:45 London time on Friday morning, July 27, 1945, I first set eyes on beautiful Ireland, specifically Londonderry—the green fields, the white cottages, the lakes and the streams. We passed over Ulster and it too stood out, beautiful, beneath us. Then the turbulent Irish sea and the coast of Scotland. At 7:45 a.m., we arrived at Prestwick. After [we passed through] British customs, we had a good English breakfast. I had exchanged my American dollars first before eating and so I had my first experience with the coin of the realm in paying two shillings six pence for the meal.

At ten o'clock we got on the plane for Bovingdon airport—some twenty five miles from London. The trip took us over Liverpool and some of the bomb damage could be seen from the air.

At noon we arrived at Bovingdon and immediately left by bus for London. The left hand side of the road gave me a queer sensation for only a short while. We rode through what appeared to be a typical English countryside with neat cottages, hedges, gardens, many bicycles and little inns. At 1:30 we arrived at our terminal on Quebec Street. A taxi to our headquarters at 49 Mount Street and the trip was over. I met Gordon Dean[2] at once. He had not received my letter and was sur-

1. Churchill lost to Labour's Clement Atlee. Churchill created many political enemies by opposing health care and education proposals, and the public seemed to have more confidence in Labour's plan to rebuild the country.
2. Dean was Dodd's colleague in the Department of Justice and served as Chief Prosecutor Robert H. Jackson's press spokesman in Nuremberg. He later became chair of the Atomic Energy Commission.

prised to see me. He told me that Brien McMahon[3] had written to him urging the selection of one Sam Kaufman, a New York lawyer, but strangely enough had not mentioned my appointment!

I am living in a very good hotel, the Cumberland, at the Marble Arch entrance to Hyde Park. As soon as I had my bags in the room I took a good bath. Gordon Dean and I had dinner together. We talked about many things — including his separation from his former law partners. After dinner I retired promptly at 9 p.m. and did not awaken until 11 a.m. this Saturday morning.

I ate lunch in the hotel, and then hired a cab — and the hotel doorman, by way of introduction maybe or perhaps in giving certain information in code, or even in polite acknowledgment of the six pence I put in his palm, told the cabbie, "This is a right good 'gov'nor' you have, boy." The cabbie beamed — got out and put the top down.

First I visited St. Paul's — saw the damage done to that beautiful edifice. I could smell smoke — or more accurately that after-fire odor that one detects in a building that has burned — this after five years! Later in the day I noticed the same odor in the ruins of the old city, in Guild Hall, in London's terribly afflicted East End. My dear, the damage is appalling — the rockets and buzz bombs did an awesome job. The cabbie pointed out places hit only a few months ago where hundreds died. The East End is a desolate ruin — miles of it — the poor lived there by the thousands. Many are still there in partly demolished areas, some in little prefabricated huts put up by the government. They stared at the cab from eyes that I could not meet. [They were] attired in clothing that made me wince. So many buildings are destroyed over all of London it will be years before they can be rebuilt. Stores are open with boarded up show windows — on every street there is wreckage of one kind or another. I tell you these English really took it. The air raid shelters are still here — England is still a war stricken country. As I rode through the destruction of the East End, I saw many political posters

3. McMahon, a Democrat, was elected to the U.S. Senate from Connecticut in 1944.

urging the election of this or that man to Parliament. Some said "Support Churchill, Vote National." One said "Elect Phil Piratin — Communist." He won![4]

I sighed at the ruins of St. Clement's Church, the destruction of St. Mary's, the cemeteries that were bombed leaving blasted monuments all a heap of stones with "here lies" showing a curiously macabre exterior every now and then. I was sad to see the shell of the Guild Hall library originally built in 1299 and the few stones that remain of a chapel that men worked on in 1425. The damage to Parliament is being repaired. Even Petticoat Lane — that legendary street — has its terrible scars. Westminster Abbey was wonderfully preserved and as I walked there I found a monument to a man born in Norwich, Connecticut. I enjoyed the Abbey — the resting place of kings and the great. I tarried in the poets' corner.

The cabbie showed me 10 Downing Street, the Admiralty, the War Office. We drove on London Bridge and on Waterloo, too. We paused at the Nelson monument at Trafalgar Square and rode down the Stand, to Piccadilly, and through Mayfair. We stopped at Berkeley Square — where they say the nightingales sing. I couldn't hear them. I didn't expect to. I never will until you and I sit in that park together.

I returned to the hotel about 5:30 p.m. and rested until 7 when I ate dinner in the officer's mess at Grosvenor House. [Then] I strolled in Hyde Park and listened to speakers. There was a great crowd around the Catholic Evidence Guild[5] speaker — a few feet away a very charming Irishman named Murphy kept the attention of hundreds while he condemned Jew-baiting. Another told a large group about the evils of free masonry. Another thumped for Communists. Still another condemned it and so it went, with vast numbers of people listening, heckling,

4. Piratin was one of two Communists elected in 1945. At the time the Communist Party had about 60,000 members in Great Britain (compared with 800,000 in France and 1.7 million in Italy). Piratin and Willie Gallacher were defeated in 1950.
5. The Catholic Evidence Guild was founded in 1918 and developed "the mass production of competent outdoor exponents of Catholicism."

applauding—what a nation!—and they show what they have been through. Their clothing is so shabby—on men and women. The lack of cosmetics is at once noticed. I really feel ashamed when these people stare, for they recognize an American by the quality of his clothing. Even the best restaurants have little food. It will be a long hard pull for Britain.

So, thus runs my story up to now. I am happy because I know you will be well and contented until I return. Give the children my most tender and affectionate salute. I have no new address as yet—but the mail situation is desperate so your letters may not reach me for weeks.

My darling, do take good care of yourself—for I need you so badly and so do the children.[6] This old heart of mine is just filled up with the deepest love for you.

Tom

London, England
July 29, 1945

Grace, my dearest one,

After breakfast today I went to Petticoat Lane to see the Sunday morning spectacle. It defies description. Fishmongers, dry goods, furs, shoes, jewelry, herring, bands playing, auctions—a strange and exotic place, comparable to nothing else in the world.

At high noon I was at holy mass at Westminster Cathedral, a remarkable church—Byzantine architecture. I forgot to say that I met a young New Zealand soldier on the way to church—one Frank Griffin—intelligent and obviously well bred, from Auckland. After mass we had lunch together and I was fascinated by his stories of life in New Zealand—the bigotries and the hardships that Catholics have had to face.

6. At this point, there are five children: Tom, age ten; Carolyn, age nine; Jeremy, age six, Martha, age four, and Christopher, fourteen months. Nicholas was born in 1948.

In the evening I had some sandwiches and coffee — which reminds me I must tell you how scarce and how expensive food is here. One peach costs $1.20. A few plums $2, a few — very few — raw potatoes, 60 cents. Everything is rationed but prices are crazy. Oranges are not to be had.

Somehow I am terribly aware, already, of the blessings that we have in America. We are very fortunate, my dearest, fortunate not only by virtue of goods and materials, but mostly because we have a certain indescribable freedom from the worries and the fears that are a part and parcel of this old world. It would be good for all of us if every American could spend one weekend abroad. I am confused about the newer arrivals in America — I mean those who find so many faults. What strange people. What lack of appreciation. Oh how I shall relish telling them off! And then too I think of our native malcontents — the Roosevelt haters. Well, today's London *Times* says the new government will likely take over the steel industry, the railroads, etc. Can't you picture the coupon clippers at Watch Hill[7] if such a proposal ever appeared in the press back home? We are now the only really conservative nation in the world. I am preaching — but if you were here you would do likewise.

Tonight I miss you dearly — your picture is before me — your truly beautiful face, your wonderful eyes. Do preserve it all just as I left it until I am home and you are in my arms.

Tom

London, England
July 31, 1945

Grace, my dearest one,

It has occurred to me that air mail postage is really too much for a daily letter. If you do not hear from me for a few days you will know that letters are in regular mail.

Yesterday it drizzled a bit and I felt that I was in London after all.

7. **A summer resort on Rhode Island's shoreline.**

I went to the office on Mount Street and sat in on a conference between Commander [James B.] Donovan,[8] some field photo officers and Dr. Jacoby. It seemed very silly to me as the whole matter could have been settled in five minutes — some nonsense about how many stenographers were to be asked for. The field photo men Majors Patterson and Hamilton of the Marine Corps have the responsibility for reviewing captured German film and also are required to take some new photos. Jacoby is supposed to examine the captured film for the purpose of identifying such Nazis as may be in the pictures. Jacoby says he was district attorney in Berlin — he doesn't look it to me. He is a refugee and like [his colleague] Dr. Valentin, I fear he is more interested in returning to Germany with some authority than he is in getting this job done. Some of these continentals are impossible. Valentin — the bearded, refugee professor — upbraided a colonel because there was some delay in obtaining room space.

I had lunch yesterday at the Connaught with Lt. Col. Robert Alcorn. A nice enough young man who is a little cocky and a bit puffed up about having studied at Cambridge and in France. A climber, too, I think who has the habit of referring to Junius Morgan[9] and other money bags with an offhand way. Commander Donovan joined us and we talked at some length about the FBI. Donovan told me that Hoover has been very envious of the O.S.S. [Office of Strategic Services] and has on one occasion given a confidential report to the papers. The report was the one to Roosevelt on the need for a U.S. Intelligence Service abroad after this war is over.

In the afternoon, I met Col. John Harlan Amen in Gordon Dean's office. I am to work for Amen in Paris. He is in charge of interrogations. At five o'clock, Amen, Dean and I went to Dean's apartment on Berkeley Square for cocktails. We had a long chat and I am pleased

8. Two Donovans are prominent at Nuremberg: Commander James B. Donovan, who served in the Office of Strategic Services (O.S.S.), predecessor of the CIA, and General William J. "Wild Bill" Donovan, who headed the O.S.S.
9. Junius Spencer Morgan, an American banker and financier, was the father of J. P. Morgan.

because I am to work with Amen. We got along very well. [He is] the former Special Prosecutor in Brooklyn, N.Y. Gordon and I had dinner at Grosvenor Square and afterwards we met [U.S. chief prosecutor, Justice Robert H.] Jackson, his secretary and military aide. We saw a preview of a one-reeler that will be shown in the theaters at home. It is intended to give the public an idea of the purpose of these trials. Jackson is a very human man and a very warm man.

After the showing of the one-reeler we then saw some captured German films of the invasion of Poland and some German propaganda film against Jews, also one about the Russian Kharkov trials[10] — which is to say the least fantastic, certainly insofar as jurisprudence is concerned. Afterwards, Gordon and I went back to his apartment and talked until 1 a.m.

On Tuesday I arose late and after a visit to the office made arrangements to see Colonel Amen again. He asked me to get reservations on the plane for both of us tomorrow afternoon — for Paris. After lunch at the officer's mess in Grosvenor House, the Scotland Yard man in the office arranged for me to see the Bow Street Court, the oldest in London. I went there to be greeted by Inspector Rogers, a handsome Englishman. Sir Bertram Watson, the chief magistrate of London, presided and I heard a few interesting cases. Give me the U.S. — with our "Yes, your honor" — in preference to "Yes, m'Lord."

[Later] at Gordon Dean's invitation, I joined him and a Major Lawrence Coleman, military aide to Justice Jackson, at Gordon's apartment where we had cocktails and conversation. Coleman is a boor. He made some remarks about "these damn civilians who come over here when the shooting is over." So I made some point about the "tin" soldiers who to avoid conscription grabbed administrative commissions.

Coleman, Donovan and Alcorn are all from O.S.S. and certainly they are of a type: supercilious, arrogant, social climbing clowns with military rank. General Donovan is a good society Republican, so they

10. **A Soviet military court sentenced three officials of the Kharkov Gestapo to death by hanging.**

say. Very Republican, very "good family" — i.e., political, social, wealthy. What a story can be written on that crowd, if half of what I hear is true. And my own experience thus far makes me believe it. The poor, obscure G.I. boys who really fought this war and won it will never get the credit with this mob of ballroom military men on the loose — unless someone spills the beans.

Much gossip is abroad about friction between the U.S., Great Britain, France and Russia over these trials. The truth is there is no trouble between U.S., Britain and France — but the Russians are just holding up the whole proceeding. They are impossible, in my opinion. I do not know the details but I do know they are not cooperative on this problem so far. I believe they want to put on another Russian farce for a trial. If that happens, I go home, and promptly! The English appointed their chief counsel 21 days after the U.S. appointed Jackson (who was the first to be appointed). The French followed soon after. Thus far no one has been appointed for Russia. Our people meet with certain Russian representatives but nothing happens. When representatives of the United Nations went to Nürnberg[11] to look it over as a possible site for the trial only the Russians failed to make the trip.

Well, so it goes. Tomorrow night I will be in Paris. So, my dearest, good-bye for now. My love to you and the children.

Devotedly,
Tom

P.S. No mail from you as yet.

August 3, 1945
Paris, France

Grace, my dearest one,

I left London Tuesday at 8 p.m. and arrived at Orly field just outside of Paris at 10:45 p.m., Paris time. I rode a bus into town

11. **Dodd used the traditional German spelling of the city's name.**

and visited Colonel Amen in his rooms at the Ritz where I met a Colonel Williams and a Major Monigan. I was taken to the Powers Hotel on Rue Manbourg where I have very poor quarters. Everything is gold braid here — best rooms, best of everything [for the military] — and you know I just cannot stomach military protocol. Oh, I know the necessity in the service. But I just feel that any American is as good as another and the temporary need for rank and all that rank implies does not rid me of that thought. Many of these military men are splendid fellows — some of them are little men in big uniforms. Ho hum! We will saw wood and do our job.

Yesterday a.m., I came to the office, 7 Rue Presbourg, met some of the staff—all military—got located and have been doing some background reading. I share offices with a Colonel Brundage from Chicago—a fine man, a lawyer. I asked him if he knew Joe Guimond.[12] He said, "He is only one block away." So we had dinner with Joe last night. I was glad to see him—he has gained weight—but is the same old Joe. I shall see him tonight. Neil Andrews[13] is here. We compared observations—we are in complete agreement about the gold braid. Please do not misunderstand this—Colonel Amen, Colonel Storey, Colonel Gill, Colonel Brundage—I must say are top-flight people. There is a general gold braid atmosphere about the office that no working lawyer likes. Also, I feel that I have been really "added on" to this staff. And, after some years of preparing and trying cases, it is a new experience to have some officer of doubtful legal ability act like Chief Justice Stone.[14]

I eat my meals in LeDoucet restaurant, an officers' mess, near the hotel. I am surprised at my French. I have discovered more of a vocabulary than I knew I had.

12. Guimond was married to one of Grace Murphy Dodd's old school friends.
13. Neil Andrews was a colleague of Dodd's at the U.S. Attorney's Office.
14. Harlan Fiske Stone was appointed chief justice by Franklin D. Roosevelt in 1941.

Paris is crowded. Prices are impossible. Soap is unknown. Both pairs of shoes are killing me — I should have taken your advice about shoes. I would be happier. But that is all on the unpleasant side. Paris is beautiful — romantic, fascinating. I shall see the city this weekend.

I am dying to get a letter from you — but so far not a word. I know it is delayed somewhere. I do have your picture and my thoughts of you. Give my love to the children and keep your share for me.

Tom

APO 887
C/o Postmaster, NY City
Paris, France
August 4, 1945

Grace, my most beloved one,

Please forgive pencil but I am anxious to get this letter off on time.

It was good to see Neil Andrews — he has been away. Neil and I are fellow civilians, of course, and we are in complete agreement about our observations with respect to the present and future. We both think things will shape up eventually. We think, too, that even a pair of civilian trial lawyers may be found useful before we go home. For after all, at some point, someone will have to do a real lawyer job — I presume.

Paris is so crowded. No taxicabs at all — a few horse carriages at fabulous prices. There are some automobiles on the street — not many — and very few after dark. Some of the trucks are wood burning and one gets the odor of burning wood all the time on the streets. The French are poor-looking people — that is, on the average — but then too there are plenty of very wealthy people here. It is curious how some remain rich through thick and thin — through German occupation, through the war and widespread suffering and impoverishment. Some made money when the Germans were here. All Americans have to buy French francs at two cents each. The French and all others exchange for one quarter cent each, which is the real value. There is terrible inflation. A brief ride in a carriage costs 800 francs. So it is quite a burden for us. Eating is absolutely prohibitive except in the officers mess — at 13 francs a meal — and the food there is very good. I have been worried about my new shoes. The brown ones I have had stretched and they are a little better. I may buy some new ones at the Officers Post Exchange — just to be comfortable.

Around the Arc de Triomphe there was heavy fighting one year ago. The hotel in which I am living was, like all others, occupied by German officers — not so long ago — so you will understand what I mean when I say "There are still scars on Paris." Chunks of some buildings show it physically. But a deeper, spiritual scar shows everywhere.

My dearest, I have no mail yet and I am so anxious to hear from you — it will arrive soon, I trust.

The weather in Paris is beautiful. It reminds me of mid-September at home — of trips with you, of walks on Sundays, of your lovely face, your magnificent soul — and therefore, beautiful as Paris and the weather of Paris is this August, I shall remember it mostly because I was lonesome in Paris for my darling Grace.

Best love to *mes enfants*.

Tom

August 5, 1945
Paris, France

Grace, my beloved one,

I arose this morning about 9:30 and met Colonel Brundage at 10:30 a.m. and we attended mass at Notre Dame. The building has a few scars as a result of the fighting around it a year ago — but they are only marks which do not permanently mar the structure. After mass we walked along the Seine — visited some of the well known book stalls and arrived at our hotel about 1 p.m. After lunch, a Mr. R. W. Jacobson of Chicago, an engineer whom I met on the London–Paris plane, called on me and invited me to go sightseeing with him in his jeep. His driver, a young soldier, was Tom White of Philadelphia. We visited Napoleon's Tomb in Les Invalides, the Pantheon where Voltaire and others are buried, the Tracadero, Eiffel Tower, Bastille Place, Louvre, Opera House and then we went to Montmartre — saw the wild Bohemian section — what a sight. And then the real Montmartre, the artist colony on the hill, where the beautiful Sacred Heart Church is located, and beneath which as far as the eye can see the whole city of Paris — it is a thrilling sight. I got back to the hotel at 7:15 p.m. Jacobson took some pictures of me and I will send them to you. I have decided, too, that the jeep will never sell too well to civilians — it is a good Army car but it is rough riding.

Always and ever as I see this or that renowned landmark I find myself thinking "Wouldn't my Grace enjoy this?" And she will. For one day we will come here together and then I will really "see" Paris.

I am lonesome for you — and for the children — and how I wish I would get a letter from you. They must be snarled up somewhere.

Do write me all the news — and I send you my deepest love.

Tom

Paris
August 7, 1945

Grace, my dearest one,

Somehow or other I expected your mail to get through to me today — but the mail is in and nothing for me! It must arrive soon. It is eleven days now since I left you and I feel so completely cut off from you, the children and home. Heaven knows how I will stand weeks of this. I hope I can adjust myself to it.

This afternoon I have had some time to think and that just isn't good for me these days. I reflect on the year, since last September, really — and what a nightmare it has been: the worry, the stress, and the strain and finally the crash.[15] All so dishonest and vicious in its course. Time may heal some of it but I doubt that it will ever remove the scars. They are too deep. Sometimes I think I shall not remain in Connecticut at all — and then I think I should. It is all very difficult and my mind is still foggy and groggy about it. I realize how much it has done to you — how wonderfully you stood by me in your sweet and courageous way — so beautifully believing in ultimate decency when I lost all — or nearly all — hope or belief in it.

Please do not believe I am brooding over here, for indeed I am not. But thus far this assignment has not been very interesting. I know it is early to formulate a judgment, and I came committed to the principle of no competition — ergo no ambitions, ergo no disappointments. But the smell of the sawdust ring does something to me — it is difficult for a fireman to sit in the station when the alarm rings. Perhaps it will be better. In any event I am not alone in this — Neil [Andrews] is talking of a possible return home. I have thought of it but have decided to give myself and the job a better chance by way of time. You see it is a Colonel's clique — from top to bottom — and it is provokingly unpleasant for civilians. I believe a terrible mistake has been made in this respect. It should be run by civilians in the name of the civil population and in the interest of peace by way of contributing to the prevention of war. From every perspective it is and should be a civilian assignment — and not one entrusted to men of war. Armies fight well sometimes — they do nothing else well. Stupid distinctions of rank blight all other activities that military men get into. A good lawyer may

15. Dodd was admitted to the bar of Connecticut in early 1945 on the basis of his experience. He had failed the Connecticut bar exam after graduating from Yale in 1933 but had passed the South Dakota exam where he worked for the FBI and was also a member of the bar of the U.S. Court of Appeals, and at the U.S. Supreme Court. Dodd's admission in Connecticut was challenged by a New London lawyer, William J. Shields, who argued the experience did not meet the state standard. The Connecticut Supreme Court agreed, and Dodd lost his standing. Later, the rules were changed, and he was admitted again.

not be a full colonel. A full colonel may not be a good lawyer. But colonels must be in charge of men of lesser rank and certainly not under or on a par with civilians. Ho! Hum! Let us hope we get the job done in any event. That is the really important thing — and I do believe it will come to pass.

I got a little better room in the same hotel last night — but there is much to be desired. We cannot eat in the French restaurants. A decent meal would cost about $10 at least. It is depressing to see the lines for food. To eat in a restaurant one must have a ration card. The restaurants are classified as A, B and C. To eat in an A one must be doing heavy work, in B medium, and the rest eat in C. The menus are all uniform per class. There is no choice. The women and men wear wooden shoes — some have black market stuff, and there is a real black market here, where butter is $10 a pound and soaps a dollar per cake. O! we are a fortunate nation — and how little we appreciate it.

Germany, I am told, is chaos. You will not believe what I already have heard of what has gone on there and of how some troops in some parts of Germany have conducted themselves — and how some of the imported workers have been acting. Of course it is retribution for having forced these people to go to Germany — but it is no less awful to hear about. God help Europe — and save us from anything like it.

Good-bye for now my dearest one — my love to all the children.

Tom

Paris, France
August 7, 1945

My most beloved Grace,

Most of Paris is on vacation now. It appears to be an institution here. The shop keepers just close up — post a sign on the door and announce that the vacation is on.

My evenings have been very quiet. I am again a teetotaler — after a few lapses in Washington. For one thing, drinking cognac is a bad business in my judgment and it is expensive. Consequently, I walk around a bit with Neil Andrews and Jim Walsh, now a lieutenant in the Army, formerly an assistant U.S. attorney in New York City. We promenade the Champs Elysées and look the French dames over — just "look," my dear, no more. The hats are wonderful — wedding cake types. The French girls are always all dressed up and made up as contrasted with the English girls, who seemed so plain and so drab.

Soon I hope to attend a session of the Pétain trial[16] — to observe the procedure and see the drama — in part. I shall write you my observations.

Neil Andrews is not feeling well and I think part of his trouble is founded in disappointment over the setup here. I am plugging along and will try very hard to make it work out. I have abhorrence for this Army caste system, having seen all I want to in the past ten days. I shall oppose any and all compulsory military training programs now suggested. I do not want our boys indoctrinated with such nonsense. As a matter of fact, in my judgment a compulsory program is just another step away from the peace and the freedom that we believe in. The results of it in Europe are all around us.

I am struck by the absence of children in Paris. I never see [a child]. There are none in the parks. I have asked about it and am told, "O, Parisians do not have children" — and I believe it is so. What a symptom of their awful decadence. It is said here that the Germans planned to make Paris the amusement center for the continent — some say the brothel city. In any event, the French certainly laid the foundation for such a place.

The *Herald Tribune* puts out a small Paris edition every day and I read it every morning. This morning's news of the new atomic bomb was headlined in all the papers here. I recall being told in Santa Fe about a mysterious government project there. This morning's paper explained that this new bomb was developed there.

16. Marshal Philippe Pétain, the World War I hero who became head of the Vichy government, was charged with collaboration with the Nazis and treason.

No mail so far — it must come soon. You must write me very long letters. Tell Tommie I use his billfold every day and I like it very much. Tell Carolyn I miss my dear little rose. Tell Jeremy I miss my little "commissioner" and hope he gets some fish. Tell Martha I miss my sweet little "Miss Butter." Tell Christopher to keep looking at my picture.

> *To all my deep love,*
> *Tom*

> Paris, France
> August 7, 1945

Grace, my dearest one,

Do you mind if I write to you twice on the same day? I won't have much to say but I will be with you for a while before retiring and tomorrow I will continue on.

This evening I passed with Colonel Max Trainig of Waterbury and a French major, at the major's home here in Paris. It was very pleasant indeed. I am trying to be sophisticated about this trip, but the truth is, my dearest, I am truly lonely without you. This is the last separation. I have known, always, how deeply I love you. I have never been unaware of how I need you with me, but this long distance separation just cuts my heart.

Tonight Colonel Trainig and Major Garbois talked of the war, of France, of Paris, Egypt, Syria, and America and every once in awhile I found my eyes on my watch and my thoughts with you in Coventry Lake.[17] It is now 11 p.m. here. It is 5 p.m. at the lake, and you are expecting the children and preparing supper. O! Devote your prayers to my return so that I will never be away again without you.

---

17. **A resort community in eastern Connecticut where the Dodd family rented a summerhouse.**

Continued — August 8, 1945

This morning I thought there might be a letter — but no luck so far. I would give a great deal for a postcard from you.

Everyone is talking about the atomic bomb. It has startled Europe, as well it might. Someone has said, "We now have the instrument which will really destroy mankind — or make it." And that expresses my own fear.

This afternoon I attended the trial of Marshal Pétain. It is a spectacle. The courtroom in the Palais de Justice is crowded to the doors. I sat in the diplomatic section — immediately behind the judges, who are attired in crimson robes with ermine capes. The jury is in two sections on both sides of the courtroom. The press sits inside the rail as does the aged Marshal. His lawyers sit just outside the rail, immediately behind him. The prosecutor, Andre Mornet, attired in crimson and ermine, sits in a special box (he prosecuted Mata Hari). The court attendants are in full dress suits. General Bergeret is the witness — a drama apparent even though I do not understand the testimony. The jurors ask questions. The Chief Judge Mongebeaux asks questions. Defense counsel impresses me — again, even though I do not understand what is said.

It is a tragic scene to me. Pétain, a marshal of France, the hero of Verdun, 89 years old, sits almost indifferently, slouched in his seat. The jury seems prejudiced to me. It is all a sorry spectacle and I wonder if it is good for France. I stayed on fascinated by the whole picture — drinking in every detail — for it is an historic occasion.

Continued Thursday, August 9, 1945

What news! Russia is in the war against Japan. It is headline material here. All think the war will soon be over. Russia and the new bomb will put *finis* on the Japs. It is really wonderful.

What news! Your letter — the first one arrived today. O! What a thrill to read your wonderful lines. I have read and re-read the letter all morning. I am glad you had a good trip home. Be sure to save all mail, and if you can, write me a brief summary of important letters.

What is your financial situation? Find out what my bank balance is in Manchester and use one of the checks to draw what you want. Are my paychecks reaching you on time? Are all the children well and happy? How is your precious self? O! I could go on asking questions for pages. For now, *au revoir* — my love to all.

Tom

Paris, France
August 10, 1945

Grace, my beloved one,

It is a rainy cold day here — the first poor day since my arrival. The temperature is very low and generally the weather is like what we get in October. Lord help us in the fall — for the fuel situation is bad, so I have been told.

I am not at all happy here — mostly because I am ignored and made to feel unimportant. Also because I detest this army caste system. I have been told to "screen" reports, which is a dull second-rate FBI job.

You will recall that I came here with the intention of doing a job and that was all — no ambition, etc. I still feel that way but I know I have had more experience than any of these people — and that I have some ability, and to treat me like a five-year-old law clerk is irritating. Neil Andrews is in the same spot. It presents a real problem. We do not want to quit, but certainly we cannot accept this kind of work. It is an insult to the Department of Justice and to us as individuals. We will have to do something about it — maybe I will be home much sooner than I expected to be. After all, I do want to get started and clerical work in Europe is hardly a justification for delay.[18] Do you mind all

18. At this point, Dodd has notions of a run for public office.

this griping? I have to tell you all I do — you are so important in my world of affairs.

By the way, on my insurance, I completely forgot it. I think there is enough of a balance in Manchester to pay it. Send me a few blank checks so I can sign them and return them to you and you can cash them.

News! We just heard that Japan has surrendered. It is a great relief and we should all be very happy. It makes me want to get home soon, too. No mail today. That letter of yesterday — your first letter — just whetted my appetite. Do take good care of your precious self — and kiss the children for me.

Tom

Sunday, August 11, 1945
Paris, France

Grace, my most beloved one,

Your letter of August 4th reached me today — it was very uplifting. I was lonesome this morning — I do get spells of lonesomeness. I just cannot help it. Write long letters. I treasure them so.

Things picked up a bit in the office yesterday — to the extent of learning that I am assigned to the "staff" for the interrogation of some of the Nazi bigwigs. That should be of interest — with a question mark, the question being whom I shall be assigned to question and what I shall do when that job is done. Neil is still very discouraged — I am hoping to work it out somehow.

Joe Guimond leaves tomorrow for Frankfurt, so I shall not have his good company. We will be in Nürnberg soon and I will cable the new APO to you.

The news about Japan has been received calmly here. I suppose it has brought great joyous outbursts at home. Somehow, the atomic bomb, the collapse of Japan and the attendant circumstances have been a shock. One feels bewildered and confused — yet glad that the war is over. The *Stars and Stripes* for this morning tells of expected vast unemployment at home — of no more gas rationing, and of new radios, automobiles, and other commodities. What a disordered period of history we live in. What does the future mean for us and for the children? I think our love and devotion is the only hope for us as individuals, as human beings who believe in God. Perhaps this separation — so painful now — will make us cherish the more our wonderful love and life together. I should be a better lover, a better husband, and better parent for it.

The Pétain trial is nearly over. I believe he will be convicted and sentenced to death. France is an explosive country. There may be violent reactions to this trial.

I hope, somehow, that the Farleys[19] do not move [from Lebanon] to Norwich. I guess because it is another tie broken that I would like to see remain. At the same time I am aware that we should not remain in Lebanon — but I have no immediate plans, of course, for a change. I simply believe that we will find it necessary to live elsewhere eventually — we can have a country place, or a camp somewhere. And my, won't we enjoy it.

Tom

Sunday night
August 11, 1945
Paris, France

Grace, my dearest one,

This is the second letter since this day dawned — but I shall only start it tonight and continue it tomorrow. While having dinner tonight

19. Helen Farley, Grace's sister, was married to John Farley, and lived in Lebanon, Connecticut, near the Dodds' pre-Revolutionary house on the town's historic green.

I met Colonel Amen and Colonel Hinkel and they asked me to go to Nürnberg with them tomorrow. I will be there all week, until Saturday. The Nazi big shots are arriving there today and tomorrow, so I will have my first glimpse of Göring, von Ribbentrop, Keitel, etc. I will write you from Nürnberg. It may be that I cannot write as fully from there — so you will understand if the tone of my letters is changed.

Joe Guimond has been very decent to me here — most gracious, friendly and downright hospitable. He is his old self. The men in the Army think very highly of him and he has been decorated with the Bronze Star. If you write to Margie (and I hope you do) tell her about his good record and how pleased I have been with his company. Max Trainig has been grand, too. I have to admit that some of these Colonels are all right. Some are stuffed shirts.

To walk on the Champs Elysées on a Sunday afternoon is an experience. The sidewalk cafes are packed and Paris seems to be trying very hard to be gay. Someday we will do all of this together and won't I have fun showing you around (to get even for Montreal and Miami).

Tomorrow I will get my weekly rations at the officers post exchange. Tobacco for my pipes, a few cigars and cigarettes, chewing gum, candy (four bars), soap. I give the cigarettes, candy and gum as tips in the hotel — and how the maid and the bellboy appreciate them. They cannot be bought except for terrific prices in Paris. The black market is open and notorious here, with unbelievable prices. Even some old stores run both a legitimate line and a black market line. Is it any wonder that France is weak? The stores are open on set schedules so many hours on certain days — and lines form in the streets outside the markets and bakeries and food shops. Milk is unseen. We get some for coffee at the mess, and that is all. The waitresses still marvel at our requests for "de l'eau" — poor French but it brings the water bottle to the table. We can drink it in Paris and the Americans cling to it and pass up the table wine. I have to turn in now — until the morning — *au revoir.*

August 13, 1945

Good morning, my sweet. The *Stars and Stripes* reports that the Japs are expected to surrender at any minute. Paris does not seem too excited about it. The soldiers think of it in terms of getting home, of course — but otherwise the war in the Pacific has been too remote for France to hold great interest. I suppose there will be big celebrations at home — give a shout for me.

I hope you will try to get a girl to work for us. There should be some available with the war's end. Hugh[20] will have to be carried on — but just that and no more, so do not worry about him. The chickens should be laying soon. What will you do with the milk this fall? Aren't you smart, doing so much canning?

I had hoped for a letter this morning — but nothing arrived. There must be some tie up in the mails. Just keep writing. It will reach me eventually. In the meantime I send you all my love.

To the children:

I have heard about a wonderful dog named Snowball. He is a little dog — all wooly and white. An armored division of the U.S. Army was traveling from Kentucky to New York and the train stopped along the way. Some of the soldiers saw a man who was being mean to Snowball. The soldiers got off of the train and bought the dog. They took him on their boat in a duffle bag and he kept very quiet as it was against the rules to take him to Europe. They fed him, kept him hidden, and took turns taking him for secret walks at night on the boat. He arrived in France and was with the soldiers in all their battles. They all love him and he did many wonderful things. I will tell you more about him in another letter.

Daddy

20. Hugh Carney, whom the children loved for his thick brogue and good stories, had been employed in the Dodd household as handyman and household helper.

CHAPTER 5

Jailbird in the Ruins

DODD ARRIVES IN WHAT IS LEFT of Nuremberg, an enormous rubble once home to four hundred thousand and where the laws against the Jews were written. He describes for Grace many of the key defendants held in the prison next to the Palace of Justice: the "sly, cagy" Rosenberg, the "Bowery character" von Ribbentrop, the strutting and shouting Göring. Jodl explains why Germany did not invade Britain in 1940 when it seemed to have the military might and desire to do so. Tom tells Grace of his fears for the future; because of the awful destruction, the Germans "may hate us for a thousand years," though their leaders "must be made to suffer and pay" for the atrocities they committed. Noting all the competition for advancement among the prosecution staff, Dodd simply decides to "saw wood." He visits Hitler's Munich apartment. He questions Keitel, who reveals that the Nazi high command trumped up evidence against Czechoslovakia meant to prove Germany would be attacked by the Czechs. This gave the Nazis an excuse to march into the Sudetenland. Keitel also asks Dodd for a personal favor — to find his wife and give her an important message.

August 14, 1945
Nürnberg, Germany

Grace, my dearest one,

Here I am in the dead city of Nürnberg. Flying up we saw many scars of the war — bridges down, buildings in ruins — but when we entered Nürnberg I saw for the first time in my life the awful ruin that comes with war. This city is devastated — the buildings, houses and streets are a complete mess. Streetcars piled up, a mass of burned and twisted steel, the rubble is everywhere. Soldiers in helmets and armed on patrol. Nothing but army vehicles on the roads and streets — not even bicycles. The people look pretty well fed but cowed. One sees countless families — all their belongings in a baby carriage or other such conveyance — walking along the roads to a home they left during the war. One sees innumerable German soldiers — in uniform and with packs but without weapons, trudging back home.

I am living in what was the Grand Hotel — the finest in the city. I am in Hitler's guest annex, where he housed his guests when the Nazi party congress was held.[1] The main part of the hotel is not habitable. My room is quite comfortable. The walls are all ripped out — bullet holes in them — no glass in the windows. The ceiling is half gone, but compared to some rooms it is in good shape. It is awesome to walk along the corridor and have to walk on a plank over an opening three stories up, or to walk down a bit further and pass a whole section of the building that is one gaping hole — no walls, just space. There is no hot water, no heat, nothing, and this is the best in this city that was once home to 400,000 people. I am told that 30,000 people were killed here in thirty minutes only a few months ago. It is not hard to believe. There is a strange odor everywhere; there are many bodies still in the ruins. Ten thousand former Storm Troopers are cleaning the place up as are the civilians.

1. The Nuremberg Rallies were held in the city every September from 1927 on, under the title of *Reichsparteitage des deutschen Volkes*, or National Day of the (Nazi) Party of the German People.

The food here is good and well prepared. After supper last night we went to what is called "the night club," a room in the hotel, where beer and cognac are served. Some German civilians put on some entertainment. Girls sang "Lily Marlene" and danced — and one former opera singer rendered a few numbers. I inquired about them and was told they are given a free meal for doing it. The girls were theater stars before the surrender. All of them work all day cleaning up debris — they live in cellars, etc., at night, as does the rest of the population. The people look sullen to me. I do not trust them. You will recall what I wrote about the absence of children in Paris. I never saw so many children as there are here. Just everywhere.

Grace, it will be years and years before this country will be even cleaned up. I wish I could describe the destruction more adequately. Believe me when I tell you it is terrific.

Today we started talking to the Nazi big boys who were brought here yesterday. I was interrupted [while writing] at this point and besides my ink is gone. I doubt that there is any in the hotel — for there is not much available. The drinking water is contaminated, probably because of the many bodies buried in the ruins. The natives carry water. There is no gas or electricity. There is a curfew at 10:30 p.m. Tell Lincoln Opper[2] that this city is said to be ninety percent destroyed — and to see it is to believe it. I walked down one street — or what was a street — and for more than one mile there isn't a thing standing. The odor is sickening. All along were wrecked Red Cross ambulances, autos and all kinds of vehicles. The endless procession of refugees — carrying a few belongings — goes on all day. Food is terribly scarce. There is no rail service. Not even mail service, nor has there been any since December. Over 80,000 people

2. **Dr. Lincoln Opper, a Norwich pathologist, and his wife, Charlotte, were friends of the Dodds. The Oppers' daughter, Carolyn, recalls that it was her father who talked a reluctant Tom Dodd into accepting the Nuremberg post. Dodd had worried about leaving five young children, including a baby (Christopher), for Grace to take care of. According to Carolyn, Lincoln Opper assured him that he would check in regularly, and he did.**

were killed in this city in all. Three air raids and the battle for the city did this. It must have been hell. All the historic "old city" — the so-called "walled city" — is gone. It had been here for 800 or 900 years. All the famous landmarks are rubble — including the place where the artist [Albrecht] Dürer lived. And this is only one such place in Germany. There are many others, so I am told. I will see them soon enough I guess.

Today, I visited the jail where Göring and the others are kept. After lunch we went to the Justice Building — or what is left of it — and we interrogated Alfred Rosenberg all afternoon. He was the minister in charge of culture and occupied countries and he directed the stealing of art treasures. He was a notorious anti-Semite. He is short, plump, blue-eyed, fair, very keen minded, sly, cagy. He is dressed in an old brown suit, khaki shirt, no tie, heavy shoes. I thought how the mighty have fallen. Here is this city, where he strutted in his fancy Nazi clothes. He is now a jailbird in the ruins. He once called this "the heart of Nazism" — the most German of all German cities. We talked with him all afternoon and believe me it was a most interesting session. I was aware of the drama of it — and of the importance of it — and we heard some interesting statements. Some day I will tell you about it.[3] Tomorrow we talk with General Keitel, the head of the German general staff, then with Göring and von Ribbentrop. The others will come later. The trip has been worthwhile just for today. I thought London was damaged — and it was — this, though, is beyond description.

Of course no mail from you will reach me this week — and I am so anxious to hear from you. My dearest I miss you terribly — do take good care of your precious self. I shall bid you good night at the close of a day I shall never forget.

Tom

3. In early letters from Nuremberg, Dodd was reluctant to provide interrogation details, but that soon changed.

August 15, 1945
Nürnberg, Germany

Grace, my dearest one,

This is your father's birthday — and the well remembered feast day[4] when all of us near the coast were sure to have a swim. I suppose all my dear ones were at mass very early this morning.

For myself, I am able to report the most fascinating days of my life. After breakfast I went to the Palace of Justice. Colonel Amen, Colonel Brundage, Lt. Col. Hinkel, representatives of the Norwegian government and an interpreter started our interrogation of Field Marshal Wilhelm Keitel. The chief of staff of the German army. He came in under guard, dressed in a long blue field coat, a pale green tunic with red and gold trimming, light blue whip cord breeches, black riding boots. He has an unusual countenance — light hair, blue eyes, a light mustache. We talked with him for three hours about the invasion of Norway — the preparations, etc. I cannot give you details but I knew I was sitting in on and participating in a history making occasion. I can only tell you that he claims the Germans invaded Norway only a few hours before the English intended to do so. Remind me to tell you what two Norwegian army officers said when we asked them if there was anything to Keitel's story. Keitel had five children when the war started. Two sons are missing in battle, one was killed in Russia, one daughter is dead and one daughter is living. He is a German officer of the old school, Hitler's close military advisor. Also remind me to tell you of his attitude towards Hitler.

After lunch at the hotel we returned to the Palace of Justice and began our questioning of Lieutenant General Alfred Jodl. He was in charge of operations — a post like that occupied by Eisenhower. He came in under guard, attired in a long black leather outside coat, high crowned cap, a tunic of blue trimmed in red and gold, pale green breeches of whip cord and shining black riding boots. He is a well built

4. Reference to a holy day of obligation and the Assumption of the Virgin.

man of 53 years. A lean hard face, thin lips, blue eyes, light thin hair, very erect in carriage. (Kietel is more dumpy, particularly about the hips, but also very military in his bearing). Jodl has a deep rumbling voice. Kietel's too is deep but softer.

Jodl was every inch and every moment the Prussian general — arrogant and haughty. We discussed the Norwegian campaign. He talked freely but sternly. He too told of the impending British invasion.

Next we questioned Joachim von Ribbentrop, who was the Nazi foreign minister. He came in under guard wearing an old brown over-coat, khaki shirt, no tie, army shoes (no laces), unshaven and seedy looking. He is of light complexion, blue eyes, light graying hair. He speaks some English. He was nervous, despondent, shaken. Here sat the man who paraded all over Europe in fancy dress with the Nazi might and power as a threat behind his diplomacy. He looked like a Bowery character to me. His answers were of great interest because in part they revealed something of Hitler's method of doing things and the competition — the jealousies among the Nazi top men. Remind me to tell you of the feeling between Rosenberg and von Ribbentrop. It fascinated me to hear this man tell of his talks with Hitler.

Finally, at about 4 p.m., in strutted Hermann Göring — wearing a long light blue outside coat, a cap, and a light blue tunic and trousers, and black shoes. He has lost a lot of weight, his color is good, eyes blue, thin brown hair, thin lips, a hard mouth. He was in a bad mood — shouted and pounded the desk — calmed down some when he learned our attitude about his loud voice and his desk pounding. Our time with him will interest you.

We returned to the Grand Hotel, set off a celebration, and the officers and everyone else celebrated until far into the night.

So came to a close this day I shall never forget. It was a miserable day weather-wise, raining all the time. It was depressing to see the beaten German soldiers trudging through this ruined city back home in the rain — to see the refugees, the deportees all winding a weary way through the wreckage. One-legged soldiers, soldiers with women, bedraggled and worn looking — families pulling little carts or pushing baby carriages loaded with a few miserable possessions. I ask — where do they come from? Where are they going? How do they eat? Where do they sleep? No one knows. It has been an endless procession every day. God spare our people from any such fate.

So my dearest one, I come to the end wishing I could tell you all of this now — there is so much that I want you to know. We will have long talks by the fire next winter — and when we are tired I will crush you with affection.

All my love to you,
Tom

Nürnberg, Germany
August 16, 1945

Grace, my beloved one,

On the way to the finance office this morning I had my first view of the Polish people who were forced laborers in Germany. They are now in a camp enclosure — living in tents awaiting either removal or other disposition. Many of them refuse to return to Poland now. What a terrible tragedy. Forced to leave home — now afraid to return there.

Late in the morning we all worked on the preparation of some papers for the Norwegians, who were with us the last two days. After lunch we again worked on these same papers and late in the afternoon I called on Colonel Andrews, the military governor here.

The boy who is driving me about is from Bridgeport, Conn. — a private in the 26th Infantry. He was captured at Aachen and later released. He fought in many famous engagements. His name is Trumpfeller. He told me how the Germans shot all prisoners at one time.

There is an expression here — "liberated." If a soldier gets a souvenir he has liberated something. I heard of a Russian soldier who was seen wearing eight wrist watches, all "liberated" from Germans. When one would run down, he would throw it away. He didn't know how to wind the stem. That's why he took eight. He wore them on both arms!

Colonel Andrews fears a terrible winter here. There is no fuel, little food. Thousands are living in cellars. There is no work. He is trying to start some toy factories and the like. I too believe it will be a terrible winter in Europe, and particularly so in Germany. There is real danger of pestilence, mostly from the decomposed bodies still in the ruins. I have heard details of the last months of the war here. It was hell on earth — fire, destruction, panic, and hysteria. Yet no revolt and a blind belief by some considerable number that Germany could still win. Up to two weeks before the surrender Goebbels kept telling the Germans that they would win with a new, secret weapon.

I have heard some wonderful accounts of the last hours in Berlin — of the very last, so it is said, of Hitler and Eva Braun. Some day it will all be written down as history. Many do not believe Hitler is dead. Some do. But some of the accounts of the end — real or imaginary — are indeed Wagnerian.

So my dearest I bring to an end another all too brief few minutes with you — a most unsatisfactory visit, by mail, but so necessary if I am to survive our separation. I have had no mail in Nürnberg. I so hope there is some in Paris. I return there tomorrow for two days — then back here.

I send all my love to you.

Tom

Nürnberg, Germany
August 18, 1945

Grace, my dearest one,

Four letters arrived today via Paris — dated July 30, August 3, August 6 and August 7. Apparently the mail is all mixed up. I was surprised to learn that my cable from Scotland took so long. In any event, it was delightful to receive mail from you. But I suggest you use both sides of the paper — and write longer letters. I read your letters over and over again.

Yesterday our group and two British colonels interviewed General Jodl again. The questions were all on strategy and tactics. He answered all of them and no matter what else may be said about him it is perfectly clear that he knows his business. He explained the war moves from almost every angle.

He said that Germany failed to invade England in 1940 simply because no one expected France to fall in less than one year. The Germans had no plans ready. Said Jodl: "If I had instructed my staff to draw up an invasion plan for Britain in 1940 they would have said I was mad."

With respect to Spain he stated that Hitler met Franco in May or June of 1940, at the Spanish–French frontier for the purpose of arranging the talks of Gibraltar. Franco refused — and as a result Germany was not able to lock the Mediterranean to the British. Jodl said, "We had the plans ready — we could have taken Gibraltar easily." He told us that no one knew of Italy's plan to invade Greece. Hitler heard of it the day it started — when he met Mussolini at Florence. As Hitler stepped from his plane, Mussolini greeted him with the news. Hitler and the German generals were furious. O! I could write pages on all of this. Jodl said, "After all, Hindenburg was right when he said, 'Even Mussolini can do no more than make Italians out of Italians.'" When did Jodl realize the war was lost? "I first thought it possible that we could lose in 1942. I felt quite sure that we would after the Americans landed in Normandy. I was positive after the Americans crossed the Remagen bridge on the Rhine." Of course it is only one side but of this I feel sure — these professional German militarists respected Hitler. They say he really ran the war![5] To hear Jodl tell of his last hours with Hitler is moving — if not anything else. After lunch yesterday, we had

---

5. During Dodd's later interrogations of Keitel, the field marshal confided that Hitler "was full of ideas . . . it was very difficult to report to him. When you reported, he started talking very soon. After the second or third sentence, he interrupted me and started talking to himself. Then lots of ideas came up. After such a report, one was very confused about what he really wanted."

a discussion about our problems. Later Col. Hinkel and I called at a supply depot and I now have a uniform. A complete one if you please, from toe to head. I will wear it only when we are traveling about Germany. It will be easier. Everything is under military control, and it will save endless stops and questions. I confess I never thought I would be in uniform in Europe.

Last night, we had a state dinner. Jackson, the vice president of the Russian Supreme Court, the Attorney General of Britain, the French representative, and many military were present. Many toasts, much speech making. All in English except the Russian, who spoke a few phrases, then his interpreter spoke in English — a few more phrases, more interpretation. The toasts came thick and fast from the King to Joe Stalin and back again. We did it in "clubs" (Rhine wine). I am glad it wasn't in "spades" (vodka). We broke up about midnight.

Grace, I am afraid of what has happened here. The awful destruction — the terrible losses of all kinds — they may hate us for one thousand years. I am sorry too because I know now from eyesight and from the lips of our own men in arms that all the atrocities, all the sinning, was not on one side. I am sorry because I know some of these things. It is not that I fear German hatred, or because I am forgetting their terrible deeds, their unspeakable horrors and cruelties and indecencies — for which they must be made to suffer and to pay. Rather that there is no sure sign of a better day in Europe or in the world because I have learned that all who carried our righteous banner did not live in its righteous way. Many did. Some did not. It is very depressing to see all this ruin, want, suffering, injury and pain and not really be hopeful for the future. Europe is a mess. I do not think it will be cleaned up for a long time, and surely the shocking conduct of French colored troops, and the savage and vicious butchery of some Russians gives one little to build on for an optimistic view. I know of these things from men who have seen and dealt with these problems — and they are not isolated incidents in a very big and hard war.

Already time and events are turning the blade of memory. A new edge, I think, is emerging. I hope it will be sharp enough to make me capable and strong enough to make me honorable. After all — it has been tempered in a fire of meanness, smallness and bigotry. Thus I explain my present attitude about the bar incident.

Kiss the children for me and give them my affection and devotion. To you, I send again the most tender message of love.

Tom

Nürnberg, Germany
August 19, 1945

Grace, my beloved one,

It is Sunday and a very rainy one here in the ruins of ancient Nürnberg. I heard mass at the military government building this morning. Colonel Brundage and I went together. Afterwards, we rode about the town a little and obtained three sets of heavy underwear from the supply depot. We have been warned that the cold weather will set in early and with the fuel situation as it is we decided to get the heavy underclothing. (You can wear it under your snowsuit some day.)

Yesterday, we again talked with General Jodl about the organization of the German Army. We also talked briefly again with Marshal Keitel. At noon we joined Jackson and his party at lunch, and bade them good-bye as they left for London by plane in midafternoon. I changed my plans and did not return to Paris, arranging instead to have my possessions brought up here.

Last night, Colonel Brundage and I were dinner guests of Colonel Charlie Andrews, the military governor of the area. He is from Little Rock, Ark., and we had a good time discussing mutual Arkansas friends. He is a very able man and a very humane man, ideally suited for his present job. I must say some of these Army colonels are splendid people. Howard Brundage is one of the best. He is a very successful lawyer from Chicago, age 53 years, and the father of six children, one of whom is in the service. He and I have become good friends and as a result the minor brass around here is very respectful.

Neil Andrews is still in Paris but expected here by midweek. We are hoping that our trial will get under way in October and I am thinking of December shipping space already.

As you have gathered I am better situated than I was a week or more past. I like the assignment — it is an important and worthwhile one — and I like the men who are working with me. Four or five of us will do all the interrogating out of a staff of nearly 200. I have good office space and fair living space. "Fair" only because there is really nothing "good" in this city.

So, my dearest one — this is the latest report from one who loves you beyond his power to express it.

Tom

Nürnberg, Germany

August 21, 1945

Grace, my dearest one,

The sunshine has finally broken through the rain clouds. But for me it is still bad weather for I have not had a letter since the fifteenth or sixteenth of this month — and then only those mailed some time back. I am hopeful for a veritable shower of letters one of these days.

Yesterday Colonel Brundage and I saw the stadium — where the Nazi party congresses were held. It is tremendous in size, and I recognized it from moving pictures we have seen of it at home. In going to the stadium and traveling about the city on two other missions yesterday, I have had a rather good view of the whole city, and am convinced that this is ninety percent destruction — probably the worst in Germany.

After lunch we were at the courthouse conferring with the maintenance and supply people about our office situation. The building is badly damaged — but good old Uncle Sam is restoring it so the trial can be held here. Ten thousand Storm Troopers, prisoners of war, are here to do the labor job. Some of us believe that the selection of Nürnberg was a bad mistake because of the extensive damage. Almost everything has to be restored for a trial of this kind — and to do it in a hurry costs even more money. The city of Heidelberg is intact and would have been ideal, but the Army never suggests a simple solution, and it never suggested that city for use.

Last night Lt. Col. John Corley had dinner with Brundage and me. He is a grand young fellow who has seen all kinds of action. He was in command at Aachen and won that city after a bitter battle, as you will recall.

After dinner we went to his quarters, a lovely home — or better — a small estate outside of the city. It is beautifully and completely furnished, and Corley with six or seven other officers reside there. We met Father Flynn, a captain who is the chaplain for the regiment. He is a passionate and a splendid man and from what we were told he has been through it all from beginning to end. We talked until midnight, mostly about the war, about the trials, and about the peace. These soldiers are all troubled about prosecuting Keitel and Jodl. And well they may worry for professional soldiers have never been considered as liable for war crimes prosecutions — and if such a precedent is established here the Army and Navy people are in a new and difficult position.

I hear so much about the Russians — none of it good — from our soldiers. Everyone has the same attitude toward them and all feel that it is high time we stopped backing down at every turn. This interests me as do the stories about the way the Russians wage war — the awful consequences to civilian populations. However, I do not feel that there is any need of talk about fighting Russia. Not only is there no need for it, but more importantly it should not be said for out of all such conversations come some of the causes of war — and I have seen and I heard too much of war — all the horrible little indecencies, the minor viciousness, the small brutalities let alone the big awfulness of war. Grace, it really is hell.

Well, so it goes — so it has been in the past. Wars bring changes — lasting changes for the worse. I know of nothing good from war. All that silly talk about the advance of science and such leaves me cold. Give me peace and a retarded science.

For now, my dearest one, I bid you adieu — kiss the children for me and give them my affection.

Tom

Nürnberg, Germany
August 22, 1945

Grace, my most beloved one,

Yesterday, like so many other days, was one of preparation in the courthouse. There is so much to be done before we get at our principal job. Tomorrow, Lt. Col. Dick Owens of New Haven and I are going to Munich for a day or two. Later in the week I hope to be in Salzburg and Vienna. The music festival is on in Salzburg and I am anxious to pass a day or more there. I feel that one in my position should get around and see these places while there is an opportunity to do so.

Still no mail — not even a postcard in more than ten days. If I do not hear soon I will send a cable as I am wondering if you are ill — or if any of the children are ill. Lack of word from you causes some anxiety even though I know there are delays. I know you are not neglecting me and consequently I worry about you. If you were flighty or unreliable I would not be so concerned — it is part of the price of having one so dear and sweet and wonderful for my wife.

I am in a dry spell mentally. The shock of seeing all this tragedy day after day makes one a little numb. I walked around recently in the ruins of the ancient Church of St. Martha — which was built in 1200 — and it made me sick to see the destruction of that cultural monument. It is the same on every side — and still the refugees plod through town. The defeated soldiers trudge on in rain and in sunshine. They seem dazed and broken. This is a woeful place, and it will be generations before there is recovery.

Our own organization is not very efficient or effective. Too much army for either. I wonder how we will ever prepare this case. There is terrific jockeying for position. Everyone wants to be in the act. A lot of little people in big uniforms frantically seeking a place in the sun. However I am sawing wood — and I refuse to get excited — or ambitious. I am enjoying the experience and I will get as much out of it as one can get.

Unless we move along, I doubt that we will be through by Christmas. But I am determined to leave here so as to be home for the holidays. It seems queer, though, to be writing of the holidays at home when the calendar says it is only August.

I often think of what I will do when I return [for good], but I am not ready to make a decision yet. More time and more thought must be given to that question. As I listen to soldiers talk I am convinced — more or less — that a public career is probably not possible for me now.

The *Stars and Stripes* (the only paper we see) tells of vast unemployment in the near future at home. This too will have bearing on my decision. In any event I am always dreaming of my return — of you and the children. What a wonderful day it will be when I see your lovely face again.

Tom

Nürnberg, Germany
August 23, 1945

Grace, my dearest one,

Another day, another night and no mail. This silence is wearing me down. Please forgive my complaints. I know you are writing. However we have never been out of reach of each other for this length of time, and I am very lonesome. A letter would do much for my morale. Besides I cannot avoid some anxiety about you and the children.

Yesterday [some of us] attended a U.S.O. show — the Strauss operetta, *Rosalinda*, in the Nürnberg opera house. It was very well done. The opera house was damaged. It is in fair shape — good enough for a good performance.

We hope to start intensive work very shortly and then I will have much to tell you. I may be in Munich tomorrow and I will write you all about it. The weather is bad and the fall has really set in. There is no heat, of course, and no hot water. I dread October and November. I fear there will be great suffering in Germany, and indeed all of Europe.

The Russians are stripping Germany of everything — that is, in that part occupied by the Russians. I hear from many who have been in Berlin that it appears that the Russians will have almost nothing and that starvation is a certainty in their zone. I know that the Germans were terribly cruel and vicious in Russia. But from what I hear there was little choosing between them and now the Russians are really grinding the Germans under heel. You see, it is all so hopeless, a vicious circle — with nowhere an opening for a real understanding or decent recovery.

Well, my dearest — I bid you good night — and send you my deepest love.

Tom

Nürnberg, Germany
August 25, 1945

Grace, my dearest one,

Yesterday, I left early in the morning for Munich with Colonel Owens. We had a most interesting trip through the German countryside. Many of the little villages are untouched by the war — outwardly — and they are pretty and picturesque. Others are badly damaged. Bridges are down everywhere and the scars of the conflict are on all sides. A wrecked German plane, a broken gun, a tank destroyed. These are all common sights along the way. The people are all busy in the fields, or hurrying to get wood in for the winter, which all fear. The endless procession of refugees goes on — mile after mile on foot, on horse, in wagons. We passed one wagon train a mile long. It looked just like the pictures of covered wagon days in America —

even the rounded tops on the wagons—horses and oxen doing the hauling, the men walking, the women and little ones riding. All heading back to Czechoslovakia, to Romania, to Bulgaria, to Austria, to places they call home. Believe me, Grace, this movement across Europe is a pitiful thing—and it wrings my heart to see it day after day.

We reached Munich at dinnertime. It is a badly wrecked city, although nowhere near as much damaged as is Nürnberg. It is still recognizable as a beautiful city—and seventy percent of it is destroyed.

Owens and I stayed at the Excelsior Hotel, and although it is partly wrecked we were quite comfortable. This morning we arose early and drove around Munich—through the wreckage and the rubble that once made this a city that men loved for its beauty and its culture. We visited a friend of Owens, an Army colonel who is living in Hitler's house on Prizregentenplatz. It is an apartment—taking up the whole third floor. All of Hitler's furniture and furnishings are there intact. It looks like a large New York apartment. The rooms are large and sunny. Hitler's bedroom is small and fairly simple in its appointments—a connecting bath separates it from the room Eva Braun occupied. His study—with his desk and other pieces still there with a picture of Hitler, Chamberlain and Daladier—is there. The dining room is large and stately. The room of his niece, Magda—which was never opened after her death—is a small bedroom. The present maids worked for him and his housekeeper, one Frau Winter. The maids say that he was there last Christmas—as was his habit at Christmastime. He again opened the door of his niece's room and remained alone in it for more than two hours. The maids also say that Eva Braun had two children by Hitler!—one should now be about seven and the other about five years.[6] There was a child's teddy bear in one of the rooms. There is a direct telephone to Berlin and one to Berchtesgaden in the house.

6. Hitler was childless. He married Eva Braun on April 29, 1945, the day before they both committed suicide—he by pistol and she by cyanide capsule. There were rumors in the bunker that she was pregnant at the time with Hitler's child, but there has been no real evidence of this.

We left Munich in midafternoon and returned to Nürnberg on the autobahn, which is a wonderful highway, just as good as — or better than — the Merritt Parkway.

My love and devotion to you,

Tom

August 26, 1945

This Sunday morning Colonels Corley, Riordan, McMahon, Brundage and I went to mass at St. Anthony's — the only Catholic church standing in Nürnberg. It was packed with soldiers. Father Flynn said the mass and preached a splendid sermon. He spoke of the awful result of the war — and in a beautiful way he referred to the German children who sang in the choir. These little children are touching. They look at us with eyes like those of our own children. They are just as curious about soldiers and jeeps and other military accoutrements — even after all that has happened to them in the past year or more!

After mass we all drove out to the prison camp, just outside the city, where were guests of Major Clisson for lunch. He is in command there. He has 10,000 troops there — and they were the meanest of the German Nazis. It is an amazing place. Thus far, all hands are in tents — soldiers and prisoners. On the grounds are 6,000 Polish soldiers who fought with us. They are under their own officers and they are indeed a tragic lot. They will not — cannot — return to Poland. What will become of them — and thousands like them — no one knows. They are the great losers, I fear, in this awful war. The Russians will never get them alive. Many Russians who are in Germany plead to be allowed to stay — or to go anywhere — but back to Russia. But under the rules they must be shipped back. Thus far the Estonians, the Lithuanians and the Latvians have not been shipped back. None of them want to return for they all fear their fate under the Russians. What a mess!

After lunch, our party was driven to Soldiers Field — the new name of the Nazi stadium. There, with more than 40,000 soldiers, we saw double-header baseball games between the 71st Division of the Third Army — Patton's Army — and the 20th Division of the 7th Army. The 71st won both games — which was not important to me. But the sight and the significance of 40,000 Americans in baseball mood in the Nazi stadium was significant. There, where Hitler corrupted and misled the youth of Germany, I heard thousands of young American soldiers calling the umpire names, I heard players called "bums" and all the old chatter and ribaldry of every American ballpark. It made that arena ring.

After the game, we returned to the hotel for supper. This evening we sat around the lobby for a bit and now I am about to say good night.

I received two letters yesterday. I was surprised at Damien's bill.[7] I think there is money in the Manchester bank — find out how much and send me a check to sign.

My dearest — I miss you very much tonight — and I do yearn to be with you. Kiss the little ones for me.

Tom

Nürnberg, Germany
August 27, 1945

Grace, my most beloved one,

This has been a lovely day — very much like a mid-September day in [our town of] Lebanon. This morning I was at the office and very busy. After lunch I started my first formal questioning of Field Marshal Keitel. We were busy until after five o'clock. Present were my interpreter and my stenographer. I did no more than some preliminary questioning as this was our first session alone. I asked him about the military preparations and rearmament of Germany. He told me that Germany started to rearm in earnest in 1935 and that she was expected to be at full peak somewhere between 1943 and 1945. This I believe to be true as I have seen the minutes of a highly secret conference

7. A worker from the Reichard dairy farm across from the Dodd house.

between Hitler, von Blomberg, von Fritsch, Admiral Raeder, Göring, and von Neurath on November 5, 1937.[8] At that time Hitler told these men of his aim and said he could accomplish it by force. He said, "We should be ready between 1943–45. After that we will decline." He also said that an earlier opportunity might present itself — but from the tenor of his remarks on that afternoon in 1937 it seems clear that he did not expect to start until 1943 to 1945. He planned for war — and he stated the basic proposition to be, "How much can Germany get by conquest at the least cost?"

Of course Keitel was not then Chief of Staff — he was assistant to von Blomberg. However he did tell me that he considered German assistance to Franco Spain as a training opportunity for German arms.

He is a gentle appearing man, very polite, very proper. But I never forget that he was Hitler's handy man for war. And we must remember that these men actually planned for war — and nothing in this world could have stopped them. It was a matter of time only.

Tomorrow I will question him further. I realize that I am talking with one of the three or four top military men of this war and with Hitler's top military man. It is something I shall never forget.

Colonel Brundage and I had Colonel Andrews as our dinner guest tonight, and passed a pleasant evening together. So passed another day in Germany. I do hope that this case will move along so we can all be home by mid-December. There is no reason — no good reason — why we should not have completed our mission by that time.

I feel quite cut off. Even the *Stars and Stripes* is no longer with us until September 1. We see no papers, hear no radio, and consequently are not up on current events. No mail again today, my dearest — and how much brighter it would be if only a card arrived.

Do write me all the news — the big and the little news. I am quite interested in the little gossip about you and the children. Have they grown any? Have they added weight? Are they tan and fit? How big is

8. On that date, Hitler held a secret conference at which he outlined plans for *Lebensraum* — German living space at the expense of other nations.

Christopher? Does he walk or talk? Did all of them learn to swim? How are you feeling—how is your weight? Have you tried to get a girl for the fall and winter in Lebanon? What about Carolyn's schoolbooks?[9]

Kiss each of my little jewels for me.

Faithfully,
Tom

Nürnberg, Germany
August 29, 1945

Grace, my dearest one,

Yesterday a large bundle of letters arrived. Quite a few from you, but not the early ones addressed to London. Helen wrote me, Margaret, Bill McCue and Joe Blumenfeld[10]—and consequently I felt very important. Needless to say your letters were opened first and reread many times.

All day yesterday I questioned Field Marshal Keitel—a very interesting session in which we discussed plans and events from November 1937 to September 1, 1939. He insists that the order to prepare to march in Austria was issued only two or three days in advance. As to Czechoslovakia, plans were made earlier and the real order was given on May 28, 1939 by Hitler to Brauchitsch.[11] Keitel has a very considerable respect for Hitler—he shows it at frequent intervals. I am surprised at his effrontery concerning some matters. For example, when I asked why he suggested a surprise attack on Czechoslovakia, he answered, "Because the Czechs were planning to attack us." Of course he attempts to justify his every deed in the same light. Always and ever

9. Carolyn required special materials. She was born with cataracts in each eye, and at the time there was no medical procedure to address the condition.
10. Margaret Dodd McAree was Tom Dodd's sister. Dodd met Bill McCue when he was head of the National Youth Administration. Joe Blumenfeld was Dodd's friend and lawyer, and after Nuremberg became his law partner and later a federal judge.
11. Colonel Walther von Brauchitsch was Göring's senior aide-de-camp.

Germany had to act to defend herself from imminent attack! You see how these people cling to this sort of answer — much as they shouted about the Versailles treaty before this war.

This morning I questioned him again — and this afternoon I will continue. Thus you see the field marshal and I are seeing quite a bit of each other. Last night Colonel Brundage, Colonel Corley and I had dinner together and afterwards we sat around in Colonel Brundage's room talking. I believe I told you — but if I did not I will repeat now — that Colonel Brundage and I are to live in an apartment — at 26 Schlegel Strasse, but do not send mail there. My address remains [the same].

We will be more comfortable in an apartment where a good hausfrau will take care of us — prepare some meals, at least, and the like.

It is now 11 p.m. Col. Brundage and I heard "Information Please."[12] It must be a recording for it was only 4 p.m. in New York. This evening I had dinner with Colonel Brundage, Colonel Corley and Father Fabian Flynn, the chaplain.

This Corley is a remarkable man. He is one of the most decorated soldiers of the war — including five silver stars — if you please! All for gallantry in combat. His men idolize him. He walked into battle with them. Father Flynn has been the chaplain with this outfit from North Africa to Germany. They were in the Normandy invasion, too. I believe that he, Corley, will in time be recognized as a great soldier. He is only 31 years old — a West Pointer, class of 1938.[13] He wants to meet you — and to visit us in Lebanon.

This afternoon, I questioned Keitel until after 5 p.m. He insisted that Germany feared an attack by Czechoslovakia and France in 1938 — and offered this as an explanation for German occupation of Czechoslovakia. Obviously this is a weak explanation for I confronted

12. An NBC radio show that ran from 1938 to 1952, hosted by Clifton Fadiman.
13. Corley became one of twenty-one officers specifically requested by General Douglas MacArthur at the onset of the Korean War. Corley eventually earned the rank of brigadier general.

him with a letter dated May 20, 1938 which he wrote to Hitler suggesting that it must somehow appear to the world that Germany was provoked into attacking the Czechs — even if the incident had to be framed by the Germans! He was very embarrassed and flustered and made a stupid answer. I am convinced that these people were really spoiling for a war — and they intended to get their objectives by war.

You will be interested in this quotation from Hitler's speech to his general just before the attack on Poland. "For you, gentlemen, glory and honor are in the offing such as has not beckoned for centuries. Be tough. Be without compassion! Act more quickly than the others. And NOW at the enemy! In Warsaw we shall meet again and celebrate."

I am writing along and forget that that a faithful husband should also be a successful — if not ardent — lover. But we know how deeply we love one another and repetition — while like an old and well loved tune — does not strengthen the bond. I have considered these letters as first of all my chance to talk with you every day and secondly as an opportunity to record my thoughts and experiences for your benefit and perhaps for mine at another time.

Be sure to write me all the news — and by the way my new correspondent in New Britain, Bill McCue, sent me a clipping from the *Hartford Courant*. My most affectionate sentiments to the children — and all of my love to you.

Faithfully,
Tom

Nürnberg, Germany
August 30, 1945

Grace, my dearest one,

I was at the office all day questioning Field Marshal Keitel. We are getting along very well together. Sometimes I find myself liking him — and feeling sorry for him. He is a very bright man — in my opinion — and a very charming one too. This afternoon he was in good spirits and he told me what he thought of the Italians. It was really humorous. He blames much of Germany's defeat on Italy. For example, Keitel, Hitler and Jodl were in Hendaye, France, in a conference with Pétain when word reached them that Italy was about to attack Greece. They immediately left for Florence and arrived the next morning at 6 a.m. Mussolini greeted them by announcing he had invaded Greece. Hitler was wild. So was Keitel — and of course Mussolini was cocky. Keitel said: "How can you defeat the Greeks?" Mussolini said, "There will be no battles — Ciano[14] has bought up the opposition with a little gold." Hitler told Keitel once, "I never tell Mussolini anything important" for what Mussolini knows, Ciano knows, London knows and Washington knows.

About the Finns: Keitel and Jodl met with the Finnish Chief of Staff at Salzburg in May of 1941. They made a proposal to the Finns. Keitel said, "The Finns gave us their answer with action — they were brave soldiers — our most faithful allies. They never asked for anything and they desired only to preserve their country."

Well, my dearest, it must be very clear that I am enjoying this assignment. Nothing could be of more interest. If I do no more than talk with these characters — hear their stories, question them about the past events, observe them as men — then my time has been and will be very well spent. Books — volumes — will be written about all of this, for it is history.

In the last few days I have had little time. You see I have to prepare a line of questioning for each day and review that of the day before. So my hours are well filled.

Take good care of yourself and of the children. Please watch Tom and Jeremy on the bicycles.

All my love to you.

Tom

14. **Galeazzo Ciano was Italy's foreign minister until the start of the war, when he became ambassador to the Vatican.**

Nürnberg, Germany
August 31, 1945

Grace my dearest one,

It is eleven o'clock here — five o'clock at Coventry Lake — just about the "children's hour" in more ways than Longfellow made memorable in verse. I think of all of you there and long to be in your midst.

This day passes somewhat uneventfully. I continued to question Keitel. We talked of the plans for the attack on Russia and he told me that Hitler wished to attack in the summer of 1941, but the troops could not be moved from France to the East in time. Then he talked of the diplomatic moves in Berlin in October of 1940 — the conferences with Molotov and with the Japanese, and the Russo-Japanese agreement. From late fall or surely early winter it was clear that the attack on Russia would come in the spring. He discussed the failure of the Japanese to attack Russia in the summer and fall of 1941 and then he said, "But in the fall of 1941 I realized that Japan could be most helpful against the U.S." This afternoon, he told me the story of von Blomberg's marriage and the resultant dismissal as Minister of War. Said he, "This woman was of easy virtue — his second wife to be — and what made it worse was his invitation to Hitler to be his best man. This upset the Führer very much and the officer corps would not stand for it." [Keitel] agreed that the charges against von Fritsch were probably framed up — degrading charges of homosexuality. But even with respect to this he clings to his defense of Hitler. It is always the same — admiration, respect, affection for Hitler. I cannot understand it. At the time of the attempt on Hitler's life on July 20, 1944, Keitel was in the room where the bomb exploded. An eyewitness who survived tells us that Keitel called out, "Where is the Führer — where is the Führer?"

Keitel leaned toward me across the desk and said, "Now I will tell you something that few people know. Hitler was no mere corporal in the German Army of the last war. After the war he was an instructor of officers in Munich!" Finally, he said to me, "I wish you would see my wife in Berchtesgaden. Tell her I am well and to go to our country home in Hanover. If you will do this for me and tell me that she is well I can stand anything." He stood very erect and handsome as he said these words — and his eyes glistened with a slight trace of water. I admit it touched me some. I assured him I would see what could be done. He asked for paper. I handed him my small notebook and in it he wrote his wife's name — Frau Lisa Keitel, and her address. *Sic transit Gloria mundi.*

No letters today, and besides it rained steadily and the temperature fell. Not a pleasant day amid these ruins. I had intended to leave on a weekend jaunt today, but the weather caused us to postpone it until tomorrow.

You have my love — all of it — always and ever. Good night to my lovely Grace.

Tom

CHAPTER 6

"The Most Brutal Measures"

KEITEL ADMITS TO DODD that he ordered "the most brutal measures even against women and children" and yet defends his actions. Dodd tries to get von Papen to take responsibility for his role in bringing Hitler to power. Seyss-Inquart provides much detail about the Anschluss but then argues that he had no real role in it—a theme developing among the Nazi defendants. Dodd becomes ill with strep throat, is hospitalized, and must write his letters to Grace from bed. After his return, he writes about his fears concerning the Soviets, who "are looting Germany of everything." The indictments, Dodd declares, are still "wretched," and he lobbies Jackson to become more involved in writing them. Dodd questions a German military historian, who first says that certain key records were burned but finally admits that he buried the most important ones in Berchtesgaden. Another Dodd interrogation uncovers the German plot to murder two high-ranking French generals. Even so, he complains to Grace about the staff, which has "so much jealousy and petty rivalry." In his final flourish, he sends Grace drawings of Hitler's bunker made by the führer's chauffeur.

Nürnberg, Germany
September 1, 1945

Grace, my dearest one,

Monday is Labor Day. Such a thought makes me slightly homesick. The summer is over and despite all my plans of last spring for passing most of the summer season with you and with the children the arrival of fall and a look backwards shows that it was one summer of our happy life together when I had but a few days with you. So goes the plan of man.

This Saturday, I continued with Field Marshal Keitel. We discussed the killing of hostages: men, women and children in Poland and Russia and Italy. He admitted that he gave such orders but only after terrible attacks had been made on German soldiers. He even verified the wording of his order as calling for "the most brutal measures even against women and children." Whole towns were slaughtered and burned. Some few able bodied [people] were shipped back to Germany as slave labor. It is a degrading business for these once proud Prussians to admit these orders. Yet Keitel is adamant. He said, "I would do it all over again if the situation presented itself as it did then." The horror of it all is that to a very large extent all armies do a certain amount of it! Not the wholesale killing of women and children and men — but certainly most commanders have at one time or another ordered the complete destruction of a town where sabotage or sniping was prevalent. Mussolini objected to Hitler about the excesses of the Germans in Italy on one occasion at least. And Hitler issued an order saying in effect that not so much of it should be done — and no Fascist Party members should be included. A mild little fellow — eh?

I did not go away this weekend as it was raining this morning and the outlook for fair weather was not good. It is just as well as I have many odds and ends to clear up. I must prepare to question von Papen next week and he's a wily gentleman.[1]

1. Dodd's intent in this interrogation was to discover the backroom politics of Hitler's rise to power and how he gained widespread support, even among men like von Papen, who had been skeptical of the Nazis.

I suppose Christopher is growing rapidly. Did I understand correctly, from a brief sentence in one of your letters, that he is now walking? It doesn't seem possible. Tell me more personal news about yourself and the children. Can't you write on both sides of the paper? It really works very well! Yet I must admit that your letters are wonderful — so cheery and so much like you. Sometimes I wonder if everything can be as smooth and easy as your letter indicated. Do not spare me the news — I want it all — because it is about you and the children. Of course I am soft about this separation, I know. After all, I have been away only five weeks — some families separate every summer. Unfortunately, I am not constructed that way — and neither are you. Thank God for that.

I find myself becoming quite accustomed to all the ruin and wreckage. By the way, it was Nürnberg, among other places that a great number of victims of German cruelty were found. Hundreds of unburied bodies of slave laborers were here. Our troops made the civilians clean up that mess and bury the dead. Four civilian Germans were assigned to carry each corpse one and one half miles to be buried. I think it was good educational treatment. Many of the Germans say they were ignorant of what went on. This I do not believe. Howard Brundage — who was here in those days — saw freight cars full of dead bodies on railroad sidings. I cannot believe that even one such shipment could be in Franklin[2] for even a few minutes without widespread knowledge — at least by nose! It is a terrible page in the history of the human race. The Germans can never live it down. Believe it when you read about the use of slave labor and internees for medical experiments — such as freezing. These were performed for the benefit of the German air corps, which wished to obtain information to be related to high-altitude flying in sub zero weather. Isn't it sickening?

So, my darling — cherish what we have. And pray and live so that our children will never be faced with a similar situation. I send you all of my love —

Tom

2. Franklin is a town near Lebanon, Connecticut.

Nürnberg, Germany
September 3, 1945

Grace, my dearest one,

One letter arrived this morning dated August 25. I am amazed to read that no letter from Germany has reached you. I have written every day. In fact I did the same in Paris. This mail business is a mess, and I am very unhappy about it.

[This morning] I was at the courthouse before nine. At 10:30 I began to question von Papen. He is a lean, gray man with a monkey-shaped face. His appearance is sharp and manner cunning. He speaks English so we conducted the interrogation in English. I started with his earliest background and brought him down to 1934. He insisted that he was willing to compromise on the naming of Hitler to the Chancellorship in 1933 — only because there was no other way out. He claims that von Hindenburg suggested it to him. I pressed him on this point for we know that von Papen induced Hindenburg to name Hitler — only after von Papen and Hitler had made a bargain which included, among other things, the naming of von Papen as vice-chancellor. However, he would not admit this to me. He made reference to his Catholic faith — and I resented this. Consequently, I said, "What did you do to help Klausner, the fine Catholic leader who was butchered by the Nazis in 1934?" He answered, "I was almost killed myself."[3] I replied, "You must have been in very bad with Hitler at that time because six weeks later he sent you to Austria as his ambassador — the most important diplomatic post that Hitler had to offer." His face colored ever so slightly but years of diplomatic deceit have given him excellent self control. He is a politician of the worst type and a professional Catholic — and he is as much responsible for the rise and power of

3. Von Papen was referring to his arrest in 1934, in the purge of Ernst Röhm, chief of the SA (Storm Troopers). Von Papen was confined to quarters for three days. Hitler decided that executing the country's vice chancellor might backfire.

Hitler and the Nazis as any man in the world. So it went all day — with a break for lunch. I adjourned our session at 4:45 p.m. and I will see him again tomorrow.

It is now 8 p.m. here — 2 p.m. at Coventry Lake on Labor Day. It has been no holiday here — and not even a suggestion of one. It is strange about these days. Time and circumstance can so change one's thinking even about great holidays.

Your letter of this morning was very sweet — but so short. How can I get you to write on both sides of the paper?

So comes to a close another day on this mission — and another day which brings me nearer to home.

Tom

Nürnberg, Germany
September 4, 1945

Grace, my most beloved one,

No mail — and that makes any day dull. Besides the interviews were not particularly exciting. In the forenoon we talked with Keitel — Colonels Amen and Brundage and I. It was a little painful for Colonel Amen who felt that Keitel was lying. I do not think so. It all grew out of some questions I asked Keitel about the Japanese and what plans the Germans and Japanese had. He answered by saying that there were no plans — and that he, Keitel — did not even think of the Japs with reference to the U.S. until the late summer of 1941. Well, we found an order which Keitel had issued on March 5, 1941 — discussing the Japanese and stating that early intervention by the Japs was desirable. It made reference to an attack on American naval vessels. Keitel freely admitted having written it when confronted but claimed he had forgotten about it. I believe him because in my judgment he is not as bright as legend has tried to make him. He told me that in July of 1941 he, Admiral Nomura [of Japan] and General Marras of Italy met as the representatives of the three countries and decided on the line 70 degrees [longitude] as a line of demarcation between German-Italian and Japanese influence.[4]

Yesterday afternoon I talked with Hildegarde Bruninghoff, secretary to Robert Ley, the head of the German Labor Division. She is a girl of about 30, married, one child — husband missing in the war. She was Ley's secretary for a long time. Frequently Hitler visited the Ley home in the evening and she was present on most of these occasions. Mrs. Ley was very beautiful — Hitler admired her very much. She says that Hitler would stay two or three hours — and talk of art, music or the theater. She often heard him say "No politics" in the conversations at the Ley home. She believes Hitler was a great man. Later in the afternoon I talked with Helen Krassezyk, formerly secretary to Hans Frank, the governor general of Poland — "the bloody butcher." She painted Frank as a man who was forced to put these vicious measures into effect, and forced to take all the steps he did take in Poland by Himmler and Hitler. She insists that he wanted to resign and Hitler refused to permit it. Well — the same old song. It would be relieving to hear one of them admit some blame for something. They blame everything on the dead or missing. I sometimes believe they do not include Hitler only because they are not certain he is dead.

For now — good-bye, my sweet. I send you all of my love.

Tom

September 6, 1945
Nürnberg, Germany

Grace, my dearest one,

Today, I questioned again Dr. Arthur Seyss-Inquart, the Austrian, and he told me in some considerable detail the story of his deeds in Austria. He persists in saying that he was no party to a deeply laid plan

---

4. The East-West line in the Indian Ocean intended to divide operations of Japanese and German naval operations.

to have the Nazis take over Austria. On the contrary, he gives me this account of his meeting of February 17, 1938 with Hitler in Berlin. He meets Hitler by giving the Nazi salute, and says to Hitler, "You may think it strange that I do it because I recognize you as the leader of all Germans." Then, Seyss-Inquart and Hitler talk for two hours, and the Austrian tells Hitler, "I am for Anschluss, but by a slow evolution-ary process, and I will be no Trojan horse." To all of this Hitler said nothing — merely changed the subject of the conversation according to S-I [Seyss-Inquart]. Well, it goes through the last days and the last hours — S-I claiming he was as surprised as anyone else. But of course I have my very grave doubts of all this, and when we talk with Schuschnigg[5] we will get much information.

This evening after dinner, Colonel Brundage and I went to see "Dear Ruth," a USO show at the Nürnberg Opera House. It was a splendid comedy and done very well by an excellent cast. The soldier audience gave the cast a big hand, and it was well deserved.

Afterward, we returned to the hotel and by 10 I am ready for bed. We all retire early here, partly because there is a curfew, even though colonels and I are exempt, and partly because we are tired at the end of a day of questioning these Nazis.

The fall is really here in Germany. One needs heavy clothing for a bed at night and a top coat in the morning and evening. You know I love the fall season, and it reminds me of you, so this autumn in Europe I am very lonesome for you, and counting the days until I return to you and the children.

I must urge you to get my bank balance — then draw a check on it. You can send me a check for signature or sign it yourself — you can imi-tate mine. But I do think you should have the use of that money.

Good night for now, my love. Give my little ones my fond affection.

Tom

5. Von Schuschnigg became the Austrian prime minister in 1934, after the mur-der of Engelbert Dollfuss. He was arrested and imprisoned by the Nazis in 1938 during the Anschluss. After the war, he taught political science at St. Louis University and became an American citizen in 1956.

September 6, 1945
Nürnberg, Germany

Grace, my dearest one,

The date on this letter is somewhat deceptive, for while it accurately tells the time of the writing, it is one day behind the events recorded.

So yesterday was a splendid early fall day—full sunshine, crisp morning and evening air. I passed the whole day at work. In the morning I prepared for the afternoon session with Seyss-Inquart—the Austrian who was the Nazi stooge when Hitler marched in. Later, Seyss-Inquart was governor of Holland during the occupation. He is a stubborn and taciturn individual. Wears heavy glasses, is rather fair of complexion, walks with a limp. He is a Roman Catholic, a lawyer and of an old family in Austria. He told me of events leading to the murder of Dollfuss[6] and was careful to insert that on the day of the murder he—Seyss-Inquart—was many miles away in his native town. He said he saw Hitler, Himmler and Göring in February of 1938 and insisted that no arrangements were made for the march in to Austria a few weeks later.

He maintains he hoped to achieve Anschluss with Germany only by a slow, evolutionary process, and this, he states, he told Hitler. He admits that on the fateful days in March he was in constant touch with Berlin and that the day before the Nazis came, a telegram, over his signature, was sent to Hitler stating that because of the internal condition—riots, etc.—he requested Hitler to send in German troops. He claims that this telegram was sent without his permission—and over his opposition. But he says, "I was opposed to sending the telegram only because at that time I was not legally head of the government. Later in the night I became the head of the government and early the next morning I called Hitler on the telephone and asked him to send German troops and suggested

6. **Dollfuss was Austrian chancellor from 1932 to his assassination in 1934 by eight Austrian Nazis.**

that Austrian troops go to meet them — and enter Germany in token of our new union. Hitler agreed, but he said the German troops were already in Austria anyway!" Later that day Seyss-Inquart met Hitler at Linz, Austria. He has a careful mind, this man — and his story, up to this point, while obviously not true as to motive, arrangements and details does have some color of substance. His trouble lies in his attempt to have it appear that he was once a patriotic Austrian and that all these things happened without any plan on his part. He admits conversations with Hitler, Himmler and Göring; admits he was made head of the Austrian government when the Nazis came; admits that he called Hitler on the phone, and all the details of these episodes, and then tries to state with conviction that he was no part of the plan. Furthermore he will have something to explain when we get into his activities in Holland.

It now appears as if we are moving ahead for the trials. I see no reason for any delay beyond early December, but of course one cannot be certain. In any event, I think that by that time I will have made my contribution and I will feel conscience free about leaving. I am always thinking about new plans. I still am not certain that I should ever attempt the Connecticut exams — and am wondering how soon I can establish residence elsewhere. You have good judgment. Why not write me your thoughts on this problem — I do want your advice. For now, my dearest, I shall say adieu — I send you my love and long to see you soon.

Tom

September 9, 1945
Chiemsee, Germany

Grace, my most beloved one,

This letter must cover some ground so I may as well tell you at the very outset that I am writing in bed — at the 112th Evacuation Hospital. It is the usual Dodd sore throat — not as bad as some I have had — but bad enough to put me here.

Now, to return to Friday, September 7, when I left Nürnberg.[7] That morning and afternoon I questioned Keitel again very thoroughly and after confronting him with certain directives which he signed, he admitted planning an attack on Czechoslovakia. In his written memo to Hitler he suggested three ways of starting the attack, one of which would be to have the German Ambassador in Czechoslovakia assassinated! He was very uneasy about all this and his explanation is "Hitler told me what he wanted to do — and I, as a soldier, had to carry out his wishes."

Late Friday afternoon I left Nürnberg in a command car and with Lieutenant Margolies, Elizabeth Clifford, and Margaret Galvin — for Salzburg. Margolies and I were to make the trip and the two girls asked for a ride and we said yes. We arrived in Munich that night about 7:30 and after a good dinner at an old German inn — now under American auspices. We stayed at the OSS house, retiring about 9 p.m. My throat was pretty sore at this point. On Saturday, early in the morning I went to the Army dispensary and had my throat looked at and sprayed. It seemed OK. I had no temperature, so we started for Salzburg. The drive through the Alps was something I shall never forget — the mountains are magnificent. The Bavarian and the Austrian countryside is the most picturesque that I have seen. This is one part of the world I could live in. Why these people want war is beyond me.

We stopped at Berchtesgaden and went to see Hitler's berghof[8] — or what is left of it. As you know it was badly bombed — but there is enough left to show and the mountains are grand.

7. On that morning, Dodd mailed a letter to his friends, the Oppers, in which he described appalling health problems in Nuremberg, and the fear of an epidemic. "When the U.S. troops entered [the city] they had to bring in bulldozers and push bodies and debris into heaps. Also they found hundreds of bodies of newly deceased slave laborers as yet unburied. I have seen photos of Nürnbergers carrying these corpses to a common burial ground under the severe and watchful eyes of American soldiers — only three or four months ago. It is all horrible and shameful and to be in the middle of it — even now — is not a pleasant experience."

8. Hitler's vacation home, purchased with the royalties from *Mein Kampf*.

Salzburg is a lovely old city — a thing of beauty and charm — with its ancient Austrian culture, its medieval buildings and churches. I saw Mozart's birthplace and all the famous landmarks. We stayed overnight in the Gablehaus, and this morning we decided to return to Nürnberg early as my throat was getting worse by the hour. We got to this hospital about noontime. I thought I would have someone look at my throat, and right away the doctor urged me to get into bed and get under treatment. He said, "You have a very sore throat — no temperature but over here we take no chances. Now is the time to take care of it, and this is the nearest big hospital to Nürnberg." So — I am in a very comfortable room, getting A plus attention from doctors and nurses. They are loading me with sulfa and irrigating the throat, so it should be all well in a few days. Continue to write, as I will be on the job in a day or two. All my love to you and the children.

Tom

Chiemsee, Germany
September 10, 1945

Grace, my dearest one,

Well this reminds me of the time I was in the Windham Hospital[9] — for already my throat is much better and I am "enjoying poor health," as Carolyn would say. The nurses are very pleasant — professionally of course, my dear — and this hospital is in a really beautiful spot. The Chiemsee is a lake and a very large one. The hospital is right on it and behind us are the Bavarian Alps with snow on their mighty peaks. It is truly a beautiful place but I am anxious to get out and get back to Nürnberg so I can do my bit to hurry matters along. I feel quite far away from everything here. Even Nürnberg seems homelike in comparison. Yet the hospital is very cheerful and well run. Not many months ago the whole

9. In Willimantic, Connecticut, where Dodd had previously been treated for strep.

staff was under canvass — in the very front lines — doing a job for wounded soldiers. And I guess they really saw action from what I hear. These young doctors and young nurses deserve a great deal of credit for their work. Now they are all pitifully anxious to get home — and I hope they do so soon. This matter of getting our people home is no joke. It is bad for us and for Europe to keep them here. Of course we must keep an occasional force here — but I am writing about those who are just "waiting," and they are in the millions. As a result all kinds of complications arise — health, social, economic complications. The Europeans are involved too and they want us to leave. So tell your congressman — or congresswoman[10] in your case, to do her bit to get these people home soon.

This is a dull letter, my dear — a history of irrigations, pills, thermometers, pulse taking, sleep, meals, back rubs and small talk. I am much better. I had thought that I would not tell you I was here, but I rejected that thought on the theory that you and I want to tell each other the "straight" of every situation.

All my love to you.

Tom

Chiemsee, Germany
September 11, 1945

Grace, my beloved one,

Another day in the 112th Evacuation Hospital and my throat is almost normal again. The doctors tell me it was strep — the old trouble — and you know how miserable it makes me feel. I expect to leave here in another few days. But these Army doctors insist on clearing up every last bit of the infection and I believe they are right. They are all very careful about the slightest disability for they fear things getting out of hand. Sore throats are particularly alarming to them — with conditions as they are in

10. **Chase Going Woodhouse served in the House from 1945 to 1951.**

Germany. So I am well along to a good sound throat and feeling fine. Did I tell you that one of the nurses is a Lieutenant Ray of New London? A very cute little girl. Her father is a sergeant on the New London police force. She trained at Lawrence & Memorial Hospital. Most of this group of nurses and doctors are from New England or upper New York state. They all come in to see me — the most recent arrival from the States — expecting some news, when actually they know as much as I do because they get mail regularly. Yet I understand their feeling and try to tell them a few little things.

I am chuckling as I write this letter — for I can see you grinning — raising your eyebrows and saying, "The old hospital Romeo is at it again — shades of Windham Memorial and the nurses in his room."

I do not think you are really worried about my conduct. I miss you so much, particularly when I have so much time to think about you and the children. You must be all re-established in Lebanon now. Are the children back in school? Did Carolyn enter the elementary school? In what grade? Have you located a girl or woman yet? Do not be afraid to pay a good wage for a good worker — it is a good investment.

For now — good-bye again from Bavarian Germany — and all my love to the loveliest girl in the world.

Tom

Nürnberg, Germany
September 14, 1945

Grace, my dearest one,

I am back in Nürnberg and feeling fit — all cured and my throat is better than Lawrence Tibbet's[11] — my throat, not my voice. I left the hospital yesterday afternoon. Colonel Corley sent Justice Jackson's car for me — a magnificent Mercedes-Benz — and I was pleased when Neil

11. Lawrence Tibbet, a regular at the Metropolitan Opera, was a leading baritone of the time.

Andrews stepped out of it to greet me. We arrived in Nürnberg late because we ran out of gas — and as a result, Colonel Brundage, Colonel Corley, Father Golden (he is from Hartford) and a few others were left waiting. They had prepared a welcome for me — consisting of all kinds of fancy goods, wines and little delicacies which they gathered with great pains. I felt very badly because they went to great lengths to prepare it. However, it was just as well, as I was very tired and was glad to get into bed. This morning I felt very good and a little important. Everyone was very pleased — so it seemed — at my recovery. There were more handshakes and greetings than at a political convention.

So this morning I again questioned Keitel until noontime. He and I are really old friends now, you know. And he had heard — via the underground, I guess, of my illness. So he greeted me warmly this morning. At noon, Jackson, who arrived yesterday from London, came into the dining room and he walked over and greeted me, referring to my hospitalization, and remarked, "I am not going to sympathize with you — for you look better than any of us." And he is right, for I got quite a sun tan on Wednesday and Thursday at the hospital. The nurses put me out in the sun in a big chair wrapped in blankets, and my face shows it.

George Hurley wrote that he has been made a junior partner in his law firm and that the members want to know if I will join as their trial counsel in either Washington or New York. He suggested that I quote some figure as to how much I would expect. Last night, Colonel Brundage said to me, "If you will come to Chicago I will guarantee that you will never regret it." He is a very successful lawyer — he represents the telephone company and other such well-off clients. He has mentioned this to me before, but we shall wait and see. Leo Gaffney[12] writes, "You must come back and take that exam." Joe Blumenfeld writes, "You must come back and take that exam." So there you are.

All my love to the sweetest girl in the world.

Tom

12. Gaffney was the chief federal attorney for Connecticut and later became a superior court judge.

Nürnberg, Germany
September 15, 1945

Grace, my dearest one,

It is Sunday afternoon and I am at the office preparing for tomorrow's work. I thought I would try my hand at this typing and relieve you of the job of deciphering my hand script.

Yesterday morning was devoted to Keitel and the afternoon to some paperwork. Col. Amen gave a cocktail party last night in honor of his birthday. About ten of us were there including Jackson. After the cocktails we had a private dinner party at the hotel. I had a good chance to talk with the Justice as I was seated opposite him at the table.

This morning we had breakfast and then went to mass at St. Anthony's Church. There we saw a moving spectacle — the first confirmation in Nürnberg for more than eight years. The Bishop of Bamberg presided and he is a distinguished looking prelate. The children looked good and the little girls were all in white clothing! These Germans are amazing people. Where they get the soap to wash with is beyond me yet the little white dresses were white and clean. Men and women wept openly and indeed it affected us to see them. The most pitiful sights were behind — blind children with missing limbs — the awful results of the war and the air raids.

After mass, Col. Brundage and I visited with Col. Corley in his quarters until lunch. When we walked into the hotel we were introduced to Mickey Rooney. He is here this week with his show, *OK-USA*. He looks and acts as he does in his movies. We are attending the show tonight at the Opera House in Colonel Corley's box. Tomorrow night Col. Corley is giving a small dinner party. I suppose it appears as if we are social lions with all these goings on, but actually it is quite informal and it does make life in this atmosphere at least bearable.

The Russian advance party arrived yesterday. I try hard to be fair in my thinking about them but I have heard too much about them and the sight of them raises my blood pressure. You have no idea of what goes on. They are beasts and worse. Believe me when I tell you these things for I have it from officers of unquestioned integrity who have seen with their own eyes.

They are looting Germany of everything. When they occupy a town they proceed as follows: The first week all machinery and tools are moved out; the second week they strip every house of furnishings; the third week all men between 16 and 40 are shipped to Russia — and all the time rape and violence are the order of the day. This is no secret by the way — every soldier who has been near their armies tells the same story. There have been numerous shooting scrapes between our soldiers and theirs — particularly in Czechoslovakia. Recently our men have shot any Russian on sight who is found inside our lines after dark. It is all a shocking situation and until and unless we stop kowtowing to them things will not get better. The U.S. soldier, by the way, says the Russian is vastly overrated as a fighting man. But life means very little to them and they beat the Germans for many reasons, among them being the reckless use of manpower. It is said that in some battles the Germans mowed them down by the thousands and yet they still kept coming and sometimes the Germans actually killed so many they ran out of ammunition — and so they had to retreat. Of course you must understand that the Germans did the same things to the Russians — looting, raping, slave labor — and that is what bothers me. They are two of a kind. What a bright outlook for a brave new world at peace! From Norway to Africa, the communists are on the march. Make no mistake about it. And the prospect of Russian totalitarianism — Russian Gestapo, Russian concentration camps, Russian *kultur* — seems to me to be a sorry result for a world that was fighting for freedom in Europe and in the world. God help us all.

I realize that I got wound up and wrote a penny lecture — but I want to write you about these things for you should know them and besides in this fashion I can keep a record of what I hear and see. I am not keeping a diary so I hope all my letters are reaching you.

I sent the boys a few little things yesterday. John Corley gave me two 1st Division shoulder patches for them and I also sent a map of Hitler's mountain place and a program of the music festival in Salzburg. I will send the girls something very soon.

It is almost two months since I saw you waving goodbye from the RR station in Washington and, my dearest, I do miss you greatly. I know you feel as I do that if I can contribute anything to this program, which even in the smallest way will make the waging of war less likely, then our separation is indeed worthwhile.

I would love to get a long letter from you — can't you write something a little extra now and then? What is the help situation? You must get someone at once.

For now, good-bye — and all my love to you,

Tom

Nürnberg, Germany
September 17, 1945

Grace my dearest one,

Yesterday, Jackson told the press that the U.S. would be ready to start the trial on November 1. By the way, the Russian representative has been suddenly withdrawn. No explanations — mere notice that he will no longer represent Russia in this matter.[13] After weeks of negotiating, weeks of work with him as chief counsel for Russia, he simply goes home and does not come back. These Russians are impossible. What effect this will have on the trial or the trial date no one knows, but you can imagine the confusion that may arise out of it.

The whole war crimes staff is here now, headed by Francis Shea, an assistant attorney general in the Department of Justice. With him are his chief assistants, Sid Kaplan and Ben Kaplan — no relation to each other. Murray Gurfein is out of the city for a few days. Sidney Goldstein is here, so is Dan Margolies and his wife who is Shea's secretary and is employed under her maiden name. There is also a Miss Lynch here. Then too there are good people like Lt. Buchsbaum, an excellent translator, Captain Enklewitz, an excellent doctor — good

13. I. T. Nikitchenko later returned as the Russian chief judge.

men like Carl Blumenstein, Major Fox, Samuel Glick. So you see we have an interesting group here. It's wonderful, really.

A week from Thursday, Colonel Corley, Col. Brundage and I are going to Italy. First to Naples, then to Capri, then back to Naples, to Rome, to Florence and Nürnberg. It will take four or five days but we all want to see it and we may not get another chance. It will be all air travel and thus we can save much time.

All of my love to you,
Tom

Nürnberg, Germany
September 19, 1945

Grace, my beloved one,

I feel as if I have been neglectful because I did not write yesterday. But it was a difficult day and you were always in my mind.

Monday afternoon we had a conference on the rough draft of the indictment which was prepared in London. It is wretched — and we all agree on that. Some of the smart alecks did the job, headed by Commander Kaplan. We have let Jackson know how we feel about it, and I am hopeful that a new staff set up for the purpose will produce something worthwhile. After all, we are writing a rather important paper.

Monday night we went to Col. Corley's dinner party. Grace, it was something I shall not forget. We were driven out to the castle of Herr von Faber Castel. It is a show place consisting of some 80 rooms — and really in castle form. Faber is — or was — a tremendously wealthy man — the Eberhardt Faber pens and pencils you know.

As we entered the dining room — which is magnificent — an orchestra was playing softly in one corner. The meal was wonderful. In the course of it a chorus of German girls sang German folk songs and hymns, and later when Colonel Corley invited them to do so they sang "Lily Marlene" and two American songs which they have learned from the soldiers. It was a great treat. Col. Brundage and I thought it was the best evening we have had in Europe.

Yesterday, I talked with Seyss-Inquart all day. Father Ed Walsh — the head of the Georgetown Foreign Service School,[14] was with me. I met him here yesterday morning. He is traveling about Europe investigating certain atrocities against Churchmen. I like him very much and have had some good conversations. Last night, Dick Owens dropped in to see me and brought a German Army rifle for the boys. He is shipping it directly to Lebanon — but be sure to put it away until we have it looked over. I have obtained some odds and ends and I believe I will ship some things along as otherwise I will be weighted down when traveling home.

I received three wonderful letters from you yesterday. And somehow I feel like I did when we were ten years — or twelve years — younger, in those grand days before we were married. I recall sitting in law school dreaming about you — and a letter meant so much in those days. Here I am in Germany twelve years later and the same deeply burning love for you fills every waking hour — and your lovely letters mean so much.

For now — good-bye — to my lovely Grace. Tell the children I will write to them soon.

Tom

September 20, 1945
Nürnberg, Germany

Grace, my dearest one,

Yesterday was devoted to Herr Franz von Papen. He is a wily one and a very difficult man to question. He speaks English, of course, very well. He admitted great responsibility for Hitler's rise to power and said

14. **Later, Georgetown University renamed it the Edmund A. Walsh School of Foreign Service.**

he believed Hitler to be "the greatest crook in history" — so! But he was ever so vague as to when he first concluded that Herr Hitler was a knave. Father Walsh sat in while I talked with von Papen and made copious notes. I assume some of it will be sold from his lecture platform — or in book form. Maybe that is what I should do!

Howard Brundage is very serious about Chicago. I told him all about the bar incident in Connecticut. He says that he can easily handle that in Illinois. Yesterday he brought the subject up again and he said, "I'll give you ten thousand a year, for five years — and you can keep all that you make yourself." Well — I do not know. He likes me I guess — and maybe thinks I know more than I do. I will let things take their own course.

Your last letter told me of Jack Meunier's help in your move back to Lebanon. He certainly is a good friend. I am a bit worried about your finances — for apparently you have had a hard time of it, what with Damien and insurance — and what not. You see where the money goes now. Perhaps every man should go away once and turn over his entire income to his wife and let her handle everything. It would accomplish a lot. First, she would learn how to handle business affairs and second she would have a better appreciation of her husband's problems. It really isn't necessary in our case, for if ever a man had a self-denying wife I have one. And no man ever had a wife who understood him as you do me. Dear me. As I read that on paper it occurs to me that I can never tell the frauleins that I am "misunderstood" at home! Do tell me the Lebanon news. How are the children enjoying school this year? I wonder if you receive all of my letters. It is easy to know for they run in chronological order. Do let me know if some are missing.

I really yearn for the day I can hold you in my arms — not for just a few minutes — for hours and hours and hours. We will have a new honeymoon and you should start getting your torso ready. But I mean torso — as well as trousseau. Good-bye for today and all of my love to the sweetest girl in the world.

Tom

Nürnberg, Germany
September 20, 1945

Grace, my dearest one,

I finished one letter to you early this afternoon and mailed it. But dinner is over and I have retired to my own room for some quiet atmosphere and some dreams of you. How better can I spend an hour than in writing again to the girl I love?

I did not talk with any of the prisoners today. I did some reading in preparation for future discussions. Colonel Brundage and I had dinner together and he went to his room early too. He lives next door to me at the hotel. Our apartment is not ready yet — like nearly all other property in this city it was badly damaged. I sometimes think no attempt should be made to reconstruct this city. It is a hopeless task. It would seem wiser to me to build a new city on new ground. The removal of the debris is a five- or ten-year job alone.

The staff continues to grow every day. Col. Kaplan is now here, as a mate, I assume, for Commander Kaplan. Dr. Newman has arrived and I do not know how many more. It is all a silly business — but "silly" really isn't the right word. One would expect that some of these people would have sense enough to put an end to this kind of a parade. You know better than anyone how I hate race or religious prejudice. You know how I have despised anti-Semitism. You know how strongly I feel toward those who preach intolerance of any kind. With that knowledge — you will understand when I tell you that this staff is about seventy-five percent Jewish. Now my point is that the Jews should stay away from this trial — for their own sake. For — mark this well — the charge "a war for the Jews" is still being made and in the post-war years it will be made again and again.[15] The too large percentage of Jewish men and women

15. Many isolationists included this view in their objections to going to war. Most notable was Charles A. Lindbergh, the most prominent member of the America First Committee, who argued in 1941 that there were three forces pushing the United States to war: the British, President Roosevelt, and the Jews.

here will be cited as proof of this charge. Sometimes it seems that the
Jews will never learn about these things. They seem intent on bringing
new difficulties down on their own heads. I do not like to write about
this matter — it is distasteful to me — but I am disturbed about it. They
are pushing and crowding and competing with each other and with
everyone else. They will try the case I guess — the Kaplans and some others. Frankly, that is the least of my concerns because as things stand now
the trial will not be over before Christmas and I want to be home by
then. If I am not involved in the trial, then I can say, "My job is done —
much as I would like to stay for the trial, I prefer to go home now."

The Russians are very cool about this business. I told you that their
representative had been suddenly withdrawn. They have not named a
judge to represent Russia. The French are not here at all and of course
they have named no judicial officer. The English are very British about
it all, if you know what I mean. And they have not named anyone as a
judicial representative. We have certain information and certain documents in London, very secret — code named and all that nonsense —
and the Russians must not know that we have it. Likewise the story here
is that the Russians have a lot of valuable stuff but they won't tell us
about it. Isn't it nice to be "dear allies"? I heard tonight that the Poles —
the soldiers and their officers who fought for Poland and against Germans and Russians when both invaded the country — are to be shipped
back to Poland, which means to Russia and death and worse. If this
happens, it will be one of the blackest crimes of all time. If the United
States ships or allows to be shipped against his will one Pole back to
Russian occupied Poland, then I shall be tempted to go home and to
say why. The Russians are butchering the Poles everywhere — believe
that for it is so. Grace, dear, the Russian situation is really terrible.[16]

16. Reports were apparently filtering in to trial headquarters of atrocities com-
    mitted by occupying Soviet forces in Eastern Europe. It is also possible that
    Dodd's thinking was influenced by the Katyn forest massacre of thousands
    of Polish officers in 1943. The Soviets had blamed the Nazis, and vice versa.
    As later letters attest, Dodd was convinced of Soviet culpability. It wasn't
    until 1989 that the Soviet Union admitted responsibility.

Our people prefer the Germans to the English, the French and all races in Europe. At first I was very surprised to hear it. Now I am of the same mind myself. The Germans are an interesting people. They love flowers, for example. In all of this wreck and ruin, we see flowers — flowers in window boxes, flowers being sold, flowers being carried, flowers being worn. I spoke of this at a dinner recently and a young Englishman said, "Yes, it is very curious — you know when the Germans occupied Paris they bought up all the pictures and prints of flowers."

Well my sweetest one — methinks I have written enough. It has been so nice to talk with you — to have your lovely face before me all of this time. Good night to the sweetest girl in the world.

Tom

Nürnberg, Germany
September 21, 1945

Grace, my dearest one,

Situation normal — interrogations continued as follows. In the morning I questioned Major General Heinz von Gyldenfeldt, an old army man, who really should not be in prison. There is no proof of any kind of crime against him, and on the contrary it appears that he is and was persona non grata with the Nazis. I have recommended that he be taken out of the jail and placed in a residence as a material witness.

In the afternoon, I questioned Alfred Rosenberg — one of the top-flight Nazis. He is a sly, evasive and cunning man. He evaded direct answers and placed blame on Hitler whenever he could do so. He even denied, so to speak, his own book, *The Myth of the Twentieth Century*, which was next to *Mein Kampf* the most authoritative book on Nazi Germany. Dr. Walsh of Georgetown sat in to hear the questioning and he was interested when Rosenberg said, "I was not against the Catholic Church — only against the Jesuits." Why the Jesuits? "Because they represent the international political aspects of the Catholic Church."

Our staff grows larger every day. The French and English are here now — so far no Russians. However the Russian [Nikitchenko] who was the chief prosecutor has now turned up as the Russian judge! It is very hard to swallow that one — a man who acts as prosecutor in the case for months suddenly is appointed to sit as a judge in the same case. Really, he should move to America and get on the Connecticut Supreme Court!

The American staff, I have discovered, is very largely made up of bright young men who have at various times been in the Labor Board — the LaFollette Committee,[17] the OPA[18] and what not. It is interesting to observe that they are all in officer uniforms — and never got any nearer to the fighting than you did.

We have had a few bad incidents here. At night steel cables have been stretched across the roads and the jeeps are wrecked on them — some serious results. We do not travel at night unless it is absolutely necessary.

Colonel Corley is sending two SS helmets to Tom and Jeremy. Two SS prisoners painted their names on them — "Herr Tom Dodd" on one, "Herr Jerry Dodd" on the other. Do not tell them until they arrive. I think they will get a big kick out of them.

So my dearest, good-bye for now, and do take good care of your precious self.

All my love,
Tom

September 23, 1945
Nürnberg, Germany

Grace, my dearest one,

This is Jeremy's birthday. I have written him a short note which he should get soon. It is also Sunday and I am squeezing in some letters

17. Congressional committee that investigated companies accused of taking extreme measures to avoid collective bargaining with unions.
18. The Office of Price Administration set ceilings on commodities and rents at the outbreak of World War II.

between mass and lunch. Yesterday was a lovely fall day, so much like our late September weather. I worked all day, devoting the morning to office details and in the afternoon I interrogated Dr. Wilhelm Heinrich Scheidt, who was the historian for the German High Command. He is a very interesting creature with a scholastic background. He can be very helpful to us and it is my intention to develop him that way. For example, he knows a lot about Keitel and Jodl and those who were associated with them. He confirms my opinion of Keitel — i.e., a stupid opportunist with enough cunning to hold a job. But he surprised me when he said Jodl wasn't the brains either — instead General [Walther] Warlimont, a member of Hitler's personal staff. Scheidt said there was considerable friction between Keitel and Jodl on one side and Warlimont on the other, and largely because Warlimont was a strict Catholic and Keitel and Jodl did not profess any faith. Scheidt tells me that he has some authentic papers hidden away. One is a memorandum on the fight within the German Army to resist Hitler. I am taking steps to find these at once.

About five thirty, Col. Brundage and I met Melvin Purvis at the hotel. He is a colonel and is making some sort of a survey over here. With him was Sid Rubenstein, a former [FBI] agent, now a lieutenant colonel working with Purvis. We had dinner together and afterwards we saw the show in the officer's club. It was a very pleasant evening.

The staff continues to grow — but we seem "to make haste slowly." I am beginning to worry about getting away before Christmas. Somehow I cannot see any necessity for all this delay. What we need is more working hours — some night work, some applied good sense, some cooperation from our allies and in no time we can do this job. I feel that I must leave in December. I do not want to pass Christmas here alone and besides I should be getting on with my plans by January. By December I will have made a contribution and I can leave in good conscience.

I guess we will be in Rome next weekend. Father Walsh is going with Colonel Brundage, Colonel Corley and me and is arranging a private audience with the Pope. I am quite excited for it is indeed a great experience. I shall write you about it. We are also stopping at Naples and Florence and Capri. We will fly down over the Alps and through the Brenner Pass. How I wish you were with me. But some day we will do it together.

Are you getting all my letters? Are any missing? I have never received the mail you sent to London and much of what you sent to Paris. Even now your letters are spotty—for example I still do not know what happened to Hugh and what Damien did. But I love your letters— they mean so much to me. I have read them and reread them time and time again.

I dream of lovely evenings years ago when I first met you—of the time I first kissed you (and you said, when I kissed you again, "Just like a bottle of olives—get the first one and the others come easy"). I recall all our plans and ambitions as we talked about them when we knew we were in love. Sometimes I think of the many times I must have tried your lovely soul—I was hard to housebreak I guess. I long to be with you. We must plan now to meet in New York when I return—just the two of us for a few days. We can do some Xmas shopping together. I do hope you get help soon—good reliable help so you can get away and so you will not be worn out with the care of the house and of the children.

So my dearest, I bid you adieu from Nürnberg once more. Sending you my love—all of it—always. Tell the children I will have many new stories for them when I get home.

Tom

Nürnberg, Germany
September 24, 1945

Grace my most beloved one,

More people arrived from London last night. I have no idea how many are on our staff, but it must be over 250. At least 150 are superfluous and worse. We are loaded with young officers — with big rank — small experience and less judgment. Some of them are intolerable, others tolerable, a few are likeable. Sometimes I wonder if this thing will ever work out, but it must, one way or another. The petty rivalry, the minor jealousy is old stuff to me. I am more concerned about the lack of leadership and direction with the resultant confusion. So far it looks like everyone has been making a holiday out of this assignment. As you can see, my feelings about this mission are still mercurial — 'twas ever thus.

My mail has fallen off — no letters for three days now. I know it is foolish — but no news makes me worry about you and the children. I know you are well — you have to be — it just can't be otherwise. I dreamed about you last night — lovely, a real dream. I guess I am still a young man. Don't you ever have a nice dream session? I highly recommend it — but the awakening is so disappointing.

I suppose the trees are changing color now. So far nothing like it here. How I would like to take your arm and walk on a quiet road, with red and yellow foliage all about us.

Adieu for now, my dearest — I love you completely. Say hello to all and to the children — give my affection.

Tom

Nürnberg, Germany
September 25, 1945

Grace, my dearest one,

Yesterday was a bit out of the ordinary. I continued my conversations with Dr. Scheidt, the military historian. We discussed the destruction of the OKW[19] files and he told me they were burned

19. *Oberkommando der Wehrmacht,* or **High Command of the Third Reich armed forces.**

at Berchtesgaden in late April of 1945. He insisted that all the records were burned — and something in his manner or his tone made me doubt him. I pressed him and at last he said, "All right, I buried some of the most important ones at Berchtesgaden." It was quite a surprise as he has been questioned many times and he has never given in. Anyway, he drew a map for us and we are sending him there with a few men to recover the documents. They may prove to be of inestimable value. It may be a great break for the prosecution. It may be a dud. In any event it brightened my day.

I continue to try to do my work, but really there is so much petty rivalry here. Brundage and I are given the leftovers, and believe me we are the only ones who have produced any results. I will have a very unimportant role in this whole show — for many reasons: 1. I am no one's fair-haired boy. 2. I am not in the military service. 3. It is a mess anyway.

I received three letters from you a few minutes ago. [He points out that several letters arrived from friends and family.] What one do you think I read first? One guess.

Do not pay Damien until he has painted the storm window two coats. Also cleaned up any mess he left. Now do not wait too long — your storm windows must be up in another few weeks. They must be painted black.

Your letters are indeed cheerful, and you seem to be doing very well. Jack Meunier wrote the most laudatory letter about you and the children. Leo Gaffney writes a newsy letter, too. He sent me a clipping from the *Hartford Courant* quoting Judge Wynne on my bar matter. What did the Norwich paper say?

Will I really get home in another two or three months? Sometimes it seems so far off. But we will make it, dearest — and what a day that will be. For now I send you my undying love.

Tom

Nürnberg, Germany
September 26, 1945

Grace, my dearest one,

Yesterday was routine in most respects. Routine, that is, for this assignment and for what has become something in the nature of a mission. In the morning I talked with Dr. Scheidt. He told me of the last days at Berchtesgaden. Sometime in April he was told to leave Berlin and to take his files with him and go to Berchtesgaden. The army set up its headquarters there as did other branches of the government and the plan called for Hitler to make his headquarters there, too. However, Scheidt says that later on he was told that Hitler had changed his mind and decided to remain in Berlin. This is of interest as it substantiates the "Redoubt" story.[20] It would appear that it was intended to carry on from the Alpine region — but the hopelessness of the entire situation caused Hitler to decide to remain in Berlin. I believe he did so and died there. Scheidt told me that the air raid which destroyed the berghof did not kill anyone.

Scheidt impresses me as a decent sort — who can be most helpful to us — but he should not be lodged in prison. He surrendered to the Americans, later was released, was taken again by the French, released to the Americans, agreed to remain to help our people with the German military records, and accordingly went to Paris and was then returned here and placed in prison. It is typical Army handling of a situation. I marvel that we ever won this war when I observe the almost hopeless confusion and red tape in the Army administration. No one claims that Scheidt is a war criminal — at most he will be a material witness. Yet he is thrown into prison — a dreary prison — because he surrendered and because he may have some information. All kinds of valuable records have been carelessly handled or ignored. All kinds of

20. **The plan of the Nazis to hold out and set up command in hidden Alpine locations.**

valuable information obtainable from men like Scheidt have been neg-
lected. An Army is an army—nothing more—sometimes much less.
Someday competent investigators will perhaps uncover much that is
now unknown.

In the afternoon, I questioned Keitel. General Lahousen, an assistant to Admiral Canaris, told us that on Hitler's orders Keitel
instructed Canaris to have the French Generals Giraud and Weygand
assassinated.[21] Lahousen said he refused to do it and Canaris kept
stalling. Keitel kept asking about it. When Heydrich[22] was assassinated
Canaris "claimed" that he had been working it out with Heydrich. In
this fashion the proposal died. It was too dirty a job to ask anyone else
to do. Keitel violently denied this and claimed that he never had any
such intention and had no such conversations. He stated that he did
instruct Canaris and Heydrich to recapture Giraud—dead or alive—
after Giraud's escape. Hitler, said Keitel, threatened to hang him if
Giraud was not caught. I believe Keitel did as Lahousen says. I think
he did whatever his master ordered. Canaris was executed after the
attempt on Hitler's life on July 20, 1944. He was undoubtedly in the
plot and seems to have been a decent sort. He and his staff were
always at loggerheads—perhaps not openly—with Hitler, Keitel and
Jodl. They were old military men and the shooting of prisoners—
Russian and Polish—disgusted them. Incidentally, the shooting of
Russian prisoners was widespread—likewise the Poles. It was done by
the SS.

I am really very fed up with the outfit. There is so much jealousy and petty rivalry. Apparently my interrogations caused some

21. Canaris was head of the German military intelligence service. Giraud was
    captured by the Nazis, escaped, and later joined the Free French forces.
    Weygand was a high official in the Vichy government.
22. Reinhard "Hangman" Heydrich, who chaired the Wannsee Conference
    and was a primary architect of the Holocaust, was ambushed in May 1941
    by Free Czechs and later died from his wounds.

considerable favorable comment—according to Neil Andrews. Consequently I am now being frozen out. Whenever anything startling is discovered concerning Keitel or the others assigned to me, Amen takes over. Thus he looks very good on the record—for usually some important document is found bearing Keitel's signature. Amen confronts him with it and of course he, Keitel, admits it. Then it appears that Amen, by skillful work, got an important admission from Keitel and my record shows no such brilliance. Neil gets the same treatment in his section. It is clear to both of us that we are not wanted by this crowd of jokers. It is a most difficult situation. I do not like to quit in the midst of this thing—and particularly for such reasons. It will seem strange at home after all the talk. It will require some explanation and I do not care to make one. This case will work out all right—these things always do. There is just so much proof—the defendants are certainly guilty on many counts. A schoolboy could convict them. Why do I always get into these situations? I was quite discouraged when I first arrived. Then things picked up a bit—I felt rather good about it all. I thought I could make a worthwhile contribution. Now things are on the down scale again—and very discouraging. Brundage feels as I do. So you see it is not peculiar to me. Really there is not one outstanding man in an important place in this organization—saving Jackson himself. I never saw anything as bad. I can understand difficulty—personality conflicts, even some professional rivalry. But this is a maelstrom of incompetence. It is awful.

Well, that is that. You will understand if I return much sooner than we anticipated. That, of course, is nothing to be upset about. What a joy it will be to see you again—and the sooner the better. I love you so deeply—so intensely—so completely. It has occurred to me that I am writing love letters. You always said you could put my letters in the paper. Turnabout is fair enough—yours could be in the *Stars and Stripes* as models of propriety!

My dearest, take good care of yourself and kiss the children for me.

Tom

Nürnberg, Germany
September 26, 1945

Grace, my dearest one,

This will be a very brief letter. It is getting near to bed time, but I want to pass a little time with you as I am leaving early in the morning for Rome.

Father Walsh is in Munich and will not be with us because of a change in plans. However we still have hopes of the audience with the Holy Father. Colonel Corley was made Regimental Commander today, so he cannot go as he had planned. Thus, Col. Brundage and I will leave together at 8:40 a.m. tomorrow for Paris, and from thence to Rome via Marseilles. We were advised not to fly over the Alps at this time of year. I will write you from Rome — from Naples — from Capri.

This afternoon I had a wonderful session with Keitel. He admitted that he, Jodl, Hitler and others planned to attack Czechoslovakia in September of 1938.[23] Do you remember our interest at the time — you were in the hospital — Jeremy was only a few days old? You had a radio, and you told me of your radio interest. Well, my sweet, we did not know how near to war the world was then. But I know now. Keitel has told me. Just about eight years ago — in this very city of Nürnberg — Hitler and his generals had a meeting which lasted far into the night and talked of the war, the attack that they were soon to make on Czechoslovakia. They were ready, and no power on earth could have stopped them. Perhaps Chamberlain will take an honorable place yet — he got an extension of time for England — maybe for the world.

Keitel gets under my skin. I know he is terribly guilty. I know better than most men. Yet I now know him — he has a pathetic aspect to me. He is so weak. Not long ago — a week or two past — he asked if I would try to locate his wife and tell her that he is well and that she should go to their home in Hanover. We found her in Berchtesgaden.

23. At the annual Nuremberg Rally, Hitler and Göring both made provocative speeches about the Sudetenland.

I had the message delivered. She was returned to Hanover. Today I told him of this. One would think I had cleared him of all accusations, set him free with one million dollars. He was very grateful. After all he is a human being — and we are supposed to be civilized.

I am enclosing something that you must put away — in the safest place. It is a diagram showing Hitler's bunker in Berlin — and the location of Hitler's body and that of Eva Braun — when they were burned after death. That is number 1.

Number 2 and 3 show the sofa where they died and other details. These were drawn by Hitler's chauffeur. They are of great interest. Do not show them to anyone.

So my sweet, I bid you adieu as I leave for Rome. Your lovely face will be before me at all times. Your beautiful soul will be with me every hour. I love even the thought of you. Sometimes here in Nürnberg — so far from you and the things we both love, I think, "If I can only get home to her, safe and sound, I will spend the rest of my life telling her of my love."

Tom

CHAPTER 7

Audience

Dodd is granted an audience with Pope Pius XII, who shows great interest in Nuremberg. When he returns to the trial, Dodd tells Grace he is disheartened by the departure of colleagues who have been mistreated by the brass. He gets damaging admissions from Keitel about Nazi intentions regarding Poland. Dodd witnesses the bizarre arrival of the "completely balmy" Rudolf Hess, who has claimed to have lost his memory. Dodd's ability at interrogation is noted by others, and one member of the staff offers him a job in Chicago — this leads to occasional self-examinations and speculations about his professional future. On a weekend, Dodd visits Czechoslovakia and witnesses the heavy-handed Soviet influence on that country. He interviews Admiral Miklós Horthy, former head of state of Hungary. He decides to write to Jackson asking to be relieved of duty, as the indictments have been served and the interrogations of the principal defendants completed.

Rome, Italy
September 28, 1945

Grace, my dearest one,

From this ancient city of Christianity and culture I write to the only woman I have ever really loved. Two nights ago I wrote from Nürnberg and told you of our plans.

Yesterday we went to the airstrip in Nürnberg at 8 a.m. The weather was bad, and the plane from Munich for Frankfurt did not come in. At about 2 p.m., a cargo ship from Compiegne, France, was leaving, to return to its base. We decided to try it. We really got our money's worth. We flew blind most of the way through fog and finally arrived at 5:15 p.m. You will recall that the surrender of 1918 was signed at Compiegne.[1] We caught the 5:50 p.m. express for Paris and stood up all the way. It was a so-called first-class train. We arrived in Paris at Gare du Nord and were fed at a horrible mess, and I had my trouble even getting in there in civilian attire. We stayed at the Lourois Hotel, retired about midnight, and arose this morning at 5:30. We went to the airfield for breakfast in pouring rain. All other flights were cancelled, but we took off at 8:55 a.m. We had an easy trip to Marseille. The climate improved our spirits. The sun was warm, the day bright. After a very light lunch we left Marseilles at 12:45. We climbed over the mountains and in an hour or more passed over Cannes, Nice and Monte Carlo — all lying beautifully beneath us. At this point we were over the Mediterranean and in another minute we saw Elba, Napoleon's place of exile, and also Corsica, his birthplace. In a short while we landed outside of Rome and our watches said it was 3 p.m.

Rome is my city. First of all it is quite untouched by the war and for that reason it makes a good impression. But also I like its looks. We rode into Rome on the Apian Way — saw the ruins of the ancient viaduct and the walls.

We are staying at the best hotel in Rome — the Hassler. After a splendid dinner — the best since I left Lebanon — Colonel Brundage and I went to call on Father McCormick at the Vatican headquarters of the Jesuits. We had a letter of introduction from Father Walsh. McCormick is the American Jesuit in Rome. He is a remarkable man. He is arranging an audience with the Pope for Sunday or Monday morning!

1. The armistice was signed at Rethondes, outside of Compiegne, on November 11, 1918.

The stores and shops in Rome are open, and it is so refreshing after Germany with all its destruction and ruin. It has wisteria bloom on all its places. I could live here and like it — with you.

I will write you again tomorrow. For tonight I kiss your lovely lips — in mind only, alas, and bid you fond adieu. Give my most tender affection to our dear little ones.

Tom

Rome, Italy
September 28, 1945
and September 30, 1945

Grace, my dearest one,

This is the end of my first full day in Rome — and what a day it has been. My first impression of this city continues to be very good. It is perhaps due — to some extent — to the change from the ruins of Germany to this open, intact city.

In the afternoon, Colonel Brundage and I, accompanied by Capt. Anthony Albert of Santa Fe., N.M., toured the city. We stood in the balcony where Mussolini so often harangued his followers. We walked through his offices in the Piazza Venitia — which are now art galleries. We went to the beautiful English cemetery and stood at the graves of Keats and of Shelley. On Keats' tombstone this legend is written, "This grave contains all that was mortal of a young English poet who on his deathbed in the bitterness of his heart at the malicious power of his enemies desired these words to be engraved on his tombstone, 'Here lies one whose name was writ in water.'" It moved me so I wrote it down to send to you.

We drove out the Apian Way to the Church of San Sebastian where the imprint of Christ's foot is in the stone. We went through the catacombs, through the Ardreatine caves where all the new coffins are — reminding us of the massacre of 325 Italians there by the Germans in 1944. At sunset we stood on the highest of the seven hills — and looked at Rome — just as the church bells rang the Angelus. We did not go to the Vatican as all of that we are seeing tomorrow.

Colonel Brundage and I had dinner with Capt. Albert at the Ambassador Hotel and in the midst of it he suddenly asked if we would like to call home. Would we? Well, you know the rest. At 11:30 a.m. our Rome time I heard your sweet voice and then the children's voices. Oh! But you sounded so good. I guess I said many stupid things — but I was so glad to talk with you.

Sunday morning —

And it is a beautiful day again. We arose at 6:30 a.m. and went to confession at the Church of St. Susanna at 7:15 a.m. At 8 we met Father McCormick at the Gesu Church — the famous Jesuit church in Rome. He took us upstairs and he said mass for us in the room of St. Ignatius. It is a small bedroom — beautifully preserved — with a lovely altar. Colonel Brundage and I and our driver knelt only a few feet from Father McCormick. Grace dear, I shall never forget it — somehow it seemed like the most wonderful mass I have ever heard. St. Ignatius died in this room. St. Aloysius, St. Francis Xavier lived in it and often visited it.

After mass, we went to St. Peters and I was breathless at the sight of it. Grace, it is magnificent. We saw it all — Father McCormick is well versed as you can imagine.

Then we drove Father McCormick and ourselves south of Rome to the Anzio beachhead. It is still a mess. Tanks, guns, destruction on all sides — much more than a year after that fearful affair. We passed the military cemeteries — rows of crosses — it does something to me. We returned to Rome about 6 p.m.

The big thrill comes tomorrow morning at 11. Colonel Brundage and Thomas Dodd will be received by the Pope — in his study, in a very private audience. Father Walsh and Father McCormick arranged it and a special invitation was delivered to us this evening by a

Vatican messenger. We are told that we should expect to see him about ten minutes — he may keep us fifteen. Really I am terribly pleased. And I feel it is an experience that comes to few men. Save me any news items.

I entirely forgot to tell you that at 9 p.m. last night Colonel Brundage and I met with the Premier of Italy — [Ferruccio] Parri — in his private office and we talked for one and one half hours. It looks like we may have accomplished something for the war crimes commission. So you see this has been an eventful trip. Parri impresses me as being honest. He was a partisan leader during the war.[2]

I am bringing rosaries for all of us tomorrow and will ask the Pope to bless them. I intend to ask his blessing for you and the children — and I am going to mention Carolyn by name. I will send the rosaries home by mail, and I will tell you just how they were blessed.

I feel very holy tonight. Communion this morning in St. Ignatius' room does something to a man. Good night my dearest one.

Tom

Rome, Italy
October 1, 1945

Grace, my dearest one,

In about one half hour I leave here by plane for Paris and Nürnberg. This has been a wonderful trip and today was the best of it.

[This morning] I purchased some rosaries at the Catholic Women's store and at 10:30 a.m. we went to the Jesuit House where we met Father Romolo Durocher, S.J. — he is the Treasurer General of the Jesuits. With him we drove to the Vatican — by the Swiss guards through the courtyards and up in an elevator to the floor where the Pope's library is situated. A monsignor was there to greet us. He said

2. **Parri was anti-Fascist and was in the Italian underground during the war.**

we were honored with the first audience of the day — even before the Vatican officials. At 10:50 a.m. we were ushered in — Col. Brundage and I. The Pope[3] was seated behind his desk in the library — a not too large room. He smiled and said, "I am so glad to see you." I knelt and kissed his ring. We sat beside his desk and he started the conversation about matters of great interest. He spoke to us in confidence and I answered his questions in the same spirit. Some day I will tell you all about it but I feel I cannot write about it in a letter. Then the Pope said — "O! let us talk of more beautiful things. Are you married? How many children have you?" When I answered five, he smiled very broadly. We talked of Hartford and of America. At 11:30 the audience ended with the Pope holding my hand firmly — I on my knees. He blessed me. Then he said, "I bless your wife and your children." He squeezed my hand warmly and said, "Thank you for coming to see me, Mr. Dodd, thank you, it means much to me." He gave me medals for all of our family.

Grace, I walked out as if treading on air. He is a wonderful man — a simple man — a holy man. And a well-informed man. So ended my private audience. He blessed all the rosaries as I held them in my hand. I will bring them home to you and the children.

It is now 3:15 p.m. — we take off at 3:25 p.m. — first stop Marseilles, then Paris, then Frankfurt and finally Nürnberg.

I send you all of my love and devotion.

Tom

3. Pope Pius XII was elected in 1939 and served until his death in 1958. His actions during the war were later scrutinized by historians. He was credited for saving thousands of Jews but was also criticized for appeasing Hitler and for his silence about Nazi atrocities. The timing of Dodd's visit is interesting in that the Pope favored leniency for war criminals, and this may account for the unusual length of the audience.

Paris, France
October 1, 1945

Grace, my lovely one,

This is part II of the letter for today. It is not 10:30 p.m., and we arrived in Paris at 9:45. Colonel Brundage and I are staying at the officers club at the airfield and we are leaving tomorrow morning for Frankfurt and Nürnberg.

I wrote you from Rome about that wonderful half hour private audience with the Pope in his library — but I am so happy about it — I recall his blessing to you and the children. You will be interested in some of the matters we discussed and in what he said about them. You will understand that I cannot write about them, but be assured they are not trivial.

It is October and in two months I will be heading home. I plan to return by boat and to arrive in New York City no later than the 20th of December — so mark that down — and let us plan accordingly.

Good night my dearest — I send you all of my love.

Tom

Paris, France
October 2, 1945

Grace, my dearest one,

The night was rather difficult. We stayed at the officers club and these young pilots kept us awake until after two a.m. However we have had a good breakfast and we felt refreshed and ready to go.

This field is called Orly Field. It is a new one as Bourget, where Lindbergh landed, was badly damaged in the war.

France is recovering quickly — or better — more quickly than many other countries. But of course much of her improved condition is a result of forced return of property from Germany. I sometimes feel depressed about the future. Many well-informed people over here say another war is inevitable — already we are laying the foundation for it.

Russia is behaving so badly — we have won the war and substituted one headache for another, one menace for another, one dictatorship for another. Make no mistake about that. I resolved, yesterday, after talking with the Holy Father, to stand openly and firmly against this menace. If we fail to do it, who will?

So good morning, my dearest Grace — I will write tonight from Germany. I send you all of my love.

Tom

Nürnberg, Germany
October 4, 1945

Grace, my loveliest one,

On the plane yesterday were two civilians from the U.S. — both refugees returning to Europe with money to buy up jewelry! How they get the authority to travel on Army planes for such a purpose is beyond me. Grace, this is a real problem. Their behavior over here is shocking. Their desire for revenge is overwhelming. It is the talk of the Army. Will they never learn?

[Today] General Betz and I had a long talk about the future war crimes program. He believes it should be handled by a group of civilians and so do I. However the choice of the right man is of the utmost importance. Without too much trouble I might get such an assignment. It would mean more than a year over here and that is why I do not want it. Do you agree?

This morning I am back at the office. Neil Andrews is leaving next week. I do not blame him. He has been shabbily treated. I will try to stick it out for another two months, but I too will leave right after the first of December no matter what else happens. I have had a rich experience — I have already made my contribution and hope to make more. It will be so pleasant to get home. Have you had the storm windows painted, and the inside of the new ones? What about a covering for the floor of the study?

Tommie wrote a nice little letter. I will write to him this week. Do take good care of yourself. I am feeling fine. I think I have picked up a little weight — but I am never again to be at the 180-pound mark.

Do continue to write. Someday your letters will arrive, I hope. And you know I write to you every day — so I do have some golden minutes with you.

Tom

P.S. Enclosed is one of four medals the Pope handed to me last Monday morning. It is for you, dearest.

Nürnberg, Germany
October 4, 1945

Grace, my dearest one,

Yesterday's letter was dated October 4 — so you see I am so anxious to reach December I even fool myself now and then.

I passed yesterday at the office preparing for further interrogations of Keitel, von Papen and Seyss-Inquart. We must have the bulk of this work done within ten days as the indictment will be served very soon.

You know I like to retire early — every few nights. I get into bed, take all of your letters and read them over. Then I just recline comfortably and think about you. I recall all kinds of incidents — all manner of experiences that we have shared together. Then I fall off to sleep thinking of you. It is the happiest hour of the day. Sometimes I plan my return home. I see myself on the deck of a vessel — you on the dock waving to me. I rush down the gangplank and take you in my arms. We are in a taxi. We are in a hotel where you have already engaged a lovely room with a large double bed. We chat incessantly. We have reservations for dinner — champagne à la May 1934 in St. Paul. We dance. We do not talk so much now. We just look into each other's eyes. It is 10 o'clock. We return to our hotel room for the sweetest night since St. Paul. Doesn't it seem like a good plan? Perhaps you have some suggestions.

Colonel Brundage and I move to our new home tomorrow. We have a lovely house — six rooms, kitchen, bath and study, two bedrooms, two rooms for servants. We have a couple who will do all the cooking, cleaning and laundry. We also have a car and a driver! It is about 12 miles from Nürnberg in the village of Zerndoff — our address is 26 Hambrugerstrasse, but don't write to me there. There is no postal service in Germany — except the APO. We are pleased about the house — it is beautifully furnished, and was owned by a well to do German family. It has been requisitioned by the Army. This is just one of the results of losing a war. Just picture the Germans in Lebanon — they give us two hours to move out — leaving all furnishings! I feel sorry for these people — but it is war, and this mission is a result of war.

There is much talk heard about Patton's removal.[4] The Jews are blamed by the soldiers. Grace, it is really distressing — you have no idea of what is going on.

Retribution and vengeance are the motives behind so many policies. The Catholics suffered terribly, too — but they are badly off now, too. Sometimes I feel like going home. That I do not want to do — and I will see it through.

I send you all of my love —

Tom

Nürnberg, Germany
Oct. 5, 1945

[I interrogated Keitel] all afternoon. Some of the Russian staff sat in and listened. Keitel was uneasy — he kept a weary eye on the Russkies, and well he might, for they will stretch his neck. He admitted ordering the branding of Russian prisoners with a hot lancet — a

4. **General George S. Patton was removed as governor of Bavaria. He had allowed several Nazis to stay in office and, at a press conference, said, "This Nazi thing. It's just like a Democratic-Republican election fight."**

mark on the left buttocks. He also admitted ordering terrorist measures in Russia and the shooting of captured commissars.

The indictment should be filed next week. We should start the trials in November. But this is conjecture.

I had a letter from you today and it was so nice to hear from you. You should have more than 43 letters from me. I have written at least one a day — and that means well over 60. Perhaps they will arrive in a bunch.

I have gained some weight — but I will not allow myself to get heavy again. However, the table here is well set — and the life is quite sedentary.

Well, dearest, this is a sketchy letter. I much prefer to write about you and to tell you how much I love you. Write me long letters — tell me what you think.

Tom

Nürnberg, Germany
October 6, 1945

Grace, my dearest one,

I was busy talking with Keitel both in the morning and in the afternoon. We had a long heart to heart. He told me what he considered his part in the Hitler regime — and he insists that while he believes in Hitler and was a follower to some extent he did not know many of the things that were done — or knowing of them felt there was nothing he could do about them, or finally in those matters which he ordered done in Hitler's name, he was simply carrying out his orders. In any case he is a tragic figure. I think he possesses very limited ability — a certain shrewdness — and a handsome face. He was a perfect tool for Hitler.

After work this afternoon I went to the officers clothing store and bought a coat — it is an Army coat — waterproof and lined, and it is considered a very wearable garment for winter or for any other time of the year. My own top coat is too light for this climate. I believe I will ship it home with a few other things which I will not use or can do without.

Colonel Brundage is asking to be relieved of his assignment here. He is not in sympathy with this case. He believes these men should be tried by the German people — in German courts — under moderate supervision. He cannot understand how we can prosecute Germans before a court partially Russian — when the Russians are guilty of the very same crimes, and perhaps worse. He is very sincere about it — and maybe he is right.[5] I am still of the view that some of these people must be tried to establish their guilt and the guilt of others before the world. The fact that the Russians are guilty of some of the same offenses does not appeal to me as a reason for dropping this case. I wish we could prosecute them, too. It makes me boil to see these Russians living on us here at the hotel — eating like pigs, getting all kinds of things at our post exchanges, and generally making Uncle Sam the goat. I don't know why they cannot pay their own way here — it is supposed to be a joint venture. The same goes for the French and British. Jackson, I know, has no real faith in the Russians. The French and English are not too interested in this case. So again the simple Americans carry the heavy weight.

I will feel lost without Brundage. We have become good friends. Neil Andrews leaves next week — and so I feel quite alone. Although I will have plenty to do — and it is a job for only a short time. I want to stick it out as long as I can make any contribution to a cause that has merit.

Your letter today told about the rabbit and the guinea pig. Charlotte Opper's letter arrived with yours — so I felt very good with two letters. I find my letters are becoming dull. I suppose I can try to describe some battered buildings — or some of the personalities — but that would be forced, and our letters can never become such. I do like to tell you how much I love you. But that may become too commonplace, and you will tire of it. I must not lose that "light touch" as you so often described it.

5. Brundage also argued to Jackson that victors in future wars would exploit the Nuremberg precedent and invariably draft charges for war crimes.

Charlotte raves about your wonderful appearance — so does everyone else. Can it be that you needed a rest from this old goat? I like to
think you are radiant with love — and that is my own understanding. I
shall bid you good-bye for now. It is dinner time and I must get to the
dining room.

All of my love to you.

Tom

Nürnberg, Germany
October 7, 1945

Grace, my dearest one,

This has been a lovely fall Sunday — a crispness in the air and the
sun is shining brightly — a New England day if I ever saw one. I went
to mass at 10:15 a.m., and then to the office. I wrote a few letters and
then walked to the hotel. I purposely walked a circuitous route and
took plenty of time. In this way one sees the German people — the
more representative people, on the residential streets — or what is left
of them. I pulled my hat brim down, turned my top coat collar up and
discovered that I got a better reception. No cold stares but instead
smiles and greetings. On the main street, particularly in the company
of U.S. officers, I get ice water treatment. Some apparently look on me
as a faithless German who is kowtowing to the U.S. Army. Others seem
to sense that I am an American and treat me accordingly. It is interesting to watch the frauleins with the American GIs. The real Germans —
the people who amount to something — are not running around with
American soldiers. The nice girls — for want of a better term — are
frigid towards any American. They are polite, but only polite, and they
look right down their noses at American soldiers — and at the Germans
who are on their arms. After lunch today I returned to the office and
talked briefly with Keitel and von Papen until nearly 6 p.m. Von Papen
broke down and wept at one point. He, of course, speaks English and
so we got on quite well. In a few days I will write you my own conclu-

sions about Keitel, von Papen, and Seyss-Inquart — for after the indictment is served our conversations will end. The Lord High Chancellor and entourage of England came in to listen to part of my questioning of Keitel and von Papen. It struck me as odd — and very Gilbert and Sullivanish. I felt the guards should be singing something about the policeman's lot while I sang about the Chancellor.

A German rifle and bayonet and two officers swords were shipped to you today — they are in a wooden box so be careful when you open it. These are for the boys — but I think you should keep them together until we get everything home. I also have two rare dueling pistols — really valuable pieces — and they will be on the way soon. The toys will arrive before Christmas, I hope — and be careful about all of the boxes if we hope to surprise the children. As for yourself, I do hope my Italian gifts arrive before your birthday — and also hope you like my selection. In any event I am sending all of my love with it. I would like to be with you for your birthday — but we will think of each other all that day.

Tom

Nürnberg, Germany
October 8, 1945

Grace, my dearest one,

This was another day for another dollar — very much routine with a long interrogation of Keitel in which he made some damaging admissions — particularly about Poland. We showed him a document that he helped prepare in October of 1939 in which the plan to destroy all intellectuals in Poland was laid![6] However, we continue to be very good friends and I confess I feel a little sorry for him — mostly because he is so weak. I do not expect to see him again before the indictment is

6. **The Nazis targeted doctors, lawyers, politicians and anyone else with a high level of education. They were put into concentration camps or executed on the spot.**

served on him and I may not talk to him afterwards. He is worried about his family — but there is little that I can do to relieve his mind.

At noon, Father Walsh and I talked briefly with General Boettcher — former military attaché in Washington. That man should not be in jail at all. He was in Washington from 1933–1942 — he did almost nothing in Germany from 1942–45 except listen to radio broadcasts from the U.S. — a kind of sinecure of a job. He is of advanced years. His daughter is married to an American in Buffalo. His wife and another daughter are missing in Russian occupied Leipzig. I feel very badly for him — if he is a war criminal, so am I. We are trying to find out why he is here at all.

Rudolf Hess arrived today. He is gone mentally and I doubt that he can answer for his offenses. Kesselring, Schacht and some others also are new guests in the jail. It is a secret — but Dr. [Leonardo] Conti, one of those who worked medical experiments on concentration camp inmates, hung himself in the jail Saturday morning. No announcement has been made so far so keep this to yourself.[7]

After supper tonight I talked with von Papen from 8 p.m. until 10 p.m. He is a cunning old man. He makes no admissions but some of his answers are really quite silly to me. I believe he was a professional Catholic, an arch intriguer — a suave diplomat and a very ambitious man.

We hear a cut may be made in the staff soon. I suppose that I will be released as soon as our preliminary examinations are over. I have no trial assignment. That is all provided for. So I do not intend to stand around as a lackey for some lawyers of questionable competence. Actually I know the case — I have talked with the defendants and the witnesses. I have all the knowledge of the evidence and the trial is of no interest, as a trial, to me. So maybe I will see you in early December — let us hope so. This trial, even if it starts as early as Nov. 15, which I doubt today — will last for two months. I do not feel I can give that much time anyway.

7. Conti, the Reich health leader, would have gone to trial with other doctors after the initial tribunal ended.

It is now bedtime. I retire dreaming of lovely Grace and wishing she were in my arms.

All of my love,
Tom

Nürnberg, Germany
October 9, 1945

Grace, my dearest one,

It is 11:15 p.m., and I am propped up in bed just having stepped out of a red hot bathtub. Ergo excuse my somewhat worse than usual script. I have nothing substantial to lean on. It is 5:15 p.m. in Lebanon and nowhere near your bedtime. That makes me a little jealous — I wish you were in bed at this hour too. Why? Oh, just because I like to think of us doing similar things at the same time. Writing at bedtime reminds me — do you still put your nightgown on behind your closet door? Or does your new freedom give you liberties and licenses of disrobing openly? This isn't quite fair I know — so I will not kid you at this great distance.

Well, dearest, this was a fairly interesting day. For my part I was busy with Seyss-Inquart — all day — but Rudolf Hess arrived yesterday from England, so he was called up for an interview. He is completely balmy — and was when he flew to England. He has no memory at all. We had Göring, von Papen, Haushofer and Bohle — all old friends — confront him. He didn't know one of them — and it was no fake. I watched him. He has suffered a complete mental collapse. Göring said to him, "Don't you recall me, your old companion and friend?" Then he mentioned many personal experiences with no sign of recollection from Hess, who said, "I am really very sorry — I realize you must be an old friend. But I cannot remember you." It is genuine — believe that when I tell you so. And so we mark off in tragic terms another of these Nazis.

Seyss-Inquart was quite cooperative today and made some interesting admissions about his part in the Anschluss of 1938 and about his activities in Poland and Holland.

And it has been a lovely day weather-wise — but I received no mail and that spoiled it all. Are my letters arriving on time? Beginning with this letter I am placing the day of the month on the back flap of the envelope — so this one will be marked "9." Thus you can tell what ones are missing. Did you get the drawings I sent you? Be sure to answer this question. I feel like writing another ten pages — but what can I say except that I love you and miss you and just live for the day when I have you in my arms. You are the whole purpose of my life — and your beautiful soul is my greatest inspiration. So darling, I bid you good night and pleasant dreams from your lover in Nürnberg.

                                                                              Tom

---

                                                    Nürnberg, Germany
                                                         Oct. 10, 1945

Grace, my dearest one,

It is now five days since I have heard from you. I realize that it is of no avail to complain — but Grace, dear, I do need your letters.

This morning I had a most interesting interview with Keitel. He told me the most romantic story of the last days in Berlin. I feel it is of great historical significance. His eyes filled with tears, his whole facial expression was one of suppressed emotion as he spoke of his last conversation with Hitler. Surely that man, Hitler, must have possessed an amazing personality, a magnetic power and an iron will. These old soldiers believed in him and admired him.

This afternoon Keitel and I talked at great length about Hitler as a personality. Believe me it was an interesting few hours. I must admit that Keitel gets under my skin — I think I like him and I guess he rather likes me. He was a career man, of course, in the German Army — an administrative officer. Hitler made him Chief of the High Command, a job for which he was not fitted either by experience, training, or character or ability. If he had been left at his own level he would probably be a free man today. He got a big job and now he is in a big mess. You will recall that I have often spoken of the tragedy of placing incompetents in important places. Please do not think I am becoming soft about the Nazis—but in this mission, as in most realistic affairs, one knows that things are not all black and white. For nothing ever is. There are always shadings. I have learned such in these few months.

The staff here continues to grow—but for what purpose I do not know. It really is a strange organization. There isn't an experienced trial lawyer at the top or near it—nor is there one of any great litigation experience—and none with any criminal law experience. And it is all very clear that no such qualifications are here. Colonel Brundage thinks it will end in a mess—or maybe never end at all. The Russians are impossible at every turn. And it makes me sick to see them prosecuting these Germans, for they have done exactly the same things and worse. By that I do not condone this conduct. I merely suggest that we all go into court with clean hands.

John Robinson[8] writes that my friends are all saying nice things and talking politics. Joe Blumenfeld urges that I prepare for the bar. Well, my mind is still unsettled and will remain so until I return and settle down for some sober judgment. Col. Brundage has made specific offers to me in Chicago. I have told him that I will think it all over. How would you like it if I were to try some diplomatic work? It would mean living abroad and at my age a career in diplomatic affairs, once started, would most likely be permanent. It has some attraction for me. There will be opportunities I think. But I wonder if it would be fair to you and to the children. You would be far from home and the children would grow up without benefit of that priceless middle-of-the-road American background.

Be assured I will not be here for the trial itself. It will not start until December and will run for many weeks. I feel that I cannot remain here after December 1 and by that time I will have had all that this experience can give to anyone.

---

8. Robinson ran the Robinson School in West Hartford, which the Dodds' children later attended.

For now I will say adieu until tomorrow. I send you my deep, unchanging love.

Tom

Nürnberg, Germany
October 10, 1945

Grace, my dearest one,

No mail at all today — and so nearly a full week without any word of any kind from you. I sometimes think this is the hardest part of the job. The separation is extremely difficult but with letters one can rock along somehow.

The toys for the children are really very attractive. There are two little automobiles. One of them runs on a table and will NOT go over the edge. It is the most ingenious little thing. Another one stops by merely blowing on it. There are some jeeps and guns, too. The workmanship is magnificent. For the girls some Bavarian dolls that I like myself! I am sending four or five dolls. You see, there are not so many things for girls. I am also sending some hand-worked handkerchiefs and other things — such as I think you will like.

This morning I worked at my desk preparing for afternoon sessions with von Papen and Seyss-Inquart. Everyone here is asking, "When will the trial start?" Or, "When will the indictment be served?" Or, "When do you think we will get out of here?"

This afternoon I had a long and most interesting conversation with Franz von Papen. One has to be on one's toes in talking with him. I felt rather good about my von Papen conversations and I think the record will look good too. You know the satisfaction of having done a good day's work is important.

I now bid you adieu, lieber, Grace, and send you all of my undying, burning love.

Tom

October 12, 1945
Nürnberg, Germany

Grace, my dearest one,

At long last—two letters from you this good day. I am glad that
"Grace" is working out well. We must call her "Grace A" for Alcoholic.[9] The telephone strike makes my blood boil. That is an essential
service—and in my judgment no telephone employee has a right to
strike any more than a fireman or policeman.

I talked with von Papen all day today—morning and afternoon,
and he wept at both sessions. He will have grave difficulty in escaping
responsibility for much of what happened.

Tonight some of us are giving Neil Andrews a farewell dinner. It
makes me blue because I would like to be home, too. Colonel
Brundage and I are planning to sail home together in December.
Colonel Brundage has a beautiful place in Miami—his wife is there
now—and he has invited you and me to visit there in January and I am
all for it. He is a grand man—and you will like him. He still talks of
Chicago and the practice of law. I have made no decision thus far and
will not until after we get home. You and I will talk it all out. Which
reminds me—I do not want my return noised about. I want a few days
alone with you and the children.

I do not like to hear that you weigh only 119 pounds. That is not
enough. Please do not get run down. You just cannot realize how much
you mean to me. I could not live without you.

Tomorrow, Colonel Brundage, Major Connor and I are leaving for
Czechoslovakia—we will drive to Pilsen and thence to Prague. For
now—good night, my dearest—and here is my love.

Tom

9. Grace Symington had been a patient at Norwich State Hospital, where mental illness was treated, and was thought to be in recovery.

Nürnberg, Germany
October 15, 1945

Grace, my dearest one,

This is a two-day letter for Saturday the 13th and yesterday the 14th. Saturday morning I talked with von Papen until about eleven o'clock and then Colonel Brundage, Major Connor and I left for Pilsen. It was a nice day so we started out with the top down. Before long we stopped and put it up and also the side curtains with it. We drove for about 150 miles through some beautiful countryside. The German villages are picturesque and by contrast much more attractive than those in Czechoslovakia. We rode through the Sudetenland, which was as you will recall the excuse for the Munich pact. Now it is again a part of Czechoslovakia, and the Germans who are there wear arm bands. We saw more people with arm bands than without. Riding through this part of the world one reflects on all the wars and battles that have been fought to settle, allegedly, age-old disputes. Well they are still at it and in my opinion always will be and we should not take too much interest in it.

In the center of Pilsen we saw a new gallows and we were told that people are hung there every day — collaborators, etc. Peace! It's wonderful for those who win.

We stayed at the Continental Hotel. After dinner we were all quite worn out from the ride and bed felt good when we got in.

Yesterday morning we were up early and intended to drive on to Prague — that is, we all said we wanted to do so and each one was ready secretly to say "uncle." The Russians occupy all of Czechoslovakia except the part around Pilsen so it is necessary to get permission to enter their area. It couldn't be done in time and we all admitted it was a good excuse to remain in Pilsen and then return to Nürnberg. About noontime we saw a swaggering Russian parade. Ceremonies were held in the center of the city and our soldiers decorated some Russians and the Russkies decorated some of our people. Then the Russian national anthem and the good old "Star Spangled Banner." How those Russians march! Swinging their shoulders and strutting like high school drum majors. Our fellows came along with their easy gait and their more intelligent faces and one could see the difference. But the Czechs are very pro-Russian, I guess, from what we hear. And not too fond of us. That is understandable to me. The Russians are more like them in language and in custom and geographically they have much more in common. And anyway I guess I am trying to say, "They can have them." Pilsen is a drab city and more unattractive. We saw the Skoda Works[10] and the bombed out areas. We left at 2 p.m. and arrived back here last night about 7:30 p.m. very cold and tired. We agree that it is getting too cold for riding in these open army cars.

I am now in one of those dead spaces mentally. A nice long letter from you would be most stimulating. I send you all of my love and ask that you give my affection to the children. Excuse all the errors. I am still a one finger-hunt and find-man at this machine.

Tom

Zerndoff, Germany

October 17, 1945

Grace, my dearest one,

Colonel Brundage and I are in our new house tonight. It is in the very pretty little German village of Zerndoff, about 12 miles from Nürnberg. We now have our own car and a soldier-chauffeur. His name is Herbert Trumpfeller and he is from Bridgeport, Conn. A nice youngster and very pleased with his job.

This morning we moved from the hotel — and it was quite a job. I was shocked when I found that I had accumulated so many things. It is incredible that I have all the luggage I left home with and two Army trunks besides! Of course the uniform, Army boots, heavy shirts, socks

10. During the war, the Skoda Works produced armaments, including the tanks known as Panzers.

and underwear, raincoat and overcoat made up a lot of it. But even so there was more than I realized I had.

After lunch I talked with Admiral Horthy[11] of Hungary. He is a very distinguished-looking man and he speaks English very well. We had a long talk and he told me about Hitler and his relationship with him which finally culminated in Horthy's arrest and sentence to death — which was prevented when the Americans reached the Bavarian castle where he was being held. He is not a defendant in this case — at the most only a witness. These Hungarians are good people. More than once, over here, I have heard them described as possibly the best people in Europe — the only solid group on the continent. What a pity that the Russians are in there! By the way, a Russian colonel sat in on the interview and old Horthy spoke of them as Bolsheviks — with scorn in his voice — and he looked at the Russkie when he said it. I said nothing — nor did I even so much as raise an eyebrow. About 4 p.m., I had another session with Seyss-Inquart and he was distressed when I referred to an appearance he made in July of 1938 in Vienna honoring the Nazis who assassinated Dollfuss — for Dollfuss was his old-time friend. He made a lame explanation but he realized he was in a tight fix — and indeed he is for he betrayed Austria and he helped the Germans terrorize Poland and was the German Governor of Holland.

I had a letter from you today — very sweet. I am glad Tommie is taking tap dancing lessons. I always wanted to learn tap dancing when I was very young and I spent hours trying to learn it by myself. I became fairly good with one foot only!

I wonder about the chickens. You should be getting plenty of eggs by now. Are you sure they have enough food and water and good nests and are the coops clean? Check up on your two poultry men — Tom and Jeremy.

---

11. Miklós Horthy was head of state of Hungary, which became an early ally of Germany in the war.

So dearest, I say good night again with dreams of seeing you as soon as possible. Take good care of yourself and of the children.

Tom

Nürnberg, Germany
Oct. 18, 1945

Grace, my dearest one,

As you can imagine we are hurrying the trial preparation — yet there seems to be a general feeling abroad that some kind of a postponement may be in the offing. The Russians say their chief prosecutor is sick — and that a postponement is absolutely necessary. Of course the Russians and the French are living better here than they have ever lived before. Automobiles, heat, light, food, drink, cigarettes, razor blades, soap — all are theirs for Uncle Sam sees to that. Now it is difficult for you to understand, but these commodities are priceless in Europe. A package of cigarettes in some parts is worth $20 — and in any commodities are the real values. Money doesn't mean much when there is nothing to buy. So I believe the Russians and the French will make this last as long as they can. The British are insisting on a prompt trial. We should be doing the same. Unfortunately, because of a terrible management, we need a week or two for proper preparation. Therefore I assume Jackson will not oppose the Russian request.

Sunday is a dull day for us here — and until recently a day we all dreaded because with not much to do we all get lonesome and homesick. Since we have been working on Sunday it has not been so bad. At the very best this is a great ordeal — nothing more. The whole situation depresses me — and I shall be so happy to get away from it. I would give anything to be leaving here tomorrow. Then why not? Because I feel I should seize the opportunity to appear in what may be one of the great trials in history. Because I need such an opportunity having no practice — and needing as much prestige as I can obtain — because the

Connecticut Supreme Court has made me anxious to achieve a niche in the profession, because I think the job is most worthwhile, because the interest of the United States is very great, because we may do something constructive to prevent the occurrence of wars of aggression.

Are these good reasons? I do not know. What do you think of them? Had I the chance to talk with you my thinking would be clearer. However, I am still counting on a flight home for Christmas. General Donovan is going and by hook or crook so am I. There is a slim chance that my part of the case will be over by that time — which means I would not return here.

So my dearest, I bid you adieu and hope that not too many Sundays hence I will be with you and the children.

Tom

Nürnberg, Germany
Mittwoch 18 Oktober, 1945

Mein lieber Grace,

How is that for German — date, day of the week and salutation. One does pick up a few words somehow or other.

Last night I spoke to the staff on the law of conspiracy. These subjects were assigned some weeks ago — and have not been very well attended. I was surprised to find a packed house — the largest turnout thus far. It went all right I guess — no one said otherwise. People never do.

This morning I had another session with Keitel. This afternoon no interviews — a quiet time — so I left the office early and came to the house. Jackson gave a large cocktail party late this afternoon. I was not invited. About fifty were present. Colonel Brundage went and I know he was embarrassed because I was not asked. You know that I do not miss such affairs — but I rather feel that the omission is typical of the way I have been treated from the beginning. A lot of young officers —

with no legal training or ability — were there, and that seems to be the caste system. I have not been happy on this job for most of the time.

Neil Andrews did the right thing, I believe, in going home. After all he is a mature lawyer of standing — and I feel that I am entitled to some consideration, too. The indictment was handed up today and I think it is a good time for me to leave. I see no prospect of any improvement in my situation and I have enjoyed the experience — consequently I think I will notify Jackson that I wish to be released to return home. For one thing, the trial will run over into January, I feel sure. If I remain I may become involved and to leave then would be embarrassing. So, I now plan to write a letter to Jackson in a day or two. I should be home by mid-November, if all goes well. That is a month earlier than I expected to leave. I suppose some people will wonder why I left. My answer is that I did not feel I could remain for the trial — as I originally understood I would be home in November and I made plans accordingly. So comes to an end an interesting experience — but it is my last separation from my family. Grace, dearest, nothing is worth that much. I have been very lonesome — and often quite unhappy and these factors added to the manner of treatment received makes this mission no longer attractive to me. Do not misunderstand all of this — perhaps it sounds or reads worse than it is. You know how I resent social and professional distinctions — well, add military rank and you will realize that such an atmosphere is impossible for me. I will have many stories to tell about this whole situation — which I have not written out.

I received four letters from you today! And I had a letter from Leo Gaffney. He relates a conversation with Judge Munger — one who sat on my matter. Munger told him that the judges were 3–2 in my favor when they walked off the bench! Leo said he would tell me later what caused the change. Leo hints at something very sinister.

Well, dearest, this is a dreary letter. I must not write drab thoughts. I am well and so anxious to get home. Start telling our friends that I hope to be home in November — and I cannot stay for the trial. All my love to you.

Tom

Nürnberg, Germany
October 19, 1945

Grace, my dearest one,

This day is one of memory. First of all General Donovan asked me to see him. He spoke generously of my interrogations of Keitel, which he has been reading. Then we discussed Keitel and the case generally. He asked me to work along with him and this I agreed to do. He is a fine-looking man and I think he has great ability. Later in the morning I had a session with Keitel — the last one before the indictment was served on him. Shortly after noon the document had been served on all the defendants and about 4 p.m. I saw von Papen, Keitel and Seyss-Inquart — in that order. Von Papen was shaken and professed surprise. Keitel was greatly distressed — nervous and highly excited. Seyss-Inquart was obviously upset but appeared despondent and dejected. Old Keitel bothers me — I feel badly about him. We have become rather good friends — so to speak.

I have drawn up a letter to Jackson asking that I be released — now that the indictment has been served and the interrogations of the principal defendants are complete. In it I suggest departure in a few weeks. If I am to be home for Christmas, it is imperative that I so plan now. It takes time to arrange for travel — particularly at this time of year as so many in Europe want to come home for the holidays. Colonel Brundage is leaving in December also. I wish I could complete the job here with some kind of trial responsibility — it would be better that way — however I cannot see how it can be done as it will be February or later, in my judgment, before these proceedings are over. It is all right for Army and Navy personnel who are under orders and prefer this assignment to most others, but for me it would be quite foolish and silly. As a matter of fact it is my opinion that much of the delay thus far is due to the Army/Navy attitude — "Why hurry? This is a good deal. Let's make it last." A few good civilian lawyers would have had this case in shape and on trial by now.

Somehow these last few days have made me feel far away from you and the children. I have dreamed about you and the children for two or three nights and particularly about you and Christopher. It was all mixed up — one of those unsatisfactory dreams.

This morning I told Amen I wished to be released as I foresee a long drawn out trial. He tried to sell me on remaining and we finally compromised on the end of November. This means home in December and I hope by the 15th.

So I come to the close of another day and another letter. I am so anxious to get home. Indeed, I know I am a homebody myself. Travel is interesting — so are new personalities — but the deep abiding interest in one's family and home can never be replaced.

Tom

Nürnberg, Germany
Oct. 21, 1945

Grace, my dearest one,

This is again a two-day letter. Yesterday was but another work day. We had a long discussion about the interrogation of the witnesses which took about all morning. After lunch I talked with Field Marshal von Brauchitsch[12] — a real old Prussian soldier. General Donovan sat in on a good part of it as did some Russians.

Today is a very "pretty" fall day — as Tommie would say. The 1st Division football team played the 4th Division and we attended. There was a great crowd — bands and cheerleaders. It was just like any college game, and we enjoyed it very much. The 1st Division won, 7–0, so of course Colonel Corley and the other members of the 1st were very happy.

We have been sitting in the study reading this evening. I am terribly

12. **Field Marshal Walther von Brauchitsch was commander in chief of the Wehrmacht in the early years of the war, relieved of command by Hitler in 1941 after failing to take Moscow.**

lonesome for home and for you and the children. Perhaps I shouldn't write to you along such lines — but it seems to help a little to say it. Sometimes my heart really aches. I realize, too, that my last few letters have sounded a sour note or two. It is not that bad — I repeat — and knowing me as you do, I am sure you read such phrases with at least one raised eyebrow.

The mail situation is definitely not good. Some say it is a result of the dock strike in New York. We all believe that our air mail is actually delivered by boat. Thus we account for the long periods between letters. I am so anxious about the Christmas things I have sent home. They should arrive early in December. Some things I will bring with me — particularly for you.

I think the atmosphere amidst all this devastation and misery gets one down. I am sick of looking at desolation and suffering. The winter will be a grave hardship — God only knows what it will mean for this stricken country. Well, my dearest, I must say goodnight for now — I send you, as ever, all of my love. Kiss my bairns for me.

Tom

CHAPTER 8

Promotion—and Fixing "the Mess"

DODD IS UNEXPECTEDLY THRUST directly into the fray at the highest administrative levels — part of a small team that Jackson will rely on heavily. Dodd's new position, however, does not change his opinion of the rampant incompetence he has observed. "Petty men always show their mettle at such times." Dodd tells Grace the details of Robert Ley's particularly grotesque suicide. And he hints to Grace that Jackson might name him to be on the trial counsel staff. This occurs, and Dodd and nine others are appointed. He writes Grace, "The evolution of my participation has been a most amazing thing to me . . . Your prayers must be very persuasive with God." He is further promoted — becoming part of a trial team of senior lawyers, four in all.

Nürnberg, Germany
Oct. 22, 1945

Grace, my dearest one,

This has been a rather unusual day. In the first place we reallocated witnesses among our interrogation staff so as to get them ready for the trial. I told Col. Amen I wanted to leave no later than the end of November. The trial is to start November 20th or about then. He agreed to that. In the afternoon I had another talk with Keitel and he is terribly upset about his indictment. He has written a personal letter to me which is now being translated and I am told it is quite interesting. Next I talked with von Papen and he appeared to be in much better spirits. He asked my advice as to whether he should challenge the jurisdiction of the court and wanted some advice on international law. I referred him to his own lawyer. About six o'clock I was back in my own office when I got a call from Colonel Storey. He came down and showed me an order issued by Jackson today reorganizing the whole staff. I was named with three others to the top of the staff and with full authority over the whole organization!! I was really amazed. Colonel Brundage was placed in charge of a section under us. He was greatly surprised, too. Well it was a bombshell and of course it is the talk of the place now. The newspaper men have the story so you may read about it. Well, I do not know how to feel. I had not cared to get too involved. Storey said I still might be able to leave when the trial starts — and if that is so all is well. I rather think it will work that way as I do not believe I will be called to assist in trying the case.

Forgive me, dear, for being a little pleased — but I came into this organization at the bottom and have received some shabby treatment. Tonight at dinner everyone was up shaking my hand. I always felt that the staff members knew what was going on and they showed it tonight. Well so it goes — as always with me. A few days ago I was pretty low, and feeling quite down, etc. Then this happens so unexpectedly! Tomorrow we organize the whole place and start anew. Amen looked a little sheepish — but I must say he was pleasant and appeared pleased about it. I do hope I can do a good job at it. But it will not be easy and some of the soreheads will be difficult. However, it does make my experience more interesting — even if it is as far as it goes. I will cut this note short — no mail again today. I love you dear always — and I long to see you. Tell the children I will write to them soon.

All of my love,
Tom

October 24, 1945
Nürnberg, Germany

Grace, my dearest,

I must learn to write smaller if I am to use this small stationery. For with the new job and the terrific pressure to get this case ready for trial I shall now and then miss a day and follow up with one of my "two-day" letters of which this is an example.

Yesterday we started to put the new organization into operation and we worked like beavers all day. What a mess this case is in! I do not know whether we can get it ready on time or not. I knew there were many fakers here — but I did not realize how many were here. At any rate we are under way. Last night we worked until after 11 o'clock. I shall not spell out all the details of our new work — it is too involved — but it is 100 Molzahn[1] cases rolled into one.

At 5 p.m. today I saw von Papen to tell him that our interviews were over and that a new man would talk with him. He seemed very sorry — and so said. He thanked me, etc., and then he handed me his own reconstruction of the Hindenburg will. You see he drafted the original — which the Nazis either destroyed or distorted — and the document of course has disappeared. I also saw Seyss-Inquart and bade him adieu — he too was thankful, etc. Finally Keitel. He seemed very distressed about the change. He said, "I feel that you have come to know me as a personality. I am very thankful for the honorable way in which you have treated me. I am sorry that you will not continue to talk with me. I would like to feel that I may write to you or ask to see you and I shall be a soldier until the end." It was really quite moving. I pity him.

1. **Dodd prosecuted Reverend Kurt E. B. Molzahn in Hartford Federal Court for Molzahn's involvement in an espionage ring accused of spying for the Axis powers. While his four co-conspirators pled guilty, Molzahn stood trial and was convicted on August 21, 1942, of violating the Espionage Act of 1917. When the verdict was delivered, the afternoon *Hartford Times* published a rare extra edition.**

So, dearest, it goes. This is a hurry-up note. I shall write more fully tomorrow. I love you always—and ever. My tender affection to the children.

Tom

Nürnberg, Germany
Oct. 25, 1945

Grace, my dearest one,

This has been another very busy day. My new responsibilities keep me occupied all day. Up to now I have stayed at my own bench—so to speak—and enjoyed talking with these characters. Now I am beginning to see what is and what has been wrong with this show. Frank Shea and his gang—and they are a pretty greedy crowd of fakers—have been fighting with Commander Donovan and his crowd, who are of better caliber yet a bit on the ambitious prima donna side. Jackson is between the two and seems to play one off against the other—at which he does not do a good job. He is hopeless as an administrator, worse than Eliot Janeway[2] said of him. I refuse to get embroiled in their mess—for it has been difficult enough for me so far and it is all so silly anyway. However I do intend to do my best to put this case on its feet and then—like Greta—"I vant to go home." I shall be in a difficult position if by any strange chance Jackson should assign me as trial counsel—or as a member of the trial staff. I am not too concerned as that likelihood is most remote. And as you know I have never labored under any illusions about my place in this staff. So—

Your letter today was cute and peppy—and lovely. I am glad you like your new fur jacket—why don't you have a raccoon hat made with the extra pieces? I am wondering what is happening in Lebanon. I had a nice letter from Joe Blumenfeld today—he surely is a peach of a friend—and two more boxes of cigars from Sam Leviston. I have so

2. Janeway was an economist and writer.

many personal letters to write and I truly do not have the time in which to write them. To be on the safe side I will send you my birthday greet- ings in this letter — with my love to you on this very important date of November 9.

I would like to be on hand to help eat some of the cake or ice cream and watch you blow out the candles — but the children will take good care of all of that.

For now, my dearest, I send you all of my love.

Tom

Nürnberg, Germany
October 27, 1945

Grace, my dearest one,

Yesterday was a full day with our new review board in constant ses- sion. As you know, one of the defendants, Robert Ley, hung himself in his cell the night before last.[3] It was a bizarre suicide — one I find very hard to understand. He actually stuffed his own underwear in his mouth and down his throat and with the border of his towel for a noose strangled himself to death while he sat on the toilet! Colonel Andrus, a very picturesque old soldier, who is in charge of the guard detail, said to me: "What a way to die — strangled with his own loin cloth on his own dung heap." Maybe that is the way to describe it. Ley was a weak- ling — an alcoholic and a man of many mistresses and illegitimate chil- dren. I have talked rather extensively with his secretary. Mrs. Brueninghoff took his children to Berchtesgaden last April and Ley gave her some poison when she left — enough for her and for the chil- dren. Confidentially this is the second suicide. A Dr. Conti, who per- formed medical experiments on the inmates of concentration camps, hung himself in his cell a few weeks ago. Nothing was said other than

---

3. **Ley, head of the German Labour Front, remained fanatically loyal to Hitler throughout the war and its aftermath.**

he had died — but he was a suicide too. If there ever is justification for suicide these creatures have it, I guess. Their guilt is so enormous — their outlook so dark — I do not wonder that they attempt self destruction. It is a curious feature of our administration of justice which causes us to be very jealous of the right and the power to execute a death sentence. We surely work hard to keep the condemned alive long enough to permit us to kill him!

The Russians are being difficult about showing us their proof — and also about translation. They really are impossible. Yet as individuals they are quite likeable. I have had some slight association with one Russian colonel — and he is quite a decent sort. I have also had some pleasant experiences with some of the French delegation.

We continue to prepare the case, and time passes more quickly when one is so engaged. Of course you are ever in my mind — at all times of the day and of the night. I think of you and of the children — I look at my watch — count back six hours and decide what you are doing.

For now I will close and bid you adieu — and I send you all of my love.

Tom

Nürnberg, Germany
October 28, 1945

Grace, my dearest one,

It is a beautiful Sunday — so much like our own fall days. The colors are not nearly as beautiful but as a substitute they will do very well. I was at mass this morning and received communion. After a nice German breakfast with Colonel Brundage and Colonel Purvis at our own house I went to the office and worked until lunchtime. We have German girls who do all the housework — make the fires, do our laundry, shine our shoes and cook grand breakfasts for us. We do not, of course, come back for lunch and we eat dinner in the hotel. The girls

Once a city of 400,000 and the center of Nazism, Nuremberg was reduced to rubble by Allied bombing.

The Palace of Justice, one of the few Nuremberg buildings left in reasonable condition, was the site of the trial.

Geoffrey Lawrence (right) was the trial's president. He is shown here conferring with Norman Birkett, the British alternate judge.

In letters home, Tom Dodd (at front of middle table) referred to his frustration about the trial's pace and the ineptitude of the Soviet prosecutors (seated at right).

Addressing the court in his first presentation, Tom Dodd was horrified to discover a page missing from his text—and had to speak extemporaneously.

Tom Dodd with the prosecution exhibit he had kept under a sheet: the shrunken head of a Polish prisoner, used by the commandant of Buchenwald as a paperweight.

Dodd pushed Robert H. Jackson, the lead U.S. prosecutor, to emphasize the "human" evidence of genocide rather than relying so heavily on documents. Jackson recommended Dodd for the Medal of Freedom, which President Truman awarded him in 1946.

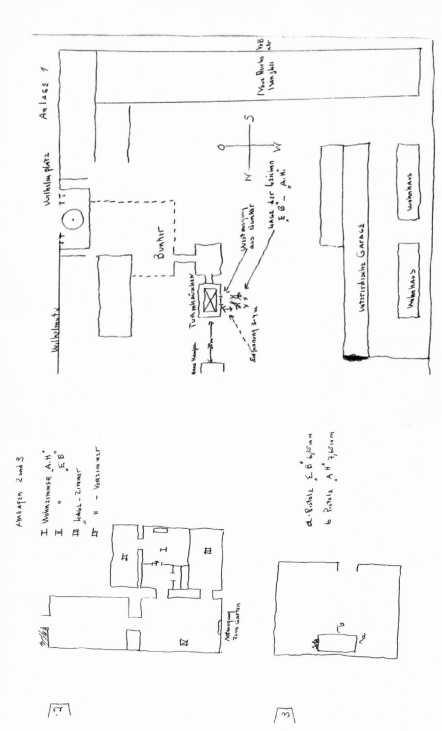

Hitler's chauffeur gave Tom Dodd his drawings of Hitler's bunker.
He specified where Hitler and Eva Braun committed suicide.

ABOVE LEFT: Wilhelm Keitel, Hitler's chief of staff, who seemed a "pathetic" figure, asked Dodd for a personal favor.

SECOND FROM LEFT: Under intense cross-examination by Dodd, Alfred Rosenberg grudgingly admitted he knew of the concentration camp atrocities.

THIRD FROM LEFT: In his autobiography, Albert Speer, the minister of war armaments (and Hitler's chief architect), referred to Tom Dodd as "sharp and aggressive."

TOP RIGHT: Dodd's interrogation of Franz von Papen, vice-chancellor under Hitler, was critical in showing how those in power acquiesced.

Walther Funk, president of the Reichsbank, was pummeled on the stand by Dodd, with evidence that gold from the teeth of murdered Jews was deposited in the bank's vaults.

RIGHT: Joachim von Ribbentrop, the foreign minister, cut a dashing figure, but by the time he became a defendant he was, in Dodd's words, "a Bowery character."

Hermann Göring, Dodd wrote home, "has been positively impish up to very recently, now gray and crest-fallen."

Tom Dodd wrote of his astonishment that little Christopher was already walking—as his sister Martha proudly helped demonstrate.

BELOW: Lebanon, Connecticut, 1946: Tom with son Christopher, whom he called his "shadow," because he followed him everywhere (even, eventually, to Washington, D.C.).

While her husband was in Nuremberg, Grace tended to the children and the family cat, Snowie. In front, Jeremy, Tom Jr., and Carolyn. Behind, Christopher and Martha.

Grace and Tom celebrating his return from Nuremberg, at a restaurant in New York City.

ABOVE: January, 1953, after the House of Representatives swearing in. The children, from left: Christopher, Martha, Jeremy, Carolyn, and Tom Jr. (Nicholas, then four years old, was not present.)

LEFT: As a senator, Tom Dodd used his Nuremberg experience in foreign policy speeches—and was a leading critic of the Soviet Union.

BELOW: The Dodd family, December 1965, North Stonington, Connecticut. Christopher is seated at left, next to his dog, Sebastian. Bernie Buonanno, his wife, Martha, and their daughter, Helena, are seated. Flanking the elder Dodds in the back row: Nicholas, Tom Jr., Carolyn, and Jeremy.

are typical Germans. Marie and Hannah — they speak no English and we speak about as much German. But we manage to understand things pretty well.

Last night we had dinner at the castle of Rowland Graf and Herren Faber. It is an incredible place. The candelabra was lit — forty candles in a magnificent crystal set. I have never seen anything like it. The German maids sang German songs from a balcony in the dining room — and their voices were lovely. Brahm's Lullaby — in German — was their closing piece. There were twelve of us present — I being the lone civilian. Many times as I see and do things worth remembering I think of you and wish you were by my side to share with me. I shall never again travel without you.

It is early November — the time is passing — and when I look back to July I wonder how I have remained this long. I couldn't make it if I had to stay another three months. Whenever I express such thoughts I think about so many of these soldiers who have been away for three years — men with wives and children, too. Surely they have given so much more than I, yet a new pain hurts as much as an old one — maybe more.

Do write me all the news about yourself and the children. How are they doing in school? Is Tom happy? What about Jeremy and Carolyn? Little Martha must be a big girl now and Christopher quite a young man? And you — tell me all about your own dear self. For now adieu — I send you my undying love.

Tom

Nürnberg, Germany
October 30, 1945

Grace, my dearest one,

Another two-day letter — after receiving two letters from you yesterday and grand letters they were. It makes me homesick to read of your walks on the country roads with all the beautiful foliage about you. I

love the fall of the year and most of all I love a New England fall — and
fall without you means nothing to me.

Yesterday was another work day trying to get this case ready for trial.
It is such a mess — mostly because of poor administration from the
beginning. Our new board is meeting all kinds of hidden opposition
from Shea and Taylor[4] and their gang. Petty men always show their
mettle at such times. I am still following my purpose not to get involved
in any of these small disputes. The struggle now is for assignment as
trial counsel and I can only repeat what I wrote yesterday — i.e., it is a
matter of great unimportance to me. I am really indifferent about it for
I am anxious to be home at the earliest possible date and such an
appointment will certainly delay my departure. I even think I may
refuse an appointment if it is tendered. You see I have worked on this
matter in two capacities. 1. As an interrogator talking with the principal defendants and witnesses. 2. As a member of the legal board of
review to prepare the case for trial. These two make up a substantial
contribution to the whole effort and I feel that I can rest at this point.
Participation as actual trial counsel is, of course, not to be dismissed
with a gesture — but weighing consideration against consideration, I
see no reason for ambition in this connection.

Colonel Brundage is adamant about going home at the end of
November and this, of course, makes me feel that I too wish to leave.
I would miss him very much if he left and I remained behind.

I sent you a package yesterday — a Nazi flag, rosaries from Rome,
some coins, odds and ends. I sent a rosary to my father and the girls
and a Nazi flag to Johnny Farley and the McArees.[5] I will say adieu —
and send you all of my love.

Tom

4. **Telford Taylor was a member of the trial staff who took over as chief prosecutor in subsequent Nuremberg trials, and later wrote *The Anatomy of the
Nuremberg Trials: A Personal Memoir*, among other books.**
5. **Charlie McAree was married to Margaret, Tom Dodd's sister.**

Nürnberg, Germany
Nov. 1, 1945

Grace, my dearest one,

A new month opens today — the severe month of November. Three months ago I was in London — it seems like three years ago.

I confess to another two-day letter. You know that I love to write to you and when I miss a day it is because I have been pressed for time. I could falsify by writing very late at night — but I prefer to keep the record straight.

Colonel Brundage and I ate our first supper at our house last night. The two frauleins were all in a dither and they prepared four times as much food as we could eat. However we enjoyed it, mostly because we are tired of the hotel, where there is so much confusion and activity.

I am glad the helmets arrived for the boys. They are real SS helmets, and they were found in Nürnberg after the fighting for this city was over.

Some of the bickering that goes on here may be relieved shortly as Shea is being sent home. He has been a source of much trouble — but one or two of his friends are just as bad and I think they should go, too. I see a lot of General Donovan — and I like him very much. He is a most colorful man. I think he likes me and he asks me to come to his office and we have some long and interesting discussions. Colonel Storey and I are also very friendly — he is a splendid lawyer from Dallas, Texas.[6] Such associations make my experience here very rich indeed. Yesterday Howard Brundage again referred to Chicago and after some talk it was left this way: If at any time I would like to go to Chicago he would like to have me. I think that is the way to leave it for now.

In your letter of yesterday you remarked that I probably was tired of having you tell me that you love me. Do you really believe that? Can

6. **Robert G. Storey served in the Army Air Corps during the war. Later he served as president of the American Bar Association, the first Civil Rights Commission, and the Panama Canal Commission.**

one ever tire of hearing that story from the only girl he loves — or ever could love?

Tom

Nürnberg, Germany
November 2, 1945

Grace, my dearest one,

I am trying to write smaller letters so I can save as much on this stationery and enjoy a good chat with you.

Yesterday was a nice fall day — clear and mild — if this weather continues these Germans will be fortunate. Let us hope they have a mild winter for if it is severe many will perish.

I worked all day on the preparation of the case for trial. I will not list the countless little and big problems — suffice it to say they are innumerable and besides there is much jealousy because we have the responsibility. What this organization needs is about six tickets — one way — to New York.

After dinner we picked up Dr. Paul Leverkuehn, a German lawyer, from Berlin and Hamburg who was formerly in the embassies in Washington and Ankara, Turkey. He is a Rhodes Scholar and speaks English as well as we do. He is an international lawyer and an old friend of General Donovan. We brought him to our house and with Colonel Brundage we had a pleasant evening. He is a most interesting fellow who was here in the war time, and we get an excellent picture of what went on inside Germany from him. He is a friend of von Papen and he is able to give us detailed information on von Papen's background, etc.

I am becoming a little disturbed about the trial. Perhaps it is all nonsense, but I have a suspicion that Jackson might name me among the trial counsel. No direct mention has been made — but there have been hints. Now that poses a problem. I want to get home. This is my most ardent wish and constant ambition. If I am a member of the trial staff my return will be delayed for two months — and the likelihood of being home for Christmas is not strong — in fact is almost nil. I have an idea that this trial will not end before February. On the other side of the ledger are the following facts: 1. It will be, perhaps, one of the greatest trials of history. 2. To actively appear as trial counsel is — or should be — a great distinction. 3. Such distinction with attendant publicity and recognition as it should bring is a great asset for us and the children. 4. It might lead to great opportunity.

There is the situation in a nutshell. You will see why I am disturbed. Please give me your views at once — and if you like ask Joe Blumenfeld what he thinks, too. It is not an easy problem. Personally, I am heartsick about my separation from you and the children and I am most anxious to get my own affairs and plans straightened out. You know I love you so intensely I can never have a really happy day without you. Thus, this work is a real personal sacrifice for me — deeper than you know. I know too that the interest of the United States is very great in this trial, and I must not — I cannot — lose sight of that most important fact.

Do give me counsel and continue to give me your love as I send you all of mine.

Tom

Nürnberg, Germany
November 4, 1945

Grace, my dearest one,

Two wonderful letters from you arrived yesterday. One written under the hair dryer! Your letters are grand — they mean so much to me.

Yesterday was Saturday on the calendar and just like every other day here. I worked steadily from 8:30 a.m. until 6 p.m. with a short break for lunch. The job of getting this case ready for trial is tremendous. Sometimes I get discouraged about it — sometimes it seems hopeless. Besides, as I have indicated before there is much effort wasted for position of prominence and the result is a lack of complete co-operative effort. When I was busy interrogating these characters I was quite removed from it all. As you know I was unhappy about many things then — and with considerably good reason. I was not well treated and it was an uphill struggle all the way. Now that I have much more overall responsibility new headaches come with it. Lately I have wished I was left alone on the interrogation job — my course would be clear — I could finish my work shortly and go home happily. Strangely, I did not even know that a reorganization was contemplated here — and this job was one I never so much as dreamed of much less sought. Perhaps the best will happen for the best and in another few weeks — two or three — I can sail home. If Jackson will announce his trial staff — and not include me — everything will be simple. If he asks me to help try the case I will be completely perplexed. I shall do nothing to further that appointment — not even by a glance or side look.

Last night Colonel Andrews had dinner with us at our house. We had baked chicken stuffed with port! I did not like it. I will take your dressing any time. The German girls were very proud of their dinner so we had to sing their praises. Afterwards, two German boys in the neighborhood came in and played German songs on their accordions. Very noisy I thought.

This morning, we were joined by Captain Frank and Captain Armsely of the British staff and we all drove out to meet Count Faber-Kastel at his hunting lodge outside the city. Poor fellow — it is an estate of acres — with all kinds of tenants and servants. The lodge itself is beautiful with all manner of game trophies, etc. It is wonderfully furnished, too. We sat before a beautiful fireplace and talked. His wife is very lovely. They have a pretty daughter, 16, and a son missing on the Russian front. So passed two more days in Germany. By all measurement I am two days nearer to you — and to the children. I loved the pictures you sent to me — send more. I also like Jeremy's letter — tell him he does very well. I send you all my love.

Tom

P.S. Don't get upset about plumbers or the well — or anything else — do the best you can under the circumstances.

November 5, 1945
Nürnberg, Germany

Grace, my dearest one,

The pressure is on for fair now. Today Jackson published a memorandum naming trial counsel — and — I was included with nine others. By this time it has probably been made public so you know all about it. As I wrote yesterday, this is one place I did not seek — or covet — and furthermore I did nothing to advance my name but on the contrary I discouraged it. The reaction was extremely interesting. Commander Kaplan, Mr. Dienhard and some of that clique have all asked to be relieved by the middle of this month. Surely such action does show motive. These people have been most aggressive about the preparation of this case with respect to their own personalities — they tried to monopolize the case and succeeded up to this point in doing so. Now because they are not given first places they hope to wreck the organization. What a pity that grown lawyers should so behave! 'twas ever thus.

We had a meeting tonight of trial counsel. It was a long and arduous session. As yet I do not know what my assignment will be. So passed another day — a rather eventful day. It seems strange to me that I should be catapulted onto this trial staff. Maybe it is a great opportunity. The world will watch this case — and in my judgment it will make history. For you — for the children — I hope I can do a job that will be worthwhile.

I must close suddenly — but I send you my deep and unfailing love. You are ever in my thoughts — always in my dreams. Kiss my bairns for me.

Tom

Nürnberg
Nov. 7, 1945

Grace, my dearest one,

Work all day and the problems are many. General Donovan is very peeved about the way things are going — and there is quite a breach between Donovan and Jackson, and it is a most difficult situation. As I understand it, Jackson does not believe Donovan knows enough about the case because he has been away too much. Donovan is upset and every day he asks me to see him and tell me what he thinks, etc.[7] So you see it is more than ordinary work that keeps me busy. I like Donovan — and he is an able trial lawyer. On the other hand he has been away most of the time. Yet he could be prepared if given the assignment.

This noon I had lunch with Amen and Gordon Dean. Amen is on the trial staff — but in my judgment he should not be. He thinks of this case in terms of some New York racket case — and it just is something more than that. He is worried for fear of not being a leading light, I think.

I walk from the office to the hotel, for lunch, when I can. It is only one and a half miles but I do need some air and exercise. I walk only one way — mostly because I do not have time to walk both ways.

We had dinner at the hotel tonight for a change — and afterwards we had Kurt Schuschnigg — the former chancellor of Austria — come out to our house for the evening. He told us all about the time in 1938 when Hitler took over Austria — of the famous meeting at Berchtesgaden, of von Papen, of Seyss-Inquart, of the attitudes of the other powers at the time, of his resignation, of his arrest and long confinement by the Nazis. He is a quiet, intelligent man who gives an impression of great honesty and strength of character. He has a good sense of humor and a pleasing manner.

Your letter of today told about the cocktail party in New York — I am so glad you went. I had two letters from Tommie today and I am very proud of his writing. He suggested that I take tap dancing lessons! The old man is too far along to learn such tricks now. There was a day when I had the same opinion — and I know what Tommie means.

7. The rift between Jackson and Donovan included differing views on presenting the case — Donovan persistently expressed the opinion that the case should not be tried largely on documentary evidence, and should rely more heavily on witnesses. He also wanted a larger role than Jackson was willing to give him.

So, my dearest, again I bid you a fond adieu and send you my deepest love and devotion.

Tom

November 9, 1945
Nürnberg, Germany

Grace, my dearest one,

Today is one of the most important days in the history of the world. It is the most important day in my own career. For this is the anniversary of the day you were born. What a difference if it had not happened. You have been on my mind very much — I love you so much, so completely. And it is wonderful to be married to you.

There is nothing new but work — and more work. The trial staff had a meeting with Jackson today and it now seems fairly certain that the trial will start on Nov. 29. I hope to fly home for Xmas and fly back again. It is worth that much to me and the children too — and I know to you. I think General Donovan will be flying in his plane and I am sure I can go along. If I arrive about the 20th and leave the 28th I will feel that we have had our holiday together. You know I had a great mental distress over my assignment to the trial staff. I guess it is an honor no lawyer would refuse — but I was so set to leave here by the end of this month that the appointment left me cold. Now I feel a little better because I am quite sure I will be home for Xmas as the court is to take a two-week recess.

Last night I was at the office until 11, talking with Howard Brundage, who is leaving December 1. He still suggests Chicago to me and I am still of an open mind. I will not make any decision now.

As you know we have two German frauleins who cook, clean, do our laundry, etc. They speak no English but they are very pleasant. Last night I opened the closet in my room and was startled to see two or three dresses on hangers. I called Hannah and finally we discovered that since she did not have a closet on the third floor and because I had some space in my closet she just moved her stuff in! Well out it went and this morning the two of us got very cool treatment! So you see we have our little problems as well as our big ones.

I will be at your birthday party in spirit and I know you will get all of the candles in one blow.

Tom

November 11, 1945
Nürnberg, Germany

Grace, my dearest one,

This is Armistice Day — and I suppose a holiday at home. The first peace-time Armistice day in a long time. Here it is another day — another mark on the calendar. That is how I feel about all the days over here. The place depresses me — I need to get home and I need it badly — so pray for my early return.

This morning we attended mass for the Germans. Heretofore we have always gone to the soldier's mass. We were very much impressed with the German fervor. They sing hymns — the whole congregation — and they sing well. Many women were hatless! It must be a local custom.

This afternoon Colonel Brundage is at the football game and I am here at the office. It is too cold and raw for me to sit at a football game between two service teams — and besides I have work to do. Anything I can do to hasten these proceedings along is what I want to do. I feel sure that the American case will be over with before Christmas — and I may not return for the rest of it. However that is all speculation as of now — and when I have more definite information I can make that judgment.

No mail from you for some days now — and it is so heartbreaking to wait and wait for your letters. I suppose with the bad winter weather the mail will be slower — particularly the air mail. I wrote notes to Tommie, Jeremy, Carolyn and Martha. I typed the one for Carolyn in capital letters and I am wondering if she will be able to read it. Be sure to let me know how she does with it. Does Christopher still know my picture? I can't believe he is walking around — he was such a baby last July — and I wonder what his reaction will be to me. He might recognize me as the man in the picture!

Joe Guimond arrives tomorrow for a few days. I am looking forward to his visit.

Sometimes I think it can never be pleasant for me here — and mostly because you are not here. I need you very badly dearest, and I must get home to you. For now I send you all of my love.

Tom

Nürnberg, Germany
Nov. 13, 1945

Grace, my dearest,

This has been a long and dreary day. Snow fell for a short time, the temperature has been low and the skies are dull gray. Amidst all the ruins and desolation one needs sunshine, and some of it comes in your wonderful letters — two of which arrived today. Otherwise, I repeat, it was a day of work — including a night session until about 11 p.m. Our trial staff met with Jackson and we battled and argued about the presentation of the proof. General Donovan and Jackson do not get along very well. Donovan is a very strong-minded man — and I must say I like the cut of his jib. Jackson is also a man of tough mind and it is quite understandable that two such personalities will clash. Also there is much struggling for positions of prominence. I continue to saw wood. In a few days a special board of senior trial lawyers is to be formed and it now looks like I shall again be named to it. Really Grace, the evolution of my participation has been a most amazing thing to me. I suppose I have had as much to do with this case as anyone here when one considers that I have questioned and talked with the defendants and witnesses, was a member of the four-man Board of Review supervising the preparation for the trail, am a member of the trial staff, and now a member of the senior trial staff. Well maybe there is a pattern to it all — there must be some purpose. Your prayers must be very persuasive with God — He must look after me, physically and mentally and spiritually. It is a great responsibility — I must carry my part of it and want to do it well but most of all I want to do it with decency, fairness and with justice.

From your letters it appears that you are doing some pleasant things. I am so pleased when you tell me of your trips to New York, New Haven and Hartford — of your bridge parties and social events. Do continue, dearest — it makes me feel better about our separation.

The pictures of the children are a great joy to me. Do send me more — and try to get better ones of Tommie and Carolyn. And please send me one of you — I have worn the old one out with looking and longing.

I send you all of my love.

Tom

Nürnberg, Germany
Nov. 15, 1945

Grace, my dearest one,

This is a two-day letter for yesterday and today. Tuesday night Joe Guimond and Colonel MacClain arrived in Nürnberg — they had been in Vienna. They got here in time for dinner at our place and we passed a most pleasant evening in conversation. They both stayed overnight with us and as a result we acted like girls at boarding school — we talked in our bedrooms until very late. As you know Joe is a full colonel now and he is pleased as punch and I am too.

Yesterday, we had a court session — really, the first one — but only preliminary matters were raised. We tried out the interpreting system. It works quite well. We all wear earphones in the courtroom — and by turning a dial we can hear anything that is said in English, in French, in Russian or in German. As I thought, today Jackson named a board of senior trail lawyers consisting of himself, Colonel Story, General Donovan, Mr. Alderman and yours truly. However I am not so sure it will work. Jackson is an administrative impossibility — and worse he compromises at all turns on questions of personnel and personal responsibility. I may work into the case but the struggles for position are terrific and I doubt that I will play any very important part. Believe me Grace I would like to leave here. I wonder if I shouldn't say I have done my share and go home. Of course people will wonder why I suppose — but that is very unimportant to me. I shall never again allow public interest or public curiosity to bother me in the least. However, a few more days will tell the story. I am never happy in a secondary trial role. You will recall how difficult it was for me in Providence and in other places. I like to run my own trials — my own way. So far it has always worked and too often here I have been forced to pull chestnuts out of the fire for others.

This morning Joe Guimond and Colonel MacClain left for Frankfurt and of course I have been at work all day. We had another court session — again preliminary matters. Krupp, one of the defendants, is too ill to stand trial. Jackson wants to substitute his son.[8] I am unalterably opposed to this because I think it is a capricious way to proceed. If young Krupp should be a defendant, then he should have been included from the beginning. There are no substitutes in criminal cases. It is not a game.

Tonight I worked until 10:30 p.m. and now I close by sending you all of my love — and my affection to the children.

Tom

8. **Gustav Krupp von Bolen und Halbach, head of the Krupp steel and armaments empire, was too ill to stand trial, having suffered a number of strokes. He was the only industrialist among the defendants, so Jackson proposed that Krupp's son, Alfred, should be substituted. The judges denied the request. The younger Krupp was tried at a later tribunal and sentenced to twelve years in prison but released in 1951, after which his inherited factories were restored to him.**

Nürnberg, Germany
Nov. 17, 1945

Grace, my dearest one,

Yesterday was a busy work day. Our Board of Review went out of existence and the new Trial Committee was organized — so I passed from one headache to another. As I wrote to you General Donovan, Colonel Storey, Sidney Alderman and I make up the Trial Committee. We are attempting to get the case ready and it now seems sure to start on Nov. 20. How, I do not know — we simply are not ready. But I do believe we can improvise along and somehow make a good presentation. I now have the so-called economic section of the case — which I will handle in court. I will also examine witnesses and defendants.

The British have a ceremonial guard here now — also the Russians and the French. The Americans look good to me in GI dress. They will alternate on duty throughout the trial. This is a great experience — just to observe the day to day play that goes on is interesting. For example the Russians are very devious and difficult. Now there is a rumor that the trial will be postponed because the Russian prosecutor is ill. It would not surprise me if they pulled something at the last minute.

I received a letter from Ed Lonergan today in which he told me about the defeat of Spellacy and Murphy[9] in New Haven. It is a great and good thing for the Democratic Party.

It is now four months ago that I left Coventry Lake — it now seems like four years. All of my love to you, dearest,

Tom

9. Thomas J. Spellacy and John W. Murphy were longtime Democratic office-holders in Connecticut.

CHAPTER 9

Inhumanity on Trial

THE TRIAL BEGINS, AND DODD PREPARES his part of the case — German rearmament, slave labor used in industry, finance, as well as persecution of the Jews. Dodd considers Jackson's opening statement "a great piece of work." He discovers to his horror that, in the midst of his own opening statement, a page of his remarks is missing. He complains to Grace about Judge Biddle, who is "doing the Nazi handiwork." Hess is ruled fit to stand trial. Dodd tries to convince Jackson that there should be less reliance on documents and a greater use of evidence that shows the human stakes. Dodd presents to the court the lampshades made of human skin and the shrunken head used as a paperweight by Buchenwald's commandant.

November 19, 1945
Nürnberg, Germany

Grace, my dearest one,

This is a date to be remembered. For the trial actually started at ten this morning. The courtroom was crowded. The defendants made quite an appearance. I suppose it has all been very fully carried in the press. I had the feeling that I was witnessing and participating in a history making event. As I walked into the courtroom, the defendants were all in the dock. Keitel, von Papen and Seyss-Inquart all smiled at me. I bowed in acknowledgment. Soon the preliminaries began. The German lawyers were all gowned — some in academic or semi-academic attire. The judges, except for the Russians, were robed. The Russians were in uniform. Behind the judges were the four flags. The American counsel table is in the midst of the other counsel tables. The British is to our right, the Russians to our left, the French to our far left.

The press was heavily represented — from all over the world. Cameramen were everywhere. High above the courtroom a radio booth was crowded with operators and broadcasters. A heavy military guard was in attendance. The indictment was read by representatives of the four powers — each taking a separate part. It lasted all day and truth to tell it was very dull for all hands.

After dinner, I returned to the office for work — a meeting of senior trial counsel — which lasted until 10:30 p.m. Then I returned home. So went the first day and if matters proceed as they started we will finish our part of this case in three weeks.

I expect to present a part of this case on Friday of this week. It will be the so called economic part having to do with industry and rearmament and finance. It is a very difficult part of the case. I realize that I can be a great success or a great failure before an international tribunal. Later — I shall present the persecution of the Jews. Also, "forced labor" or "slave labor" and also concentration camps.[1] I have the heaviest part of the trial work — and the greatest amount of it.

Thus, my dearest, you will understand if for the next two weeks my letters are brief and even tardy. I reiterate that the evolution of my part

1. When he addressed the tribunal on slave labor, Dodd said, "The Nazi foreign labor policy was a policy of mass deportation and mass enslavement . . . of underfeeding and overworking foreign laborers, of subjecting them to every form of degradation, brutality and inhumanity."

in this case is a strange thing. It seems as if some force is pushing me to the fore. I trust it is for the best. I have not sought it.

I send you all my love and devotion.

Tom

Nürnberg, Germany
Nov. 26, 1945

Grace, my dearest one,

Please do not think I am becoming careless, thoughtless or neglectful. The simple truth is I have been completely overwhelmed with work from early morning until late at night. The case is a madhouse. I appeared before the court last Friday — perhaps it was in the papers at home — in any event here is a clipping from the local *Stars and Stripes*.

It is so hard to know whether I have made a bad judgment on staying on. Right now I would give anything to get away — and I may do it very soon. I can get little out of this except some public recognition and maybe not that.

I want to tell you something about the way the trial has been going. It was a very impressive opening of the Tribunal. Jackson's opening statement was, I think, a great piece of work. The whole second and third days having been taken up with the reading of the indictment by the representatives of the four nations. As you have heard me say Jackson is a great lawyer but I was a little sorry that he does not possess more oratorical talent. He concluded his opening late on the afternoon of Wednesday the 21st. [That night] I returned to the office for a meeting of the trial planning committee and thereafter to work on my own preparation for the economic aspects of the conspiracy. The trial opened on schedule at 10 on Thursday morning and after Colonel Storey explained to the Court the source of most of our documentary proof as having been obtained through our capture by the American and British Armies. Then Commander Ralph Albrecht of New York addressed the court and explained the Nazi Party and State organization. He made a very clear exposition and he also used some very impressive charts. He was followed by Major Frank Wallis of Boston who presented the proof under the charge of the Common Plan or conspiracy. He continued throughout the entire day on Thursday and of course that night we worked until 1 or 2 o'clock in the morning getting the economic case ready. On Friday the 23rd, Major Wallis completed his presentation. At about 11 o'clock I think I started to present [my case]. I had written out the statement that I was to make to the court and was greatly surprised on turning the second page to find the third page missing. With some difficulty I got along all right[2] and continued after the noon recess till shortly after 3 o'clock. Sidney Alderman then started his presentation of that part of the case called Aggressive War. Alderman did not get very far because difficulty arose with respect to the use of documents and use of trial briefs and the offering of an opportunity for the Defense to examine [them].

Saturday morning the court was in recess and I worked all day in the office. During the afternoon I witnessed the showing of the film on the concentration camps. I have already seen it once and that is too much.

Sunday morning John Corley left for the United States and I doubt very much if he will be back. I regretted seeing him go because I developed a very great liking for him and considerable admiration for him.

Colonel Brundage was quite sick all day Sunday. He has not been well now for some weeks. I went to Mass and spent the day working. It

2. A review of Dodd's presentation on that day indicates the following was offered extemporaneously: "I will not take the time of this Tribunal to prove what the world already knows: that the Nazi conspirators re-armed Germany on a vast scale. I propose to place in evidence the secret records of the plans and deliberations of the inner councils of the Nazis, which prove that the reorganization of the German Government, the financial wizardry of the Defendant Schacht, and the total mobilization of the German economy largely under the Defendant Schacht, Göring, and Funk, were directed at a single goal: aggressive war."

was a very depressing day. The weather was gloomy and so many people are leaving here and with the coming of the Christmas season it is very hard to keep one's spirits up. I worked Sunday night until after 11 o'clock so this gives you some idea of how my days are occupied.

Yesterday, Monday, was another day of labor. I went to the opening of the court then returned to the office. I am trying to prepare the slave labor feature of the case but the fact of the matter is that they have loaded too much on my back.

Last night Jackson gave a dinner party for the Russian judges and prosecutors at the hotel and I was invited and attended. As usual we drank toasts to Stalin, the King, De Gaulle and Truman. Present were the American judges, French judges, English judges and the Russian judges and all of the prosecutors. The highlight of the evening and perhaps of many a day came when one of the Russians, after making an impassioned speech about the war criminals, then proposed a toast. We all arose, judges as well as lawyers, and his toast was "May the road for these war criminals from the courthouse to the grave be a very short one." I winced and I could see that Judge Parker, the American Alternate, was certainly embarrassed, and certainly the Lord Justice was in a stew. These Russians certainly are realists. We talk about packing a court but they really know how to do it.

Yesterday afternoon, Jackson wrote a letter to General Donovan telling him that he felt that their views were so far apart on the case that Donovan should not plan on actively participating in the trial. As soon as the general got it he called me and he showed it to me.[3] I feel very badly about it because I like Donovan and I think he is a great lawyer. The whole trouble is a clash of personalities but there has been too much of that throughout this whole organization.

Donovan is leaving tomorrow and so is Colonel Brundage. You can well imagine it makes me very blue to see Brundage go. He and I

3. Jackson wrote, in part, "Frankly, Bill, your views and mine appear to be so far apart that I do not consider it possible to assign you to examination or cross-examination of witnesses."

have lived together since last July and I have developed a great affection for him. He is a truly remarkable man and I know you will like him. You know how easy I get down about things and therefore you understand if I seem a little depressed with all of these people leaving for home. I am planning to make a valiant effort to leave here myself within a week or ten days. I propose to suggest that I will return after the holidays if it is necessary that I do so, but I would much prefer to remain at home. Apparently I have received little press value from this affair so far and the struggle for whatever may follow in the future is not worth the sacrifices involved. Besides I am terribly anxious, as I keep repeating, to get home and to see you and the children.

You asked me to look for some china for you and I intend to do so but it will probably not arrive for two or three months. As for silverware, I do not know of any in this neighborhood. It is not so easy to find these things in Germany today because of the economic conditions of the country. You see everyone is on a barter basis and goods are worth much more than money. The more scarce the goods the more difficult it is to buy.

I have been so busy and so tired at the end of a day as to make my schedule for letter writing impossible. But at all times you and only you have been in my mind. No hour passes without thoughts of you and a terrible longing to be home. Sometimes I do not feel I can stay another hour.

[Judge] Biddle is as nasty as he can be — but everyone here knows he is a faker and worse, a man without character. He will make a farce of this case yet and he is doing the Nazi handiwork now. This is no usual trial — and usual procedures will not work. The responsibilities of judges and prosecutors are not at all very different. Yet we are harried at every turn.

So, dearest, I close a not too pleasant letter — with the hope and the dream that I will see you soon. I will cable when I have more definite plans — for now I send you all of my love.

Tom

Nürnberg, Germany
Thursday, Nov. 29, 1945

Grace, my dearest one,

The dark days are here again. After a very short half day of sunshine — the gloom has descended again. Some say it will be like this almost all of the time until spring. A letter from you would help to brighten things — but the mail is all mixed up and no one knows what is wrong with it.

Yesterday morning Colonel Brundage and I were up at the crack of dawn. We drove to the airport at 7 a.m. but the weather was very bad and about 8:30 Colonel Brundage left by automobile for Frankfurt and thence to Paris and Le Havre.[4] I felt very badly about his departure — and I too packed up and moved out of the house in Zerndoff. I am living with Gordon Dean and Colonel Gill on 30 Lindenstrasse. It is a beautiful house — just about the best one here — with English speaking servants. I am glad to be with Gordon and I feel better about things generally.

Yesterday I worked in and out of the courtroom, part of the time at my desk trying to get ready for the future aspects of the case, and part of the time in court. Last night Jackson asked trial counsel to have dinner with him at the hotel and we discussed the case until 9 p.m. Then Gordon and I went to our house. About 10 p.m. we went over to Jackson's, which is just across the street from us — and we talked with Jackson and his son Bill until nearly midnight. It is really my first personal conversation with Jackson and it was very interesting.

Now dearest, I want you to use your influence for me. If all goes well — that is if the case moves along — I can leave here about the 13th of December and sail from Le Havre or from England on a fast boat — which will put me in New York a day or two before Christmas. Your

4. Brundage went back to his law firm of Brundage and Short, which represented major Chicago retailers and the Chicago Bears and its longtime coach, George Halas. He died in 1961.

prayers can do the trick. I will return here by boat just after the first of the year. It is all in the hands of fate and good luck. The transportation people are making the boat reservations, and the only question is whether or not my part of the case can be put on the 10th and 11th, and that depends on how fast the proof moves along next week. Let us hope for the best. Frankly, I do not want to fly at this time of the year. There have been a number of plane accidents lately.

If and when I know certainly that I will sail for New York I will send you a cablegram. For now I will make this brief and send you all of my love.

Tom

Nürnberg, Germany
December 1, 1945

Grace, my dearest,

Yesterday, we put our first witness on the stand — General Lahousen.[5] He was examined by John Amen who did only a fair job at it. Late yesterday the tribunal held a hearing on the mental condition of Hess. After two hours of argument, Hess suddenly and dramatically announced that his loss of memory is and was a fraud, etc. I believe he is of unsound mind — and I have great doubt that he should be on trial.

General Donovan left yesterday by plane for Berlin, thence to Paris, to Belgrade, back to Paris and New York. I went to the airport and saw him off. His plane is leaving Paris for New York on the 15th and he has invited me along. I shall try desperately to make it — so by the time this reaches you I may be on my way to you.

It is now Saturday afternoon and I am sitting in the living room and the servants are putting evergreen and tinsel around the house. Nürnberg has been famed as a Christmas city and we are told that the

---

5. Erwin von Lahousen was part of the plot to assassinate Hitler. He testified here on the murder of thousands of Soviet prisoners of war.

pre-war Christmas holiday here was beautiful and memorable. What a shame that this once lovely place is now in ruins.

I miss you terribly these days — and suppress a terrible aching to walk out of this whole business and go home. If the publicity has not been good then I get very little out of the effort — that is, little recognition. I send you all of my love and devotion.

Tom

December 4, 1945
Nürnberg, Germany

Grace, my dearest one,

Two grand letters arrived today. They were so very helpful. Your courage is steadfast as it always has been. I have known how disappointing it is for all of us to know that my stay here must be prolonged — but your wonderful attitude makes it possible for me to do my job. I am very doubtful about getting home for Christmas. The case is behind schedule and may be more so in another week. To get home means a flight across the Atlantic and the weather at this time of year is not good. Do not plan on me for Christmas. If by any strange chance I do get away it will be a pleasant surprise for all of us. I will be thinking of you — of the children and of home — and I will be happier to know you are having Christmas as we all love it. It is better that I finish this work — for there will be other years and we can make up for this separation in many ways.

On Saturday, the Court held a session lasting until nearly 2 o'clock — the first Saturday session that has been held. A witness, Major General Lahousen, was under cross-examination by the German lawyers on Saturday morning. The German attorneys obviously are completely unfamiliar with the art of cross-examination as it is known in English and American procedure and consequently they did a miserable job as a whole. Von Papen's lawyer did succeed in getting in a good stroke for von Papen by getting an admission from the witness that von Papen was not in sympathy with Hitler's policies and that he had remained in Hitler's service in the hope of restraining Hitler and his cohorts to some extent at least. This has been von Papen's principle of defense as I understand it from my conversations with him and I feel that the case against him is extremely weak. I was distressed when the witness ventured this opinion from the stand. I feel that it was a result of poor preparation on the part of Colonel Amen who presented the witness and it undoubtedly will come back to haunt us later in the case.

The presentation for the witness did give the case a certain change in gait which is desirable in any trial and particularly so here because Sidney Alderman who has been presenting the Aggressive War case is a slow motion attorney who takes longer by far than most lawyers would take to present any given subject. As a consequence of his slow presentation over a matter of two or three days which took on a certain monotony the necessity for putting a live witness on the stand was very real.

A high point of the Saturday session was the request by the attorney for Göring to permit Göring to cross-examine the witness. We strenuously objected and the Tribunal held that no defendant who had counsel could cross-examine except through his counsel. If defendants were permitted to personally cross-examine, this case would be very likely to fall to the level of the sedition trials of unhappy memory in Washington last summer.[6]

I am continuing now after another interruption and without a typewriter. There is more petty envy and competition in this staff to an extent that is disgusting. For many reasons I will be happy when this business is over but the least of them is by no means this one of personality conflicts. Strangely, I am not involved. But all of us are affected to some extent by it — and under all the circumstances we need as much cooperation as we can get.

---

6. "The Great Sedition Trial," as it became known, was of more than thirty individuals accused of violating the Smith Act by being part of a Nazi conspiracy. No one was convicted.

On Monday, the Tribunal convened again and Sidney Alderman took up his presentation. I did not remain in court as it was more of the same sort of presentation that had been put on for a considerable number of days. It lasted all day with only one interesting incident which amounted to the court refusing to admit affidavits of witnesses who are available in Nürnberg. This throws a serious crimp in our plans of execution of the trial since we had understood an affidavit would be acceptable by the court under the terms of the court charter. Use of affidavits is particularly important in this hearing as most of the prospective witnesses for our case are Germans and Nazis and we do not wish to put them on the stand as witnesses in the usual sense of the term, which ordinarily means that the side presenting a witness vouches for him and is bound by his statements. It also means a considerable slowing up of the presentation of proof since live witnesses take much longer from the point of view of time than the introduction of affidavits which may be read into the record and also because with 20 defendants and 20 lawyers[7] reading them, the cross-examination of one witness takes a very great length of time.

Somewhat as a result of this ruling and because of other factors, Justice Jackson called a few of us to a dinner meeting at the hotel — not a very satisfactory meeting because it developed into a general discussion about the matter of witnesses and affidavits. Mr. Jackson stated that the British were in agreement with us that a motion should be made in open court to permit documents to be introduced in evidence as they were ordinarily introduced in trials without respect to the necessity of reading them into the record, and we discovered as a result of the discussion that this strange rule is the result of the insistence of the Russians and the French that these matters be read because they had not provided the translation facilities for themselves they promised to provide before the trial started.

We are still being defeated by all the personality difficulties that

7. Actually, there were twenty-two defendants, including Martin Bormann, in absentia.

have upset this organization since I came into it. Colonel Storey, who has been acting as Executive Counsel, has been more or less disregarded over the order of proof and general control of the trial, and Colonel Amen, who is interested in personally presenting witnesses, has been violently opposing Storey with the result that this afternoon they had a serious and, perhaps, final, wrangle about their respective positions. Storey has been overworked anyway and has not received the co-operation that he was entitled to from Amen and from others on the staff. As a consequence he did not attend the dinner meeting tonight but went home to bed with the complaint that he had the grippe but he also told me that he was feeling very low mentally and was seriously considering asking to be relieved of any responsibility in this case. It would make another fatality in the organization, following close on the heels of the departure of General Donovan which I do not think would be a good thing for the interests of the United States and the nations allied with it. First of all because I think Storey has done a job that no one else was prepared or willing to do in getting this case ready and secondly because I do not believe that Amen and some others here are capable of handling any large part of this case in a satisfactory manner. When I consider that Colonel Bernays, who was in the organization in London last July, was a fatality[8] and Francis Shea, who was in the organization from May, was a fatality and that General Donovan is the latest to fall into this class, I am somewhat distressed about the turn of events of the last few hours and I am aware that much of it is the result of poor selection of personalities at the beginning.

[After dinner] I returned to our own house and discussed the events of the day with Gordon Dean. Gordon agrees with my analysis of the situation and feels as I do that we should make an effort to keep Colonel Storey here but he also feels that Amen, who has been in the organization from the earliest days, should go on to put a few

8. Lieutenant Colonel Murray C. Bernays, who developed the initial plan to try the defendants and provided much of the momentum, was assigned no meaningful trial duties by Jackson and, devastated, resigned for health reasons.

live witnesses on the stand. I find no difficulty with this latter suggestion except that I do not want him putting on any witnesses which
have to do with that part of the case which has been assigned to me.
And I would not be surprised if other lawyers with similar responsibilities took the same stand. The matter will probably come to a head
the latter part of this week. [Amen] does not know this part of the case
and I do not think he is qualified to examine a witness who will testify with respect to any particular part of the case.

Once again I am half typing and half writing a letter. You see I am
finding it most difficult to keep up my schedule. I write parts of letters
over a period of time. With the trial on and the great amount of work
after court hours I am indeed sorely pressed for time. You know it is a
hardship for me not to be able to write every day — for the hour or so
spent is an hour of unbroken thoughts of you, whom I love beyond all
else in the world.

I hope you have Christmas in Lebanon — and all the trimmings
with it. I think it is better for you and the children that way. I will be
with you in spirit, helping with the tree, setting out the presents, fixing
up the house, and I will be at the table helping you carve and loving
you every minute.

Tom

December 6, 1945
Nürnberg, Germany

Grace, my dearest one,

Another two-day letter — and again the same cause for the passing
of a day without writing a few lines to you — work and more work. Tuesday, the Chief British Prosecutor made his opening statement — Sir
Harley Shawcross, who is also Attorney General of Britain. He did a
very lawyer-like job and his presentation was well received. The British
began presenting proof of aggression as to Poland and other countries.
It is very dull as it is mostly a recital of the then existing Treaty obligations. This will continue for all of this week — I fear. Then again on

Monday, Sidney Alderman will finish up on Japan and the aggression against the U.S., and German aggression against Russia. Then I will begin to present the case on slave labor — next concentration camps and under my supervision Major Bill Walsh will present the persecution of the Jews. I would have done this myself but there is too much for a lawyer to handle in these three aspects of the case. We will be through in about three days. I still do not know about Christmas. I wrote a memorandum to Jackson suggesting that I be allowed to make a hurried trip over and back. Of course much depends on what progress we make between now and the time I should leave.

We received a copy of last Sunday's *New York Times* — and the picture in the magazine section should interest you — yes, that is me, not easily recognized, with my hand holding my face, in the first occupied seat on the right of our counsel table and my back to the Russians. Please save it, and anything else of interest.

Colonel Amen is becoming most difficult — he is a real fat head and a publicity hound. He wants to examine all witnesses. I say nothing doing with respect to those related to my part of the case. We shall see what happens.

I cannot understand why Joe Blumenfeld was unaware that I am on the trial staff. It was in the *New York Times*, but maybe not in the Connecticut papers. I am not over-anxious about publicity but on the other hand there is a decent public relations situation which permits some public notice when one participates in a trial of this importance.

Well, dearest, do keep your fingers crossed about Christmas. By the time this letter reaches you it will be decided. I send you all of my never ending love and devotion.

Tom

[After this letter was sent, Dodd received permission to go home for Christmas.]

CHAPTER 10

Czech War Crimes

AFTER A BRIEF PERSONAL BREAK IN CONNECTICUT, Dodd
returns to the trial in time to witness the French put on its part of the prosecution's case, to await the turn of the Soviets — and to be named Jackson's
chief assistant. Dodd travels to Prague to witness the war crimes trial of
three Czech generals who collaborated with the Nazis. The former president of the Republic, Edvard Beneš, tells him that in 1938 the British and
French advised him to cooperate with the Nazis, and reveals that he
warned FDR early on as to Germany's plans to conquer Europe. Dodd
meets often with Jackson trying to find ways to shorten the case. The Soviet
case, he tells Grace, "sounds like the report on a Chinese flood." All the
while, he worries over Grace's mysterious illness.

London, England
January 6, 1945

Dearest Grace,

I slept about two hours [last night] and woke up after dreaming of
you and the children. I arose about an hour ago. It is 5 a.m. We leave
at six for the airport, so I will not have too long to wait here in the lobby
where I am writing this letter.

You see sometimes I get almost overwhelmed with loneliness for you — my heart actually aches. Then I cannot sleep, or do much else. Last night was such a time. It seems weak and silly — I suppose — but I love you so, and to be separated from you is an ordeal and a trial for me. I miss the children so much and I do not think I saw nearly enough of them while at home. The memories that stick are not of parties with friends but those of you and the children — your smile, your eyes, and your lovely soul.

It has made me feel so much better to have these few minutes with you. I send my love as ever unchanging and unending.

Tom

Nürnberg, Germany
January 16, 1946

Grace, my dearest one,

My spirits jumped ahead ten points when your two letters of January 2nd and 3rd arrived a few minutes ago. I was really getting low about the lack of mail. The letters today were grand — to know that you love me as enthusiastically as ever makes me feel better. I thought you were disappointed with me when I was home. You know it wasn't my fault, altogether, that we did not have more time alone. And then that silly spat — over nothing. It was so wonderful to see you and to be with you and the children.

Don't be fooled by this political talk about the governorship or the Senate.[1] Time may change the whole outlook, and those who talk the most now will do something else later. I am not at all enthusiastic about it. I much prefer a good law practice — and now is the time for me to strike, I think. Gordon Dean asked me to open one with him in California. Of course that is not possible, but I did appre-

1. **Dodd's name was being put forward by Democratic Party leaders.**

ciate the compliment. I have heard nothing from Washington. I still have hopes, very slim ones, but some hopes. However, things will work out for the best. My new philosophy is to saw wood and let things work out.

Do take good care of yourself — and of the children. I send you my constant love and devotion.

Tom

Nürnberg, Germany
January 17, 1946

Grace, my dearest one,

Two more wonderful letters arrived from you today — and I feel like a new man. Strange, your letter of January 6th tells how blue you are — that was the night I was in London, and I wrote you a letter telling how blue I felt. We are so close to each other even our moods are in unison.

Tonight Colonel Gill is entertaining the judges and Justice Jackson at dinner at our house — so we must all be on hand to help out. For my own part I expect a dull evening — but it is one of those things one must do.

I have been dreaming about you and the children very often of late, and, strangely, about your mother — about your home on Narragansett Avenue. I am really not a believer in dreams but I need for you to realistically explain them for me. [In last night's dream] you and the children were crying — had tears in your eyes. It must be the Irish in me causing me to ponder on dreams — when psychologists explain them so easily.

Soon there will be a transatlantic phone connection here in Nürnberg and I will surprise you someday with a call. Just to hear your lovely voice will mean so much to me.

Tom

Nürnberg, Germany
January 18, 1946

Grace, my dearest one,

The French continue to state their case. We are not too interested as most of their proof came from our files. I try to understand the French — but they are so "Frenchie," if you know what I mean. The Russkies will be even worse I suppose with all manner of exaggerations — thousands murdered, millions missing, everything colossal. We will weather it out somehow and get a judgment one way or another, but it is an endurance contest among other things.

By the way, how is your health? I will return pronto if you are considering any little pink booties and such. Be so careful of your dear self — I worry about you sometimes. You are so slight, and you have so many responsibilities. Little wonder that you're tired so much of the time. Someday soon I hope we can all take things a little easier.

George Hurley's death[2] is often on my mind — somehow I feel it more now — he was such a great fellow and so good a friend. I shall miss him greatly — and no trip to Washington will ever mean as much again. I know what has been lost.

Dearest, I send you, as ever, all of my eternal love and devotion. Give my affection to the children.

Tom

Prague, Czechoslovakia
January 18, 1946

Grace, my dearest one,

This has been a memorable day — but before I begin the story of it I must tell you of the very interesting dinner party we had at our house

2. **Hurley was staying at a hotel with his ailing father. While helping his father up the stairs, he fell backward, tumbled down the stairwell, and died from his injuries.**

in Nürnberg last night. Lord Justice Lawrence, Francis Biddle, Judge John Parker, Justice Jackson and Bill Jackson were our guests. Everything went very well and after dinner we had a very interesting conversation about the case—staying clear and well away from any real discussion of the merits. Yet it was a revealing talk for it demonstrated the great interest the judges have in this case. They suggested that we should publish—now—the evidence that we have presented and such additional proof as we have but which we did not offer in evidence. Biddle is very entertaining but he is a very insincere man—a shallow man, an opportunist. Sir Geoffrey Lawrence is a great man of depth and wisdom and Parker is a wholesome, practical man of ability. Jackson is, as ever, a most unusual man of ideas and character.

This morning Father Walsh, Lt. Col. Bill Baldwin, Dr. Franz Blaha and Captain Honack (the latter two Czechs—Blaha the physician who was confined in Dachau for four years)—and I left by plane for Prague. We knew we should reach the city by about 11:45. That time came and passed. At 1 p.m., still no Prague. Then we knew we were lost. There was a rather heavy haze, but the visibility was not too bad. We flew low over two or three small communities—and Blaha said he recognized two and we were well north of Prague and headed away from it. The pilot, Dick Thompson, did not agree. After awhile a plane came in sight and we turned and flew alongside. It was fearful. We tried to communicate with its pilot but to no avail. We swooped and started in Blaha's direction. Then Thompson said our gas was low and in fifteen minutes he would have to go down. Father Walsh was in the rear seat—I was in the front. I turned and looked at him and he was very composed. In ten minutes we sighted Prague. Everyone was happy. I turned to look at Father Walsh. He smiled and took his hand out of his pocket—it was holding his rosary. I tipped my hat.

When we landed we were met by the chief war crimes prosecutor for Czechoslovakia, Foreign Office representatives, saluting army officers and whatnot. A huge limousine whisked us to this magnificent hotel—the finest in the city. I have a four-room suite with two baths! We were tendered a beautiful luncheon, then a sightseeing trip, tea at the National Club, back to the hotel for a wash up and so on — thence for dinner at Lippett's, a famous restaurant here, and at 11 p.m., we returned to our hotel and here I am. This is a magnificent city — the finest I have seen — excepting Rome, yet it is more appealing than Rome. It is medieval, yet there is a gaiety in the air. The girls are most attractive. The men, many of them, well dressed and good looking. The city looks smart. The old part of it is fascinating. The cathedral, the castle, the St. Charles Bridge — all are beautiful. But more, they are so much a part of the Middle Ages. We also visited the oldest Jewish synagogue in Central Europe — just about 6 p.m. while services were on. Probably twenty-five Jewish men — no women — attending the service.

As I sit writing this letter young people are singing Czech songs in the street. It is Saturday night, of course — but I am sure they did not sing one year ago. The Nazis were still here then.

I am surprised to learn that this country is 98 percent literate. How little we know about other people — no wonder we have misunderstandings.

My dearest, only one thing is missing to make this trip complete — your own dear self. Some day you and I will come to Prague — and you will love it as I do. I again send you my heart full of love for you.

Tom

P.S. I saw something for you — it will be sent from here.

Prague, Czechoslovakia
January 20, 1946

Grace, my dearest one,

[This morning] we saw Strahov Convent and its wonderful library, something absolutely out of the Middle Ages. Two monks showed us about. One was a very handsome young man.

I attended Mass in the wonderful St. Vitus Cathedral. We visited the Loretto Church — on the hour the chimes played a hymn. We were shown the scenes of the terrible street fighting with the Germans last May. We walked on the Street of the Alchemists which once housed alchemists seeking the way to make gold for a king.

[After a luncheon] we stopped at Ambassador Steinhardt's home — a magnificent place — just in time for a wedding! A Miss Connelly, of the Embassy staff, was married to a young air corps man. The ceremony was performed by a Catholic priest. I like Steinhardt — he was formerly ambassador to Russia, later to Turkey. I am to see him again tomorrow. We left there about 6 p.m. and went to the beautiful Prague Opera house where *Libussa* was playing. We were in a box — the house was packed. The performance lasted until 10:45 — it is a patriotic and legendary opera, written by Smetana, and the Czechs are very proud of it. During the German occupation the playing of it was forbidden. After the opera we returned to the hotel for a lovely dinner. It is now 12:50 a.m., and the day is done.

Tomorrow I will shop, attend a war criminal trial, see Steinhardt and a few other Czechs and return to Nürnberg by air if the weather is good.

It is late, my dearest. I will end this letter by repeating the old story I love to tell and hear you tell me — I love you with all my heart.

Tom

Prague, Czechoslovakia
January 21, 1946

Grace, my dearest one,

[After breakfast] I attended the War Crimes Trial of three Czech generals who collaborated with the Nazis. We were ushered in with much pomp and circumstance. The courtroom was packed with what I judge to be 1,000 people. I was photographed innumerable times as I sat in a special seat only a few feet from the judges. The summation was in Czech. But there was an atmosphere and I understood it. The trial was dignified yet efficient. Once there was some hissing — the presiding judge called for and got order. We stayed one hour. (I heard tonight that two of the generals were sentenced to death and one got twenty-five years in prison. The two were executed by hanging at 5 p.m. this afternoon — under Czech law a death sentence is carried out three hours later.)

We visited Pankrac prison, adjoining the court. It was a melancholy experience. Many political prisoners are there now — collaborationists — or at least those accused of it. They were a sorry-looking lot of peasants — men and women and — praise God — children. I mean little children — the age of Martha and Christopher. Squatting in the corridor — in the cold, dank corridor. Maybe because there is no other place for them while their parents are confined. We were shown the Nazi guillotine. It was a gruesome sight — in a white marble-tiled room, with drains for the blood, a basket to catch the head and cheap coffins for bodies. A small "courtroom" was a few feet away. Meat hooks hung from a track — so the bodies could be moved about. Yes, meat hooks such as we see in beef houses. Thousands were beheaded in that terrible place which still smells of blood and death. Some for offenses such as "giving bread to a Russian prisoner of war." (It is a matter of record.)

We visited the cell of Karl Hermann Frank — the Nazi ruler of Czechoslovakia.[3] He is a petty-looking creature — before he became a Nazi tribune he was a small book seller!

We returned to the hotel via a shopping tour. I bought you a beautiful glass vase. Unpleasant as money matters are I must tell you I paid $27 for it. In the U.S. we would pay $100. It is small but I think truly a treasure. I also bought you a blouse for $16 — $40 in New York. I hope you like it as much as I do. Mrs. Rais — the wife of a Czech friend I met here — helped pick it out.

We thought we would leave the airport at 3 p.m. I was all packed

---

3. Frank was instrumental in the destruction of the Czech villages Lidice and Ležáky. He was hanged at Pancrak Prison on May 22, 1946.

when the phone rang and the pilot said the flight was cancelled — ice
on the wings, etc. So we went shopping again and as a result you have
a fur hat — very inexpensive — white rabbit and cloth, coonskin style,
made for German troops. I bought a grey one. Yours will look grand
with your snowsuit.

At 6 p.m., Father Walsh and I were received by the President of
Czechoslovakia, Eduard Beneš, in his office in the castle. We talked
with him for an hour. He told us about Munich in '38 — how the
French and British ambassadors called on him and said, "If you resist
the Nazis you will have the responsibility for war and more — even if
you win we will take the area that the Nazis want away from you." He
related the story of Hitler's offer of a secret pact — made through
Albrecht Haushofer[4] and an Austrian count on December 18, 1937 in
Prague. Beneš said, "But I have treaty commitments. I am a member
of the League of Nations. Said they, 'Don't worry about that. When
war comes you will simply not live up to your treaties — and in the
League you will not vote sanctions.'" He told us of a conversation with
Roosevelt in the early summer of 1939. Beneš told F.D.R., "The war
will come soon after July 15th — it will start with Poland — and will
engulf all of Europe." He told me how pleased he is with the Nürnberg trial — mostly because the proof vindicates his position. He is
made of great personal attractions — a man of courage and of strong
mind. He said, "Hitler hated me because I ignored his invitation to
Berlin — thrice made."

In the morning, if the weather is good, we fly to Nürnberg. I send
you all of my love, and ask you to kiss the children for me.

Tom

4. Haushofer worked on peace treaties with the French and the British before
turning against the Nazi regime. He was part of the bomb plot against Hitler
and was shot by an SS commando in April 1945.

Nürnberg, Germany
January 22, 1946

Grace, my dearest one,

We arrived in Nürnberg about 2:30 p.m. today after a flight from Prague. I must be a jinx for planes — we nearly crashed in landing, ran off the runway and generally had a time of it.

Your letters of January 8th and 10th were on my desk. I am upset about your illness. What manner of infection is it? When did it set in? What is it all about? Please tell me as I prefer, always, to know the whole story. I will be worried until you write me fully about it. You are so calm usually — it must have been most unusual to cause you to worry. The pity of our separation is that I am not nearby to help you, and also to be informed. So you are run down — that is from dieting too much. Maybe I wore you out while at home — is the infection the result of that? Really it worries me to think you may have something wrong — please write me fully — and please tell me the whole story. It isn't fair to mislead or withhold in such matters.

Dearest, I love you so — with all my heart — and you are so precious. Please do take good care of yourself. I live only for you and the day I have you in my arms.

Tom

Nürnberg, Germany
January 23, 1946

Grace, my dearest one,

I sent you a cable a few minutes ago because I sense that something is wrong. You made no mention of your visit [in the last letter] to the doctor on the 12th, and laconically wrote "I am fine" at the end of your letter, which is so unlike you. You see you must always tell me directly and fully about such things as it worries me to think you will not keep me completely informed. I think such a fear is much worse than any one worry. I am mystified at the whole business — and it must have been something to cause you to be in the dumps and to seek help. If I could talk to you it would be so much easier for me.

This letter will go to you via Bill Jackson who is going to the States for two weeks. It should be in your hands Monday or Tuesday — and if you will answer me soon — and I know you will, and completely — at least I will know the situation. I am really upset about you. It is all so mysterious. Please, please, take good care of yourself — you are all I really have in this world. No matter what is wrong we will straighten it out.

Give my affection to the children and I send you all of my love.

Tom

Nürnberg, Germany
January 24, 1946

Grace, my dearest one,

I am so worried about you, I can do little work. Last night I slept fitfully — fretfully — waking and thinking of you. If only I knew what is wrong and what it is all about. Your letter of the 10th said you saw the doctor — "a surface infection" — you were to see him on the 12th. Your letter of the 12th never mentioned the doctor. Your letter of the 13th made no mention of your condition but said in closing "the children are all well and so am I." That isn't like you. I know something is wrong and I must be near you if that is so.

Now I understand the dreams I had about your mother and your home in Westerly. It was so clear — Grace, dearest, you have no idea how I am pained to think of you ill. It is absolutely impossible for me to be away from you. Nothing in this world — nothing — means anything to me except you. Nothing is — or ever can be — as important, nothing. No one else matters.

I will try to call you on the transatlantic phone tonight or as soon as I can get through. The new line opened here only yesterday.[5] The cable service is bad, but I sent you one anyway.

You must be thinking of me as I simply cannot get you out of my mind — and we always have had a kind of telepathy between us. When you wrote that Lincoln Opper took your blood pressure, I wondered why. It must be that you told him you were not feeling too well. What does the doctor say? How often have you seen him? What kind of treatment are you getting? What is a surface infection? Why were you going to Hartford? For medical attention? All of these questions are plaguing me. I know you have no one in whom to confide — no one who can take you in his arms as I can — no one who really cares or could care as completely as I do. I can be home in a jiffy — and I cannot stay away if you are in need of me. I love you, Grace, with all my heart and soul.

Tom

Nürnberg, Germany
January 27, 1946

Friday, I was in court most of the morning and the French prosecutor Du Bost stalled the proceedings for one hour simply because of stupidity. During the afternoon I was in the office most of the time doing some work on a motion which if granted should materially shorten this trial. With the British I am working to have the defense make a detailed offer of proof before they start their case — we may be able to agree on some of it — some will certainly be ruled out and finally we will ask that affidavits be used for most of the testimony and thus save long oral examinations.

No mail from you since last week on Tuesday — but the telephone

5. Dodd called that night and got through, relieving his stress over the illness, although indications were that his wife was not very explicit.

call has sustained me — it was so good to hear your voice. I think I will try to call once a month for as long as I am here — it is the best investment I can make for twelve dollars.

If you agree I wish you would start early to find a spot for the summer — for I do intend to have this summer with you and the children. Tomorrow I will write notes to the children. Jerry's letter tickled me — it opened "Dear Tom."

I send you anew all of my love and all of my affection.

Tom

Nürnberg, Germany
January 28, 1946

Grace, my dearest one,

A new program started for me this morning. I arose and took a half hour walk — a good brisk one before breakfast. I have made no hard and fast rule, but I have resolved to get in shape if at all possible. I am restricting my smoking to a pipe after breakfast, lunch and dinner — and alcohol is out altogether. I expect to do it for six months or at least until I get home and perhaps for much longer.

Today I was in court about all the time. The French put three witnesses on the stand who told of the terrible sufferings and tortures of the concentration camps. It was shocking — but we have heard so much of it. All are tired of it. These Frenchmen are really terribly hard to get on with — they are terribly thin-skinned and touchy, and somewhat stupid. I make allowances for them. Their defeat and humiliation has made them sensitive — they have suffered greatly. Besides, their witnesses are about all French communists — and that is something they can avoid. For actually the communists did not suffer as did so many others and anyway I doubt their basic French patriotism. I do not like to prove a case against Nazism by using communist witnesses. A plague on both your houses, say I.

Tonight Colonel Gill and I had Colonel Dostert and Mr. Sere-brenekov — a Russian/English interpreter — for dinner and a game of bridge. I played with Gill and we won three dollars — but I was really nervous about the game. Gill is former president of the National Bridge Association — has played and won tournaments all over the U.S. and is one of the top players. Dostert and his partner were good, too. Gill is teaching me — we are to play every week — so beware of your laurels when I return.

Kiss the bairns for me — do write me long letters and do let me know how you are.

Tom

Nürnberg, Germany
January 28, 1946

Grace, my dearest one,

A nice letter from you this afternoon — a very courageous one too congratulating me on the appointment as chief assistant, when I know how you feel and how I feel about it because of the separation.

This is otherwise a dark and dreary day. I have been in court most of the time. At lunch, I met with Justice Jackson and we discussed ways and means of shortening the case. It seems as if we are sure to do it by the end of April — if all goes well. I had dinner with Sidney Alderman at the hotel tonight. I felt it was a duty dinner for he seems quite lonesome — all excepting Sidney have left the house where he lives. I suppose the trial gets little press attention at home, which is not strange at this stage of the game. My only aim is to bring it to a successful and speedy conclusion — if I do that then my job will have been a success.

I send you all of my never ceasing love and my endless devotion.

Tom

Nürnberg, Germany
January 31, 1946

Grace, my dearest one,

A long dreary day — most of it in the courtroom. The French case continued. At one point this afternoon Sir David Maxwell-Fyfe and I had to step in to extricate Monsieur Du Bost from a bad legal hole.[6] Late this afternoon Maxwell-Fyfe, Colonel Fillimore, Mr. Dean and Elwyn Jones of the British delegation met with us — Jackson and me — and we discussed plans for shortening the case. This morning I had a long talk with Justice Jackson. We covered many problems and a number of vexing questions. I have discovered that he is inclined to be rash and impetuous. He was angry at the press today and wanted to blast the AP publicly. I finally convinced him that it would not only be unwise but also futile. He calmed down and took my advice. Tomorrow night the Justice is giving a dinner party for the French and I must attend — o my! — I do hope I am not seated between two Frenchmen.

This is all the news — for it isn't new to tell you again that I love you with all my heart and soul — and I will until the end of time.

Tom

Nürnberg, Germany
February 3, 1946

Grace, my dearest one,

Yesterday at three I left for Stuttgart, after calling Major Bingham, who made a hotel reservation for me. It was more or less of a brainstorm. We drove — the chauffeur and I — through some rain and bad weather and over what seemed to be mountains and after one flat tire

6. The transcript does not indicate the precise problem, or Fyfe and Dodd's intervention.

we arrived at the Graf Zeppelin Hotel too late for dinner. However, the driver went to the Red Cross Club while Bingham took me to the residence of Colonel Dawson, the military government chief, where I had some cold cuts, but not enough. Dawson was Dean of Western Reserve Law School — Joe Guimond was one of his students. It was a dull evening, very stuffy. Bingham is an ineffectual person — so broad he is flat. Dawson, perhaps without intent, made too many slighting references to Catholics and Irishmen. A fawning ass of a lieutenant colonel said yes, yes, and laughed like a tin toy man. Well, with rare exceptions these military government people are of such dimensions. Sort of camp followers, if you know what I mean.

This morning we rode about what was once, I am sure, the beautiful center of Stuttgart. It is badly damaged — and sadly — mostly libraries, churches, museums, and old buildings. I attended Mass at the Red Cross Club. Bingham met me at 10 and we went sightseeing until 11:30. Bingham thinks he is a great candidate. I said I did not know him well. He finally asked directly if I was interested politically next year. I said, "O! I am so busy in Nürnberg. I really haven't thought about it. What about you?" said I. "O! I will look the situation over when I get home in April — but do you think we can win a Senate seat?" So the major wants to be a Senator and Bowles[7] is to be Governor! Bingham and Bowles is the new firm, ladies and gentlemen. Step up and see our fancy Yankee wares! Bingham will try to trade in on his non-combat, military, government, war service, while Bowles is the great administrator. I trust the Democrats will have more sense.

We left Stuttgart after lunch and arrived here about an hour ago, at 5 p.m. I am lonesome tonight. Seeing the Germans out walking on Sunday makes me envious. I wish I were at home with you and the children. A good walk, a cheery fire, high tea, or a good pick up Sunday night supper — rummy and go to bed. Wouldn't that be divine?

7. **Chester Bliss Bowles was cofounder of Benton and Bowles, an advertising agency. He later went into public service. He was elected governor of Connecticut for one term and served in the Kennedy and Johnson administrations. He was the U.S. ambassador to India for many years.**

I miss you, my dearest. I have had no news for three weeks. And that is a long, long time. As ever I send you all of my love and my devotion.

Tom

Nürnberg, Germany
February 5, 1946

Grace, my dearest one,

Another day without any word from you. The mail must be hopelessly bogged down somewhere. I watch every day for the mail and every day for weeks now only disappointment. I will be full of hope again tomorrow.

I was in court for most of this morning. At 11:30, Justice Jackson called a meeting of the chief prosecutors and I attended with them. General Rudenko, the Russian, is so suspicious, so distant, at times almost hostile. Sir David Maxwell-Fyfe and DeRibes of France humor him along. Even Jackson treats him somewhat patiently — but I know what he thinks of Russia and the Russians. It is so difficult to work with Russians. I am ever thinking what an enigma they are. I do believe we must try hard to get along with them but sometimes I think it is all hopeless and it can and will only be resolved by dreadful resort to arms. It may come soon — sooner than we now realize.

I am now under care of a bodyguard. A soldier who follows me everywhere. He seems like a steady young man. It is a new rule — for the judges and chief prosecuting officials. I really think it is foolish and unnecessary. I do think it will be a nuisance to have this shadow wherever I go.

I am mailing some pictures tomorrow. Some of Dodd and the human head[8] — one of me addressing the Tribunal, and a few shots of the courtroom.

---

8. The Associated Press and other news organizations photographed Dodd holding the paperweight made of the shrunken head of a hanged Polish prisoner.

Grace, dearest, I must not dwell too much on this lack of mail from you — but truly I am so lonesome over here and the absence of mail makes existence here almost unbearable. I should not complain — and it sounds or reads worse than it is, I am sure. Nevertheless, my dear, my love for you is so great — so strong — so lasting it can live on even if the mail never gets through.

Tom

Nürnberg, Germany
February 6, 1946

Grace, my dearest one,

Yet another day with no letter from you. The situation is actually getting desperate — not since last July and August have I been so out of touch with you. Everyone else is in the same boat.

I was in court part of this morning. My bodyguard is already oppressive. Everywhere I go he is right behind me — and really it gets on one's nerves. He is a nice young soldier from near Boston. His name is Tom Kerival.

After lunch I saw Justice Jackson and we had a long talk about the case. Our trip to Poland, scheduled for this weekend, was very suddenly "postponed." We were so advised by the American ambassador in Warsaw late this afternoon. Of course we know why. The Russians wouldn't allow us in Poland. The Polish delegation here is terribly embarrassed — but they are completely prisoners of the Russians. We know that. Justice Jackson invited me to go with him to Prague, Vienna and Budapest, leaving Nürnberg on February 15th. Tomorrow, the French finish their case. On Friday the Russians start in — for good or bad — no one knows which. But at least we do know we are moving ahead toward the end.

At seven tonight, Colonel Gill, Major Nimtz and I had dinner at home. Colonel Gill told me that Jackson has expressed great confidence in me. Gill said, "I told him you were not only a great lawyer but you were always on the job and always sober." The latter part is for your information. I know you will say, "That chameleon — living with a dry he becomes one." Truth is I started my own program some time back.

Well, my dearest. I need mail in order to write even fair letters. This way one engages in a soliloquy. Absence of mail does not dull my love for you. If anything it makes it sharp — more eager.

Tom

Nürnberg, Germany
February 9, 1946

Grace my dearest one,

At long last two letters have arrived — one dated January 21 and the other January 28 — and the last one prior to these two was dated January 14. It looks like someone has decided to let me have a letter once a week. I hope the back numbers arrive — for I am still without any information on your illness — and your letters weeks apart leave gaps.[9] Yet I am happy to have heard from you and I will not complain too much.

Now I must go back to Thursday, February 7th, and tell you what has been happening. I was in court most of the day — the French finished their part of the prosecution case and the British presented some proof about Rudolf Hess and his trip to England. I talked with the Justice about some problems and particularly about the assignments for cross-examination.

Yesterday, Friday, opened the Russian case. General Rudenko made his statement and the Russian photographers were all over the place. It lasted most of the day and about four o'clock the Russkies began presenting evidence. I conferred with the Justice about segregating Göring from other defendants for he is browbeating and threatening them — and particularly those who might admit some guilt. He wants all to hang together — and to try to prove that Roosevelt was the cause of the war!

9. **Grace Dodd's illness at the time remains a mystery to family members. None of her children recall her being sick during this period.**

Well, we will take care of that defense all right but I do not think he is entitled to go on intimidating people as he has done for much of his life.

This Saturday morning the Tribunal sat until 11:30 a.m. I was in court for a time and later in the office working on a motion. About noontime I met with Keitel and his counsel — at their request. He asked to see a document so as to prepare his defense. However I think he is fishing about for some kind of situation for his lawyer said he would like to have a long talk with me alone. I will see him next week. It would be quite a break if he pleads guilty.

So, I am a possible candidate for Governor — well, I am not so sure. Believe me when I tell you I am not too interested. Of course [Brien] McMahon[10] does not want me to run for the Senate or for anything else — so I might take a shot at him by helping someone else. However, we shall see.

I am sending you a Persian lamb cap made from a skin I saw in Prague. It will look very chic on you with a black suit or black dress and accessories and your leopard coat. It is really expensive fur — but you won't see many like it.

My dearest, I am so pleased because I have the two letters from you — but somehow you do not sound cheerful. I can't say why or where in your letters but I seem to feel it when I read them. Please let me know if anything is bothering you or worrying you. I send you my love — all of it — never changing, and all my devotion as well.

Tom

Nürnberg, Germany
February 9, 1946

Grace, my dearest one,

This is the second time today that I have written to you. I refused two dinner engagements tonight, so my lonesomeness is of my own choosing. I miss you terribly at times, and this is one of those times.

---

10. **In addition to his role as U.S. senator, McMahon was a party power broker.**

If it were not for a real belief in the need for the doing of this job —
and a strong feeling that our country's interest is at stake — I would not
stay here another day. Also I feel that Jackson needs my help. He has
been terribly let down by many of these lawyers who have been on this
case. They fall into one of two classes. Some Army and Navy officers,
lawyers, sought to get on the staff as a soft assignment. Some Army and
Navy officers, and some civilian lawyers, got on by exaggerated reports
about their ability — and once on the staff proceeded to seek and get
some personal publicity and then asked to be released. You will know
both groups — they will be telling everyone what they did in Nürnberg.
Jackson knows this now. And I feel badly for him. I cannot shirk this
responsibility, and you would not let me. We will see this job through —
and I know despite the sacrifices that you and I are making that we will
be glad we did it this way. Sometimes a man knows his duty so clearly,
so surely, he cannot hesitate. He dare not refuse it. Even great pain and
other sacrifices seem unimportant in such a situation. The pain is no
less for this knowledge, but the pain has a purpose at least.

So, dearest, soon I shall be abed — and dreaming, I hope, of you. I
wanted to tell you tonight how much I love you — how deeply I love
you, how earnestly, how intensely — how fiercely I love you.

Tom

Nürnberg, Germany
February 12, 1946

Grace, my dearest one,

Yesterday was one of court room and office work, and a conference
with Justice Jackson. The Russians continued to present their case and
late in the day they rather dramatically presented the German Field
Marshal von Paulus,[11] whom they captured at Stalingrad. He

11. Friedrich von Paulus commanded German forces at Stalingrad, where he
surrendered. Thereafter, he became a vocal critic of the Nazi regime.

denounced Hitler, the Nazis, and the defendants. However, his story struck me as being just a bit too well rehearsed. The German defense lawyers cross-examined von Paulus and did quite a good job of it.

Last night the Justice gave a buffet supper party for General Gill — on his promotion to general from colonel. I feel very good about living with the general.

Our Prague, Vienna, Budapest trip has also been postponed. Last week, the Polish trip was put off. However, I am not complaining as the plane trip at this time of year is not too attractive.

Monday the package arrived — weren't you sweet to get me a new cap. I enjoyed the three *Norwich Bulletins* — but one had a piece cut out of it. Are you censoring my papers? I had two letters also — one from Jeremy and one from Tommie. I will write to them in a few days.

All my love and devotion to you.

Tom

Nürnberg, Germany
February 14, 1946

Grace, my dearest year around valentine,

Yesterday was all work for dull Jack — or Tom — much of it in court. The Russians continue to present their case. It sounds like the report on a Chinese flood, if you know what I mean. And ever so gory. As much blood and many killed as you can imagine. This afternoon all of the chief and assistant prosecutors met in my office. The Russian was a young general and very difficult. He stalled us as usual simply because he did not have his orders from Moscow.

For my part I am counting the days on the calendar until May 1st, or sooner. I think we should be through by the end of April or early May — and then come to you and the children, and home for good and to stay. At least never again so far away — for so long a time — without you.

For now, love, on Valentine's Day from your lover in Nürnberg.

Tom

Nürnberg, Germany
February 15, 1946

Grace, dearest one,

I am quite inclined to agree with your views on politics. I think I have given enough time to public service. The governorship does not intrigue me. Less does the Senate. I want to practice law — to be at home with you and with the children and I want to do things, little things that we all enjoy. At least for a few years.

I send all of you my never ending love and devotion.

Tom

Nürnberg, Germany
February 16, 1946

Grace, my dearest one,

It is Saturday afternoon here but for all purposes it might just as well be Monday afternoon, except that the office building is quiet and there is an atmosphere of the tomb hereabouts. I am in the office — doing some work — and now enjoying a few minutes with you. This morning we had a long session with the tribunal — a closed session at which both the defense and the prosecution were represented. Justice Jackson and I represented the U.S. The purpose was to find ways and means to cut down the trial time without depriving the defendants of any rights to a fair trial. I think some good will come of it. After lunch I had a long chat with Jackson — we talked about cross-examination again and he has agreed to examine Göring and Schacht — at my suggestion. John Amen — who is quite a windbag and thinks he is a great lawyer — wants to do the bulk of the cross, and he has Jackson buffaloed. I will set the Justice right on that soon enough.

Well, last night I had a blowup with General Gill. He talked me into playing bridge with him again. Two strange creatures —

interpreters — arrived to play with us. One was a blousy looking old bat-tle ax, the other a down-at-the-heels bloke who speaks two languages and doesn't think in one (these interpreters are a queer lot). We started the game and Gill began that abominable post-hand scolding that he sometimes does. I said, "Let us understand each other right now — I play this game only as a time killer — it means little to me whether I play well or poorly. I do not intend to pass an evening of argument over a bridge hand. I have more interesting things to do." Gill was surprised. So were the characters. We played on and Gill and I won three dollars apiece — but he was really unhappy. He is an old goat — as is any old man who has never been married and who has devoted his whole life to making money for himself. I find that he has been disliked by about everyone who has lived with him. Major Nimtz was particularly pleased because I spoke up. He has been his assistant for most of the war years and I guess the old goat has really made it difficult for him. Being an Army officer of subordinate rank he cannot speak up — I am only a civilian, thank God.

You see what little things disturb us? Just like a girls' school or a convent. We are all fed up with this place and I suppose we fuss a good bit.

Tonight the British have invited me to dinner and I look forward to it as a break in this work-and-no-play existence. At least they are civ-ilized. I must confess I am becoming more and more pro-British. Sir Norman Birkett, one of the British judges, has invited me to dinner next Thursday night. You know the British judges have their wives here — Lady Birkett and Lady Lawrence and Lady Maxwell-Fyfe are all here and they are lovely women. Really intelligent and such good com-pany — believe me, they remind me of you. Lady Lawrence has five children — she must be fifty, and she doesn't look forty. Which is your stock in trade, too. Of course they have other attributes besides youth which remind me of you. They are all pretty, all slim, all wholesome, all unaffected. They are shy, though — something that makes you the most wonderful woman in the world — something that has made me love you for years—something that keeps me in love with you—something that makes me feel about you as I did one night on Stonington Point when you said you felt that way too. Do you remember that night? You should—you said you always would. It is wonderful to have such memories when we are apart. I dream of such times over here. I recall our wedding day and night, the morning Tommie was born, the fun we have had on our trips, the night in New York at the Stork Club and afterwards. One Sunday afternoon in St. Louis in the Coronado Hotel—do you remember that? How we laughed about the cigar I bought at Antoines in New Orleans. O so much more! All so precious to me and to you. And to no one else.

I have been rambling on here and now I find I am writing about a twelve-page letter—in longhand. You owe me a long letter—and you never write them. Why not sit down some time just as I am doing this afternoon in Nürnberg—all by yourself and write whatever you feel like—just as if we were at home talking. I am not conscious of proper grammatical construction or of word choice or of any formality—I am on the sofa and I am talking to you and I'll be darned if I will pick my words like a parson preparing a sermon. I am even chewing gum—because I haven't smoked in two weeks, and I really feel better for it. I am becoming a holy roller—no alcohol, no smoking, no wife. I'll drop the last when I get home! I mean I'll take up "wifing" again.

I had a note from McMahon—simply saying he had a note from me and to please keep in touch with him. I wonder if that job has been filled. Bowles has a new job[12]—is that a kick upstairs, or what is the dope! I do not believe in that gentleman—never have.

Well, my sweet, I shall wend my weary way to our house—I can never bring myself to use the word "home." Old Gill will be very cool. O me O my we do have our troubles. He is going to Rome with Jack-

12. Chester Bowles was appointed director of the Office of Economic Stabilization, a federal post.

son tomorrow and that will relieve the situation. I must be here to keep the ball rolling. That suits me all right. I want to get home and anything that will hasten that day is my best job.

I send you all of my burning love and all of my endless and firm devotion. Kiss the bairns for me.

Tom

CHAPTER 11

Getting to Göring

THE RUSSIANS FINISH THEIR CASE. The men in the dock present witnesses and testify in their defense. Göring's witnesses take the stand, defending him, but buckle under Jackson's cross. Göring finally takes the stand. "There was a flurry in the courtroom," Dodd writes to Grace. "Press men rushed to get the word on the wires." Göring begins with, "I am out of the Renaissance." Two days later, Dodd writes that Göring "is a supreme egotist and a consummate liar but a charming rascal." From a *New Yorker* magazine report: "It was the complicated narrative of a brain without a conscience." Those in attendance "had the awful privilege of listening to the personal recital of a man who helped tear apart millions of lives, as if with those large, white hands that gestured as he sat on the Nuremberg witness stand." In the cross-examination, Jackson tries to pummel Göring, but the defendant deftly dodges the attacks.

Nürnberg, Germany
February 17, 1946

Grace my dearest one,

This is Sunday morning. It is only five thirty in the morning in Lebanon and I can see you sleeping so peacefully.

237

Last night I was back at our place [after dinner] and in bed at midnight. Old Gill is very unpleasant and he suggested to Major Nimtz that I might want to move elsewhere — that as a result of the bridge game the other night! It has made me angry to think he has that much nerve — but actually I do not want to live there and neither does Nimtz. Gill has gone to Rome with Jackson today. He has Jackson's ear all the time and if I find any evidence of difficulty with Jackson or with my work I shall hand in my suit fast — it would give me a grand excuse to get out. I will watch carefully as Gill has boasted in my presence of how he has influenced Jackson about this one and that one. Only lately did I hear him say he advised Jackson to get rid of General Donovan — and Nimtz says Gordon Dean will not come back because of Gill. He has been a bad influence here and I think he has done much damage. Only last week he got Jackson to let Father Walsh out. Walsh came to see me and I knew how much he wanted to see this case through (he will write a book, I suppose),[1] so I wrote a memorandum asking that he be kept on and is to stay. You see it is really very difficult to be here at all and when unpleasantness is added it is intolerable. I may be home sooner than you expect. After all I have had my share and more of this case. I will not be unhappy here for Gill, Jackson or anyone else. I am unhappy enough away from home and you. Well, we will see.

Are my letters arriving? You know they are chronological — easy to tell if one is missing. I really worry about our post office — I mean the one in Lebanon.

Good-bye for now, my dearest one. I love you beyond description — always have, always will. Do take good care of yourself. I cannot live without you.

Tom

1. In 1949, Father Edmund Walsh published *Total Power: A Footnote to History.*

Nürnberg, Germany
February 19, 1946

Grace, my dearest one,

I had two letters from you yesterday—but you have left me completely in the dark about the letters I wrote to you asking about your health. You really shouldn't do that. It isn't fair to me when I am so far from home. I think you have been very evasive and that doesn't help at all—it makes matters much worse. I am not lecturing you but I do think you should answer and tell me the truth about the situation. I know that you are interested in sparing me any worry—that is a most lovable trait—but I now know that you have something wrong and failure to answer my letters is not sparing me. It is actually making me miserable. Enough said—RSVP.

Yesterday the Justice left for Rome and believe me I put in a day's work. Between the court and the office I was here until seven last night and didn't get out for lunch (I won't today either). I saw Keitel at 6 p.m, and von Papen at 6:30. Keitel looks terrible and says the trial is wearing him out—I think he is cracking up. He asked to see me. Papen has a chest buried somewhere in Turkey which we have heard about. He admitted its existence but refuses to say more than that it contains $29,000 in gold, his wife's jewels and no more. He is willing to give me the name of a man to see in Turkey who will allow me to examine the box—provided I do not disclose his name, as von Papen says he is a prominent man and it will injure him in Turkey if it is learned that he has had anything to do with von Papen! So I may make a flying trip to Turkey some weekend soon.

The court refused the defense request for a three-week adjournment today. That pleases me, for it cuts my time down three weeks—hooray! I still think we will finish in May—early May. Maybe we can celebrate our anniversary together yet. Where do you suggest as the scene for that wonderful occasion? Let's make it somewhere interesting and restful—although I can be happy with you in a sand lot.

I am glad you are getting around a bit. Do get out and enjoy your-self as much as possible. Don't be a recluse. I am very happy, too, about Carolyn's music. You are a grand mother to take her to Hartford once a week. How is she doing at school? How is Tom and his dancing? What about Jeremy? And Miss Martha — how is she and what is she doing and last but not least how is Christopher?

Now, dearest, do write me fully about everything. I love you so completely I do not want you to ever hold anything from me even though you think you are sparing me — I am jealous of your thoughts when I do not share them. I send you all of my love and devotion.

Tom

Nürnberg, Germany
February 20, 1946

My dear Grace, whom I love so much,

I suppose you think I have been neglectful, but really it is so hard to find time to do everything. I feel as if I really am fortunate to have talked with you on the phone for now it is almost impossible to list a call. The men here stay up all night at the exchange and thus are in line at six a.m. in order to reserve a call. All calls must be made four days in advance — that is, the reservation must be made that much ahead. Some of the Army people sleep in ambulances outside the exchange. This morning there were sixteen lined up and you see only nine calls can be made each day. Thus it does not appear that I will be calling again for some time.

I am moving back to the hotel at the end of the week. I wouldn't live with this old goat Gill. Poor Major Nimtz works for him and much as he hates him and hates living with him he feels he cannot move out. The junior officer just can't do that I guess. Thank god I am "Mister" — it's a grand old American title.

Gill is such a hypocrite — he was always pretending to be a good friend to Gordon Dean and since Gordon left he has done nothing but knock him. I resent it because it is not true and anyway because it is so dishonest. I wrote Gordon and told him. The worst of Gill, however, is his disloyalty to Jackson. He is always smiling and fawning at him and knocking his head off behind his back. However, I shall go on my own way and do my own job. Somehow I don't give a darn over here — I am anxious to get home and I doubt that I shall ever be thanked for staying on to the end — not that I need thanks. But what I mean is I shall be happy to let Gill be the big shot and let me go home, and the sooner the better. For one thing I do want to get into something right away. It is the law business I am interested in — no matter what John Farley [Dodd's brother-in-law] thinks about my interest in politics. I do not know what the situation may be but I do know that any man who has strengths gets more respect than does a weakling. <u>This is only for your eyes and ears.</u> Actually much of my seeming interest in politics has been born of this theory. Until I have strength of another sort I shall not throw away this spear. It is the strength of another sort that I want — the strength of an established law business — bearing fruit and built on talent. Had I been free to practice my profession in Connecticut I would long since have forsaken most political interest. But the years were hectic ones — depression and war and chaos. And besides I like our state and also it was the one place where I had a little of this strength of which I write. The other alternative would have been to be elsewhere. I do not believe in looking back — I might turn to stone! So, my dear, you will know no matter what others say — no matter what the appearance may be — that I really do not want a political career. For one thing it is an empty calling, for another it is too demanding a mistress and especially for a man who is madly in love with his wife. I want to spend this little time with you — more than ever. I want to make up for absences and separations, for carelessness and swashbuckling. I want us to be happy with our own company — to love each hour of this wonderful romance and to live it together and fully. I want to grow older with you and with your love. I send you all of that never dying love and devotion.

Tom

Nürnberg, Germany
February 22, 1946

Grace my dearest one,

Four letters from you arrived yesterday afternoon. Now, as a result of the letter of January 24, I know something of your illness and I gather you are feeling better. How long since you have seen the doctor and what did he say was wrong and what treatment did he prescribe? I am not fretting too much but as you must now realize I have had no information at all from January 14th until yesterday — except for the phone call. When one is so far away and mail is so late in arriving it is easy to let the imagination run wild.

I also had a very nice letter from Tommie yesterday. And a fine letter from Carolyn. And a very nice letter from Jeremy.

We had our dinner party last night — all but one guest British officers and lawyers — a pleasant evening. Tonight I am the dinner guest of Sir Norman Birkett and Lady Birkett. Tomorrow night we are entertaining Colonel Sutherland, Major Blalock and Captain Gilman — all American officers here with the 1st Division. Saturday night, as the enclosed invitation shows, I will help celebrate Red Army Day! So it has been a busy week from every aspect — work as well as play. It so helps to have something going on — the days pass more quickly. This is why living with Gill is out of the question.

Tomorrow Ambassador Richard C. Patterson is arriving from Yugoslavia and Justice Jackson has asked me to entertain him. His wife, daughter and Naval aide will be with him. I have arranged a luncheon with the judges and a few others and of course they will attend the trial.

I am sending you a wood cut which was presented to me by the man who did it. The artist is Richard Swarzkopf — he was from Dusseldorf before the war. His son is a nice young man who was a flier in the German air force — was forced down in Ireland and married an Irish girl in Dublin. He was returned here of course after the war and is desperately trying to get back there. I met them through Colonel Baldwin who met them at an art exhibition here in Nürnberg.

I am still working on the china deal and sooner or later it will be achieved but it is no longer easy to do. Things are tightening up now and will get much more so — all of which is natural and proper if this country is ever to get back on its feet.

This is not much of a letter but it does give me a chance again today to pass a few minutes with you. Of course you are ever in my thoughts and always in my heart.

Tom

Nürnberg, Germany
February 22, 1946

This is the second letter I have started today. I shall finish the first one tomorrow under a new date line. The trouble is I am now at home and it will not be easy to write anew without repeating some things already told. It is just after 11 p.m. and Major Nimtz and I are closing up the house after having our dinner party. Tomorrow I will move from here and be back in the Grand Hotel. Capt. Vonetes has assigned a nice suite for me so as far as comfort goes I will be well off.

Now about the politics — I think McMahon is encouraging Tone[2] and is opposed to me for any office. That makes me boil when I think of what we did for him. Please do not misunderstand me. I feel that I am not losing anything — but I do want to knock that bird into a cocked hat and I will do it at the right time — to make sure that McMahon does not run the Democratic Party as he sees fit. Well, I shall not raise my blood pressure about this business at this distance — but I have put up with this long enough. This time I will throw down the gauntlet — not for myself preferably but against the hypocrite McMahon. Then I can practice law with peace of mind.

This is hardly the kind of a letter to write to one's best girl — all

2. **Joseph M. Tone was a Democrat who lost in a race for the Senate against Republican Raymond E. Baldwin.**

fuzzy with politics and wrath and venom. I am not really as angry as I sound and nowhere near as vicious! How can I feel bitterly as I write a few lines to you? The very thought of you softens me — makes me gentle and generous and magnanimous. You whom I love with all my will and all my spirit.

Because I have the other letter in the office I will cut this one short. For this page and this night I send my renewed message of undying love and devotion to you, the loveliest girl in the world.

Tom

Nürnberg, Germany
February 26, 1946

Grace my dearest one,

Yesterday was another work day. The Justice arrived from Rome on Sunday and I forgot to mention that he called me Sunday night at the hotel and told me that he had a grand trip and how much he enjoyed seeing the country and his visit with the Pope. General Gill was in my office very early today and apologized for his conduct. I passed it off but do not trust him or like him — the man is no good. He is worried I think for fear that I might say something to the Justice — that I will not do right now, or unless necessary. I am not very much interested in feuding with anyone over here about such matters as my personal relationship with them.

I was in court most of this day — the Russians were on and the Tribunal also held a hearing on the application of Keitel, von Ribbentrop and Hess for witnesses and documents. Ambassador Richard Patterson and his wife and daughter arrived yesterday, and last night the Justice gave a dinner party for them. I like Patterson quite well. He is an old friend of the Justice — an American businessman who has made a lot of money and wants to enjoy being an ambassador. He told me that things were terrible in Yugoslavia. Americans are laughed at — and worse, they are actually in danger on the streets. The press vilifies us and the British, and praises Russia at every turn! Tito the communist is in control and it is a reign of terror. Ninety percent of the people are opposed to communism, says Patterson, but Tito and his gang have established a dictatorship. Catholics are being terribly persecuted. More than 250 priests have been killed in the last six months. Isn't that a pretty picture? There is this good sign — wherever the Reds have been the people are forever after cured of even a taint of like for them. But it is a costly medicine.

I am so busy I have to write my letters as I can — in fits and starts. I was in court all morning. The Justice called me early and said he was remaining at his house today to work on his argument concerning criminal organizations, which he must make in the next few days. The Russians put on two witnesses today and some terrible pictures sent from Yugoslavia showing hangings and worse — captured film — these Germans really left their tracks behind them.

I had a long letter from Jim Waters today and also one from Saul Budnick — you must have been buying fish.[3] Saul wants two beer steins! Also had a letter from Ed Hickey and Bill Quish.[4] But your letters are the ones I want and lots of them.

I send you all of my love.

Tom

Nürnberg, Germany
February 28, 1946

Grace my dearest one,

Things are moving very fast here (thank God) and as a result I have very little time even to write a few lines to you and that simply means

3. Budnick, a childhood friend of Dodd's, ran a fish market. There is family lore that Dodd once confronted a bully who made anti-Semitic remarks to young Budnick.
4. Quish was an undertaker in Manchester. The Dodd children were fond of him because of the humorous stories he told.

that I lose one of the great joys of my life — for next to seeing you and talking with you writing to you is my very greatest pleasure.

The Russians finished their case about 4:30 p.m. after putting on the witness stand a Russian orthodox bishop! Really — at least he said he was one, and he looked the part. A tame bishop to be sure — but a bishop in any event.[5] These Russkies are really on their toes! After the Russians finished I was before the Tribunal for the last half hour clearing up some matters that escaped us during the rush of the case. I then returned to the office and worked until 6 p.m. During the afternoon we had a chief prosecutors meeting. I saw the Justice during the day and we talked over the case with respect to the defense and our cross-examination.

(Interruption)

I received a present the other day — a beautifully engraved letter opener with my name and other appropriate legends thereon including "from an unknown victim of the Nazis." Very interesting, don't you think?

This morning we started the final argument on the criminal organizations. The Justice spoke for us and it really was a magnificent speech. He is a great writer and a great lawyer. This afternoon we continue with the British, French and Soviet speeches on the same subject and then our case is in. The defense will start Monday I am sure. The end is in sight. Quite a few of the lawyers who left here in December and January are now writing asking if they can come back. Apparently they realize that one cannot be rightfully said to have been of counsel in this case unless he was here for all of it.

I sent some material to the *Catholic Transcript* — some of the proof we put in regarding the persecution of the church by the Nazis, some

5. **The Very Reverend Nikolai Ivanovitch Lomakin, archdean of the churches of Leningrad, testified about the siege of the city by the Germans and the devastating effect on the living and even the dead. He said, "The cemetery was very often bombed by German planes. Please imagine the scene when people who have found eternal rest — their coffins, bodies, bones, skulls — all this is thrown out on the ground."**

material on the new German Cardinal von Galen and a report on Yugoslavia. I think we should let our people know what is going on. I must close here — court time — I send you all of my love and all of my devotion.

Tom

Nürnberg, Germany
March 1, 1946

Grace my dearest one,

Lord how I wish this would end — how I long to be home. I could help you so much with Grace gone. I will not be easy until I know you have good help. Pay a good price — it is the best investment we can make right now.

We had a full court session today and we are moving ahead but so very slowly. Let us hope the defense does better than we did from a time standpoint.

March 2, 1946

I did not finish this letter yesterday — did not have the time. I write when I can fit a few lines in. (New interruption.) This will read like a Chinese newspaper. Today we had another court session and by midday we had moved much nearer to the actual taking of the testimony for the defense.

This is one of those days that gets me down. My heart just aches to get home. Lately I feel that I cannot stand it much more. It really is a wearing experience and it has taken a lot out of me — some of which will never return. I look at this grand picture of you and the children and feel that I want to leave tomorrow. I cannot let Justice Jackson down but if it were not for him I wouldn't stay. It really is too much to ask me to do. Some men do not seem to mind it — others may but, they cover up well. And some of course have given up and gone home. But there, I must not write of such depressing things for I will feel better tomorrow. If only the sun would come out? It is actually grey here six out of seven days.

I envy you those walks in Lebanon. I get almost no exercise. I cannot walk about much — simply because I do not like to do it without someone with me and even then it is not easy except on Sundays. The bodyguard is a very nice young soldier but he is not exactly a walking companion. We are advised not to go out alone and so there we are.

Let us keep up courage and stout hearts for a little while longer. Do take good care of your precious self — do not try to do too much and make a big effort to get some decent help. All of my love and devotion to you.

Tom

Nürnberg, Germany
March 4, 1946

Grace my dearest one,

Today we officially closed the case for the prosecution at 10:37½ a.m. The day in court was taken up with the defense application for witnesses. Tomorrow will call for the same and by Thursday we will really be into the defense case.

I had a letter from Joe Guimond today. He said the baby was operated on for some bladder trouble but was now all right. I hope to see him when he gets over here — perhaps for a weekend. Of course I wish I had been home for as long a time but I would dread returning for as long a time, too. He will be here a year at the very least and maybe much more. He had talked about bringing Margie and the baby over and I think he will. That does not appeal to me at all. Germany is no place for anyone who doesn't have to be here. Everyone who has been here for any time agrees with that view. It is the worst place in the world right now — or at least the worst in Europe. And it will be a long, long time before it is any better. I think Jackson is terribly fed up. He stays out at his house a great part of the time. I, of course, have to be in court every day and in the office when I am not in court. That is all right with me. I just want to get this trial over with! And soon. Lord Lawrence is anxious too. Everyone is. I know it is becoming in some respects an endurance contest — all protracted litigation is to some extent and the defense knows it too. They will profit the longer it goes and they know it is difficult for us over here. Yet no matter how much we try to hurry in a matter of this magnitude much time is consumed.

Another day has slipped away since I started this letter, and so it is now March 5th. We were in court all morning working on the defense application. This afternoon the court recessed after announcing that Göring's defense would begin Thursday morning. I worked all afternoon in the office on the remaining defense applications. Jackson remained at his house again today. He is getting ready to cross-examine Göring. I will have about four of them and the rest are to be divided up between Amen and Alderman. The last two really should not be doing it as neither one of them knows this case. Amen has been away for the last month — on a rest vacation if you please. Alderman just isn't on the ball. But Jackson seems to want to get along with them and I know he wants them to participate. It is all right with me. I have more cross-examination than they do and with my other duties I have all I can handle. But I have no faith in either of them.

Tomorrow is the beginning of Lent and I must make some sacrifice. I will try to hear Mass every day — or as near to that as possible. Father Lavelle says Mass every afternoon in his billet at 5:30 p.m. I think I can make that about every day.

Thus, dearest, I bring this letter to a close. I love you completely and I am very and always devoted to you. Give my affection to the children.

Tom

Nürnberg, Germany
March 6, 1946

Grace, my dearest one,

I was in court all day until four o'clock. We were occupied with the defense application for witnesses and in the course of the day the Tribunal announced that the Göring defense would not begin tomorrow as announced but would begin as soon as we finish the examination of the defense application for witnesses. Göring's lawyer raised a fuss and said he could not be ready tomorrow. It now looks like Friday is the day. Thus far in this witness business I have thought it best to allow one man to speak for the entire prosecution and consequently we agreed to having Sir David Maxwell-Fyfe do the job. He is a nice fellow but I am disappointed in him as a lawyer — at least as a man on evidence. He also is a fence straddler and he seems terribly afraid of the Tribunal with the result that he never stands up for a viewpoint. I think it must be the long influence of serving the crown and bowing and giving obeisance and of saying "my Lord." I tell you we Americans do not half appreciate what we have. We are the free people of this world in heart, soul, mind and body and we show it. The unconsciousness of real freedom is a distinctive characteristic of real Americans — we don't even think of it and we seldom talk about it. The new citizen of the U.S. is always talking about his rights — he gets over it in time, or anyway his children do.

(First interruption) — This afternoon at 4 p.m. we had a closed session of the tribunal — present were the judges, the four prosecutors (I represented Jackson) and the defense lawyers who represent the organizations (the SS, the Gestapo, SA, etc.). The question was how to take testimony from the former members now in the prison camps. We had suggested the appointment of several masters. Well, I will not recount all the details but in the course of it, Rudenko, the Russian, voiced opposition. This after telling us he was for it! I spoke up and said we were concerned about the ones in the Russian and

French camps as we had no information on them and word of any kind on them whereas from the American and British camps 45,000 had been heard from. I was glad I said it for I will not be in this thing unless I can be honest about it. But the British — or rather Sir David, as usual — straddled the fence. These Russians will not use me for their hypocrisy and the French are as bad. Of course it was a bad day as this morning the news broke over here about the Churchill speech.[6] Everyone knows Churchill is dead right and it is high time we said so. I would not be too surprised if this trial broke up — or at least if the Russians withdrew. Of course they will probably back down — they always do when their bluff is called. Grace, they are no different from the Nazis — the same breed of cat and they are predatory and aggressive and they intend to run the world. In most of Europe where they are in control there is a veritable reign of terror and God knows what the end will be. This war has not settled things by a long shot — in my judgment we are enjoying a brief armistice and nothing more. On the other hand these Nazis hope we do get into a terrible conflict for they will thus hope to justify themselves and recover their places. We are between two terrible fires — one of which is pretty well out but the sparks and embers are still there. The other is spreading nearer and nearer to us. Maybe the good Lord will send a heavy rain and save us from the awful task of fighting it with our blood and tears.

I sent some more photos today. I love you, Grace, and my love for you never wavers, weakens or slackens. I live for the day when once again I am with you.

Tom

6. Churchill introduced the phrase *Iron Curtain* to describe the division between the West and the Communist Bloc. For captured Nazis, this speech provided hope that the United States, Britain, and France would recognize that their far more threatening enemy had always been the Soviet Union, not Germany.

Nürnberg, Germany
March 7, 1946

Grace my dearest one,

No long sheets of paper are available tonight so this letter will be shorter than usual.

We finished the applications for the defense witnesses this afternoon about three o'clock and then the court recessed until tomorrow when we will start taking testimony. I was in court all morning and until recess time this afternoon. Bill Jackson arrived this afternoon from the States. He brought a letter from Gordon Dean telling me that he is not returning. He has taken his family to California for permanent residence. He said in his letter that he got home "just in time." I understand that his wife is badly off mentally. Isn't that tragic? I think, however, that it is an old situation — you may recall, as I do, some talk about it.

Bill Jackson brought bad news about affairs at home — particularly about the strikes and all the disputes and the rising prices. Maybe I should take the job as head of the subsequent proceedings over here[7] — I can have it — and move you and the children over. I am not serious about that. I just do not want to live over here. Not these days.

Tonight Ralph Albrecht and I had dinner together and Major Finke joined us. We sat in the lobby talking until long after eleven and as a result I am up very late. It seems good to talk with someone who has so recently been at home — everyone wants to ask questions and mostly about the same subjects. Only Americans understand American interests. Many of the newspaper people are arriving in town again tonight because the defense begins tomorrow. They left in large numbers while the French and Russians were putting on their cases. I suppose we will be getting more attention in the press at home after tomorrow. Göring will be a good story when he gets on the stand — and

7. A reference to the twelve trials at Nuremberg that were to follow of lesser-known defendants.

I expect Justice Jackson will take good care of him on cross-examination. I do like Jackson, Grace, and he is truly a great advocate. I get along with him very well.

Got to the end of this paper too soon. I send you all of my love, Grace dear.

Tom

Nürnberg, Germany
March 7, 1946

Grace my dearest one,

Well, we actually did begin to take testimony this morning. I feel that we are on our way at least — although I know we have much distance to travel yet. The first witness was General [Karl] Bodenshatz, adjutant to Göring. He told a fairly good story on direct examination but Justice Jackson pounded him on cross. He had testified that he and Göring had many times interceded for the release of people from arrest and from confinement. Jackson said, "Of course you determined whether these people were guilty or innocent before interceding?" Said the witness, "O no! We knew they were innocent." By other answers he was forced to admit that people were mistreated in these concentration camps. This was important as these Germans are insisting that they did not know of concentration camps and had no real knowledge of the Gestapo. It is the party line and of course it is untrue. But it is one of the ways of fooling the world again and Grace, dear, they are at it again. The second witness was Field Marshal [Erhard] Milch also of Göring's air corps. He just completed his direct testimony at recess time — but in the course of it he indicated that he had knowledge of the medical experiments tried on the inmates of the camps for the benefit of the air corps (nice thing to have in one's record, eh?). Everyone felt that the defense looked very badly today and unless they greatly improve the defense will be worse for having offered proof. Also I am hoping that the other defendants will learn a lesson and cut down on their defenses. But these Germans are arrogant — I couldn't help thinking of the Molzahn trial. There's an earlier reference to this trial as I sat in court today — the same type of performance.

This noon I had a massage and was under the sun lamp for a few minutes. I am having a massage three days a week — with the sun lamp. The masseur is here in the hotel and has a set of rooms only for the personnel. He is a half-Swede, half-German and he is very capable. I decided that I should take advantage of the opportunity — it costs 40 cents for the whole treatment! Tonight my face is red as from sunburn and everyone is telling me how well I look — so you will understand when I arrive home with my suntan already acquired. I am also walking to the office as many mornings as possible — it is about two miles — and that should help. So you see I am taking good care of myself and I hope you are doing the same. You should take massages and steam baths. Really, they do wonders and they help to keep you young, though that is not really necessary for you, who keeps a private fountain of youth. My worry is that I will age too fast and then my young wife will tire of me and give me all sorts of pain and sorrow!

I am enclosing the address of the government printing office and I wish you would send for their publication put out by the State Department on the case. Get two or three copies and send me one and put at least one away. I wish you would save it as all these things will be of great interest as in my judgment the library on these proceedings will be very great. The entire American-British case is being published about the first of June — it will be in six volumes — one thousand pages to the volume and it will be sold for $10 per set. I will get one of course. Later the whole trial record will be published and that will run to twenty or thirty volumes.

Grace, my dearest, I must not write so much shop talk — yet I want these letters to tell some of my story about this case. But most of all I write because it is my only way of spending some time with the one girl I love and because I like to tell her how much I love her. Your picture is right before me as I write — your lovely face surrounded by those five beautiful jewels that you and I found together — and they are so rare — there are no others like them. Give all of them my love and affection.

Tom

Nürnberg, Germany
March 9, 1946

Grace my dearest one,

I was busy in the office all morning as the Tribunal did not sit. I had a long talk with Jackson about the case. We discussed his cross-examination of the witnesses and of the defendants whom he will have responsibility for. In the course of the chat he somehow got on the subject of General Donovan and he skinned him alive. He said that Donovan was shallow — that he was not well thought of in Buffalo. That he was a social climber. He said that Donovan left here intending to start a smear campaign against Jackson and the case and actually went as far as to talk to a public relations man about it. However, Jackson says he didn't dare try it as Jackson has some papers that show that Donovan was trying to get something on him by framing or faking so-called "phony orders" which it was intended Jackson should unwittingly sign! Finally he said that he, Jackson, did not like to get into urinating contests (he used another word) because only a skunk can win in such a struggle. Well, he is earthy and he is honest and that is what he said. And I must report the facts to my Lebanon correspondent. We chatted for more than an hour and afterwards I saw John Amen about his cross-examination responsibilities and later some of the other lawyers. I had lunch at the hotel and afterwards retired to my room where I puttered about most of the afternoon — took a leisurely bath, clipped toenails, manicured fingernails, read a bit, wrote a bit, slept a bit. At five p.m., I went for a walk of thirty minutes duration which was invigorating. Some of the young officers were promoted last week and they gave a joint cocktail party at 6:30 p.m., and I dropped in for a little time. At seven Paul Leverkuehn, the German lawyer I have met though Donovan, came in and he and I and Albrecht had dinner together. Afterwards we retired to my room and chatted until ten thirty when Leverkuehn left as he must be in his house before curfew.

There is a Saturday for you—but it is typical of all Saturdays in Nürnberg. Do you wonder that I am uneasy and unhappy and anxious to get home? Besides the longing for you and the children and the pain at being separated from you which is awful enough, the very dullness of the time here is killing.

Tomorrow I will find time I hope to write to each one of the children. I think Tom is doing very well with his writing. How about Carolyn—how is her school work and how is she getting on with her piano lessons? I must say a word about Jeremy and the horses—do be careful about him. He is so little to be loose with animals. I think we should watch until he is older and better able to take care of himself. Of course I am glad that he has the interest and it pleases me to know he has the courage. Can't you get Tom to take an interest—I think he would ride well and like it if once he got started—a little sales work from you and Jeremy might help. Carolyn should be good at it too. Martha is too little yet—but that dame will ride like a cavalryman when she gets ready.

Paul Leverkuehn raved about the pictures of you and the children. As a matter of fact I am basking in all the compliments about you—it is so common now that I rather expect it. After all I know how lovely you are. I know what a grand person you are. I know what a wonderful mother you are. I know your charms. But I still like to hear other people say they recognize it too—and from a picture! What would they say if they saw the original! Little wonder that I love you so strongly—so completely.

Tom

P.S. No ink—no sharp pencil—except this red one.

Nürnberg, Germany
March 10, 1946

Grace, my dearest one,

After breakfast this morning [Sunday], I walked for more than an hour through the ruins of the old city. I had not been there in some time. As a matter of fact I had not been in some parts of it since last August and I was surprised at the recovery and the reconstruction — although it is pathetically little compared to what must be done. It is still a dead city and the city of the dead. Some restaurants are open here and there — small and unpretentious places with boarded windows and makeshift arrangements, yet they are crowded, and lines form in front of some of them. I know why and so do you. Just to be able to sit and be served, to eat in the company of others, "to eat out," even though the food is poor, does something for people and particularly for distressed people. Food is of course not plentiful here but this part of Germany is much better off than other parts. Yet the real pinch will come later. It isn't only food that is missing it is as well all the little things in life that these people have learned to use and rely on. Toothpaste, soap, razor blades, combs and brushes and shoe paste and thread and needles, nails and glass, dishes, a pail and so on with a list that you can make better than I can. So a meal in a place that even resembles a café gives them a lift. I smile when I pass all the ladies' hairdressing places that are opened up — in places with equipment that would hardly entice the females under ordinary circumstances.

Albrecht and I had dinner together tonight, and afterwards we played a few games of bridge with two British fellows. We talked for a while and here I am. I am on a real sugar drunk. We had two pieces of pie for dessert tonight and as I write I have been munching two candy bars — O that "waste" line!

I do so hope that there will be some mail from you by tomorrow — I need it badly. I am in a low spot. I am just plain lonely and homesick. I look at your picture, I take my fingers from these typewriter

keys, I gaze and dream and think of you and of the children, of
Lebanon and our home, of our fireplace, of so many pleasant memories. I think of you laughing heartily and I can hear the children
laughing too. I can hear that piano after the evening meal and the
children in a gay mood after my singing. I think of the morning and
how the children join in helping fix your breakfast on a tray. My but
those are nice recollections and how I long to get home to build
some more — many more. In the courtroom, in the office, at meals,
at bridge and in conversation thoughts of you pass before my mind's
eye. Sometimes I find myself sighing and I know why.

Ten days of March are gone and soon it will be spring in Lebanon.
Do plant some new flowers and some plants and some lovely growing
things this year. Make your decision as to the garden — I wish I could
be there to help start it and to help care for it. For now, as always, at
the close of these blessed hours with you, I send you a message of love
and devotion.

Tom

Nürnberg, Germany
March 11, 1946

Grace, my dearest one,

It is the end of another day, the second of the defense and we are
gradually getting ahead. Justice Jackson cross-examined General
Milch, one of Göring's aides, after various defense attorneys had asked
questions. Jackson did well but not as well as he did Friday — he
labored some unimportant points and got into some matters where we
did not have the goods. However, towards the end he came back hard
and left Milch a discredited witness. He could have done it in much
less time. The British took over and did all right but I was surprised at
the liberties they take with a witness. Our courts would not stand for
it — argument and opinion were frequently the basis for questions. It
took all day and the Russians were still at it when the court recessed for

the day — and the Russian Rudenko was doing a terrible job. The court was annoyed most of the time, I fear, and as a result we are summoned to a meeting with the court and the defense in the morning to restrict the cross-examination.

After court this afternoon the Justice walked into my office and handed me a cable from Joe Keenan in Tokyo asking that Jackson release me to become Keenan's assistant saying that Tom Clark was willing! I was surprised. It was the first I had heard of it — and I think Jackson thought I knew about it. I assured him I would not think of it — and he seemed relieved and told me he could not agree to it. I said if he did I wouldn't go anyway. So we wound up with a laugh!

I have so much to do these days. I have to run the trial and at the same time prepare myself to cross-examine four defendants and their witnesses. The details of running this case are tremendous as you can imagine — just from an administrative standpoint let alone the legal questions. I have had to stop all letter writing except to you — I simply do not have the time, and I will not have it in the future. Of course I look upon letters to you as a pleasure.

My typing does not seem to improve — as a matter of fact it seems to be getting worse. But it does save weight for the air mail. I have a letter from John Robinson asking me to give the commencement address at Cheshire Academy[8] — I am undecided about it as I am not keen about a lot of speaking dates when I get home. I want to do all of my talking to you and O! but I do have lots of things to say to you. I want this time to be somewhere with you for at least ten days — some isolated spot — some pleasant place that you and I will enjoy, far from any telephone or telegraph, and we will do nothing but enjoy our own company. Please begin now to plan for it. You pick out the place. Let us have a real new honeymoon. I have heard they are best after about ten years. Until that day I will be living for that.

Tom

8. A private school founded in 1794 in Cheshire, Connecticut. Three Dodd brothers attended there.

Nürnberg, Germany
March 12, 1946

Grace, my dearest one,

Another day of defense is over but we are not getting ahead as we should. Everyone is taking too much time on both direct and cross-examination and related matters. We will have to do something drastic or we will never finish this trial — or at least we cannot finish for six months or more. I do think it is a matter that will improve itself after a few days — but I shall watch it closely and if it doesn't improve then I shall holler. I was in the courtroom all day. In the morning Colonel von Brauchitsch was on for Göring. He is the son of the Field Marshal who broke with Hitler. Thereafter Field Marshal Kesselring was also for Göring. Young von B. is a nice looking person and he makes a very good impression. Actually some of the defendants were looking on him with pride. It was very obvious to anyone who watched carefully. Kesselring made a good witness. He was a well thought of soldier who commanded the Germans in Italy and who made it very difficult for us. He is an air corps officer but he was placed in command of ground troops, and was in charge of the air war against Poland, France, and England. He claimed the bombing of Rotterdam was an accident but his explanation did not square with the facts. He claimed the bombing of Warsaw was a military necessity. But on this too he did not sound well. He said Coventry was a military target, and I was a bit surprised to learn that it was to some extent. For you will remember that the press releases of the time said only that it was an old, peaceful, cathedral city of Lady Godiva. Well, I asked some of the British here and they admit it was heavily engaged in war work. Of course that does not excuse the Nazis for the indiscriminate bombing. Jackson cross-examined him and did fairly well, but believe me, dear, he has much to learn of that art. Sir David for the British is not better. Nor is there anyone here who is top flight. It gives me courage. I know that I can do better and have done much better right in Hartford. I am aching to get at one of these birds. But my turn will not come for some time.

There is another indication that Keitel may admit considerable responsibility — but my own judgment is that he does not know what to do and he wavers and vacillates. He is, as I have always said, essentially a weak man. He looks at me in the courtroom sometimes with an almost pathetic attitude. We always speak to each other and my friend Papen does the same. What a pity that men must contend with one another. It is as ever not easy for me to condemn. I see something worthwhile even in these evil men. And I regret that the greatness that went to evil did not exert itself for good. These men could have made Germany a great nation and thus enriched the rest of the world. The mystery of Hitler grows upon me day by day. I mean simply that I am baffled when I consider that able minds like Kesselring and others were completely under his influence — and they are not weaklings. On the contrary they impress me as men of strong minds and of strong will. Some of them are beyond doubt personally of good character. They are men who fear God. I intend to devote some thinking and some time to this question. For in the answer lies something that we all must know.

We read in the *Stars and Stripes* of the Russian reaction to Churchill's speech — it is violent. Our colleagues have not shown any particular reaction so far. For myself I think we have been far too easy with Russia. I think we have made something of a farce of the four freedoms.[9] I think a dictatorship by the Reds is as fearful as that of the Nazis. I think the Reds are predatory and imperialistic. BUT — I do not want a war with Russia or with anyone else. I think midway or thereabouts between Churchill and Stalin there is a good firm bit of ground on which we must stand. It is not a battle ground. It is not a playground. And in time, on this ground, I think we can work out a decent way of living, as neighbors, with other people. It will take time. It will take patience. It will take honor. It requires a high mind as a people. It can be done.

9. These were articulated in FDR's third inaugural address in 1941: freedom of speech and expression, freedom of every person to worship God in his own way, freedom from want, freedom from fear.

March 13

Another day — Göring day if you please. He took the stand at 2:30 p.m. It came very suddenly. We had finished our cross-examination for the witness Kesselring just after the noon recess when Dr. Stammer, counsel for Göring, suddenly called him to the stand. There was a flurry in the courtroom. Press men rushed to get the word on the wires. People came into the courtroom in a hurry and in two minutes it was packed to the doors. Our trial table was filled up. Jackson sits in the left front seat and I sit in the right front seat. Behind us sit the lawyers in two rows on either side of the table. We all felt it was a moment of historical importance. Göring was very calm as he began his testimony. The defendants all leaned forward in the dock — the judges turned in their high chairs to stare at him. He is a charming rascal — a real buccaneer. He has said of himself, "I am out of the Renaissance" — and indeed he is. One of his witnesses said he considered him the last great figure of the same period. He dominates this scene and he is far and away the dominating character in the dock. (As a matter of interest we have had to separate him at lunch time from the other defendants because there are some who seem ready to admit some of the charges against the Nazis and he has been making life miserable for them, and in his sight and under the lash of his tongue they have no courage.) He began with the story of his life and went into his first association with Hitler and recounted the days and years up to 1933 — then we recessed for the day. He will continue tomorrow.

This was a great day. I have four letters from you! And how happy I am. I also had a letter from Howard Brundage today — I am enclosing it — what do you think of his reference to Chicago? If things do not turn to my liking at home I will think very seriously of it. I have told him that you and I felt that I have given enough time to public affairs.

I think I should tell you that I am sending a portrait which my friend Schwarzkopf has done of me. I intended to surprise you but I thought it best to warn you so you will open the package carefully. If you think it is to your liking you may have it properly framed and then put in the attic! It is in water color and should be behind glass. I sat many hours for it. Your turn comes next — and soon — we must have one of you.

My love and devotion go, as ever and always, with this letter.

Tom

Nürnberg, Germany
March 14, 1946

Grace, my dearest one,

This was the second Göring day as he was on the stand all day and he has made a most unusual witness, and I think quite a frank one. He admitted responsibility for many of the offenses and he is not cringing or crawling. He will go down as fighting — somehow he makes me think of a captured lion. Of course I am not forgetting his part in all of this business and much less am I unmindful of the facts that all of these top flight Nazis are spellbinders and fakers — that is how they did it — or part of how they did it anyway.

I was in court all day and while it was a day of interest it is tiring to sit and listen to anyone for that long. I was invited to dinner tonight at the press camp by Wes Gallagher of the A.P. but last night I got sunburned, or lamp burned, and I am too uncomfortable to go. I will pass a quiet evening here in my room and catch up on some letters and some reading.

There is a certain tenseness developing over here — many feel that another war is in the offing. Some say it is best to have it now and get it over with while we can once and for all set the Russians where they belong. Some think Russia will attack us here and elsewhere in Europe suddenly and with great strength. Some air corps units are being reestablished which only last week were getting ready to go home. What a mess — after a war to establish peace and freedom. I still believe we can work our way out in peace. The present leadership in Russia cannot live forever nor even the present political policy. If we can hold to our own way of living and do it decently and keep our heads I think we need not be at war. None of us can stand another one. The world will be a total wreck after another — every city will be a Nürnberg.

March 15, 1946

The ides of March have come and gone and all seems well except there was no mail from you and so the day was no success. I was in court all day and Göring continued on and he gets bolder and more doctrinaire with each hour. He is a supreme egoist and a consummate liar but a charming rascal. He is also a forceful talker and he knows how to tell his story. The other defendants are taking courage from him now but if Jackson does the proper job on cross they will soon get over this new found confidence.

So dearest, two more days are over and half of March and soon I will have you in my arms. I will be thinking of you at Farley's party and maybe you will feel me tweak your ear and kiss your lips in honor of the good Saint Patrick.

Tom

Nürnberg, Germany
March 18, 1946

Grace dearest one,

I so enjoyed talking to you last night. Your voice was heavenly — and I really think we got a break on the time. Maybe some good-hearted operator realized we needed more time for ourselves and our five children. The children sounded well and happy. You are such a wonderful mother. They will realize someday how lucky they have been — as I realize every day.

We are trying to move the case along but the obstacles in our way are very great. Of course we must give these defendants a fair hearing — a most fair hearing — otherwise this whole effort is a farce.

No decent lawyer feels otherwise. Yet it is the waste of time that bothers me — not the use of it.

On Monday, March 19, the Göring case went on again. Defense Counsel interrogated Göring with respect to various features of the case which involved their own clients. Of course it was lengthy and in many cases repetitive but in the long run it will probably save time.

Göring was in his element, obviously enjoying his position as a witness and particularly in his pose as the successor to Hitler and the No. 1 Nazi now alive. He readily went out of his way to take shots at the Allied countries. We all thought the examination was terribly lengthy and our spirits sank because if this was any standard then our chances of finishing this case in anything like a reasonable time are practically nil.

The Justice began his cross-examination late in the morning and for the rest of that session he had Göring pretty well on the ropes but the Tribunal simply would not curtail Göring in his answers. Immediately after the session the Justice called a meeting of the Chief Prosecutors and also invited me to attend. General Rudenko had already left the building so that the Russians were not represented.

The Justice was very much disturbed about the way the Court was permitting Göring to make speeches and it was the unanimous opinion of Sir David Maxwell-Fyfe, Champetier de Ribes and myself that the Justice was absolutely right about it. We all talked it out and I have never seen the Justice as disturbed as he appeared to be. However, it was decided that he would make a strong effort immediately in the next session to require the court to control Göring.[10]

Later that evening I ran into Ray and Tanya Daniels of the *New York Times* in the hotel and they both were aware of the fact that the

10. Jackson told the court, "I respectfully submit to the Tribunal that this witness is not being responsive . . . It is perfectly futile to spend our time if we cannot have responsible answers to our questions . . . This witness has . . . adopted in the witness box and in the dock an arrogant and contemptuous attitude toward the Tribunal, which is giving him the trial which he never gave a living soul, nor dead ones either."

Tribunal was making it very difficult for the Justice and particularly thought that Mr. Biddle was making it difficult.

Tuesday, March 19

Göring was withdrawn from the stand to permit the witness Dahlerus to testify. Dahlerus is the Swedish engineer who was an intermediary between Göring and Hitler and the British in the fateful days of August 1939. On direct examination he did very little for Göring and on cross we murdered him. Dahlerus had a note passed to me through one of the sentries during the lunch recess, attached to which was a letter that he had sent to Göring's counsel, practically warning them that he, Dahlerus, would not be a good witness for Göring. The cross-examination revealed that.

After Dahlerus had testified Göring went back on the stand. Justice Jackson resumed his cross-examination and obviously Göring was needled up, also resentful because he had been made to look badly, and he proceeded to become arrogant, impertinent and unresponsive. Things went from bad to worse and the defense lawyers ganged up to complain that they had not received copies of documents that the Justice was using in cross-examination. This, of course was senseless to us as the element of surprise in cross-examination is one of the fundamentals. But strangely the Tribunal temporized and did not take a very strong stand. This was apparently the beginnings of the difficulties and from that time on Göring really got out of hand with Biddle apparently opposing the Justice and making his cross-examination extremely difficult.

Wednesday, March 20

The Justice continued his cross-examination of Göring and gave him a good pasting with documents and with new information at our disposal. Apropos of this we discovered only the night before one document which showed Göring as advocating cruel treatment for

American and British flyers who were prisoners of war. The cross-examination continued all day with the Justice looking very good and Göring looking very poorly.[11]

Afterwards I was invited to a reception at the home of Justice Biddle and Parker given for Smith and Gregory of the Bar Association. I did not attend because I had already scheduled a telephone call to Lebanon and expected to get it about 9 p.m. I was not able to get it through of course until 1:15 in the morning so it was impossible for me to get to the reception but there was no question in my mind as to which was the more pleasant for me.

Now, dearest, I must say good night — you know I love you completely and with every fiber of my heart and soul. I send you as ever all of my never ceasing love and devotion.

Tom

P.S. No mail from you these days — I do hope you get some help soon. Isn't there some way of getting someone?

Nürnberg, Germany
March 22, 1946

Grace, my dearest one,

Today saw the end of Göring on the stand and of his defense — at last. We had a wild session again when his counsel wanted to read every document. We had them all translated into four languages and all typed and mimeographed and 250 copies of each one for the press and radio at our expense and still he wanted to take hours of time to read

11. Covering the trial for the *New Yorker* magazine, Janet Flanner had a different view. She wrote, "[I]t was, unhappily, Prosecutor Jackson who lost. When the former Reichsmarschall strode from the witness stand to the prisoners' box after his last session with Mr. Jackson, he was congratulated and smiled upon by his fellow-Nazis there, like a gladiator who had just won his fight."

them aloud! Under the rules of this court and of the charter such a procedure is outrageous. Jackson argues well for our side and the defense
put up a strong fight and one or two of them again came very close to
insolence. The court temporized again but did finally admit that
Göring had been allowed to make speeches and that it must stop. This
was a victory for us and I know now that these judges are beginning to
know that we have them licked and particularly that faker Biddle. As a
result Göring's lawyer did not read all the documents and started on
Hess. We did not get far as the day ended soon afterwards. I of course
was in the courtroom all day.

Yesterday was another tough day in court. Sir David was on until
afternoon cross-examining Göring and he did very well with it but of
course Biddle did not dare do much to him and also of course was
too much of a bootlicker to do so. Jackson is very angry still and once
today, when the defense made an objection to Sir David's line of
questions and the court sustained Sir David, Jackson turned to me
and in an audible voice said, "If I were examining the defense would
have been sustained." Everyone heard it—including Biddle. At
another point Jackson wrote me a note when Biddle began to show
signs of causing Sir David trouble. It said, "Sir David is being bid-
dled too." Late in the afternoon Rudenko began to cross-examine
Göring and Göring snarled answers at him. This morning Göring
proceeded to attack the Russians for their conduct in the war—and
while I hold no brief for them I do feel that this forum is not for the
purpose of trying the Russians and also I thought it might help the
international situation—so I suggested to Jackson that he support
Rudenko in objecting to this sort of evidence. He did it and the court
ruled it out. Rudenko came over to our table and thanked the Justice for his help.

I really believe [Biddle] is one of the poorest specimens of American judicial temperament I have ever seen and he is so small he cannot conceal his shortcomings. The press is well aware of what he is
trying to do to Jackson and I have lost no time or no opportunity to let
the reporters have the facts.

I shouldn't be in this frame of mind after having the pleasure of talking to you only so recently. Believe me, dearest, those few minutes meant more to me than you will ever know. I wanted to go on talking but I suppose I sounded stupid. I was so fearful that I would not be able to reach you. For now I send all of my love and devotion.

Tom

Political Savages

KEITEL GOES ON THE STAND and "practically admitted his guilt." Colonel Amen, Dodd complains to Grace, is butchering his cross-examinations. When Jackson becomes ill, Dodd takes over for him, even as he prepares for the most important cross-examination he has ever done, on Rosenberg. "The whole burden of this case is very much on my shoulders." A number is finally affixed to the atrocities at Auschwitz. After Dodd cross-examines Rosenberg, the *New York Times* reports, "Mr. Dodd got [Rosenberg] to acknowledge responsibility for the slave labor laws that Rosenberg had previously attempted to pin on Fritz Sauckel." He tells Grace of Rosenberg, "He was most difficult to examine — an evasive lying rogue, if ever I saw one."

Nürnberg, Germany
March 24, 1946

Grace my dearest one,

Sunday again in Nürnberg. I was up early this morning and at Mass. Fr. Walsh and Albrecht and I had lunch and then Albrecht and I rode to Bayreuth — the home of Richard Wagner. We saw the music festival house and the town. Much of the town is in ruins but much of it is also untouched. The music house is intact.

Yesterday, I was in the courtroom most of the morning as the Tribunal held an open session on requests for witnesses and some documents for some of the remaining defendants. After lunch I worked at my desk until mid afternoon but I got very little done as both the girls played ill on me. They are impossible. The Clarke girl from Middletown is a hopeless little hypochondriac and lazy to boot. The other one, Miss Low, is a British girl who is lazy and tired from too much social life. I will have to get rid of both of them and have already taken steps to do so. So many people have come over here on a personal skylark — men and women. With Gill in charge of the administrative division this place is falling apart — he is a complete faker.

Dearest, this has been a bad week for letter writing — the worst since I left last summer. I have had to write all two-day letters — but not because I want to. I miss the chance to write to you. And when I am denied the opportunity I feel like I have missed something of the greatest importance. This week I will get back on schedule. I love you every hour waking or sleeping — and you are always in my thoughts and dreams.

Tom

· Nürnberg, Germany
March 26, 1946

Grace my dearest one,

Yesterday, the Hess case was on and a sorry exhibition it was. In the first place he has no real defense and besides his lawyer is not too bright. Hess is half mad and as a result the effort was almost silly. He put two witnesses on the stand and they amounted to nothing. The British took too long at cross-exam and Amen, who wanted to get his name in the paper and who is stupid and knows almost nothing about this case, beat a dead horse to death for two hours. I gave him a good lecture afterwards but it does little good. I had a long talk with Bill Jackson tonight about the case. I told him that unless we moved it along we would never finish it. The Justice is ill in bed and will not be back for a few days. I think he is worn out from his experience with Göring—he has been on the bench too long to take the cross-examination work.

Today the Hess case ended after an all morning battle over the Versailles Treaty. Biddle was again the difficulty—he has done more to impede this trial than anyone here. After lunch the Ribbentrop case started. His lawyer said he might be too ill to take the stand. I made some inquiry and found he is very well but scared to death, so I arose and so informed the court. The afternoon passed with the offering of some documents and the direct examination of one witness.

Tonight the British gave a dinner party for Raymond Massey's brother, who is the Canadian High Commissioner in London, and I attended as a guest. Massey and I had a grand conversation. I told him that you and I saw his brother in Abe Lincoln of Illinois.

I had a letter from Ed Lonergan telling me that Tone has the backing of McMahon for the governorship. He really is no good. I actually am not interested but as far as he is concerned he is without that knowledge and he is a real ingrate if ever there was one — but mark this well that gentleman will get his comeuppance and I do not want my name even mentioned with his — he is headed for a bad end. All I want is to finish this case with a good result and to get home to you and to get into the law business — the years will be long enough for many other things and with more comfort and less bother.

I worry about you all alone with our little ones. How I wish I could be there to help you. But keep your pretty little chin up—it will all work out for the best. And soon I will be home to you — never to leave your side again.

Tom

Nürnberg, Germany
March 29, 1946

Grace, my dearest one,

I am absolutely swamped with work. It is really more than I can adequately handle with the other obligations. The Justice has been asking me to help entertain visiting celebrities and it was quite a chore.

Thursday I was in court all day — the Justice was ill and I have been in charge. We proceeded with the defense and they are doing all they can to stall us. I have been objecting right along and so you may have read about it in the press. The Tribunal just is not doing its job and unless it does very soon we will all find ourselves in a pickle.

I had a long letter from Leo Gaffney. He saw McMahon in Washington who told him Tone would be the candidate for governor. He said I refused to keep an engagement with him when he wanted me to manage his campaign. This is the third time I have heard that story. Now that makes me want to take this bird on. I am wondering if I should write to him and tell him that I know about this and give him something to think about. Let me know what you think — you might ask Joe Blumenfeld what he thinks. In some ways I am tempted to run no matter what the outcome and align a decent element in the party against him right away. It really should be done. If Bowles is serious and has some support he and I could team up and give McMahon and Golden a good licking I think. My trouble is that I have no one to manage the thing while I am here.

Today I was in court all day and von Ribbentrop went on with his defense. It is woefully weak. I again objected to the delay and the court agreed and admonished the lawyer but did no more.

Last night I had dinner with Judges Biddle and Parker and we played poker for awhile afterward and I won 16 dollars. Tomorrow Jackson goes to Paris to speak before the Paris Bar Association. I will stay on the job. Walter Lippmann[1] and his wife are arriving Sunday and the Justice asked me to meet them and entertain them. Don't be frightened about my entertaining costs — they are provided for in a special fund given to the Justice.

I haven't had a letter from you in a few days — but I know how busy you are. I had a letter from Joe Blumenfeld about the Bar — he is trying to get the rule changed. He is a great friend and we must never forget him and the children must always know all that he has done for me and the depth of his great friendship for us. I doubt that he can work the change but it would be great if he could. It would make so much difference to us.

Maybe I should forget it all anyway and go to Chicago or elsewhere. But this McMahon makes me fighting mad — and I do so want to give him a good licking. I feel certain that he is enjoying his one term in the Senate and I know now what a mistake that was. Maloney really made a mess of that — and he was to blame for temporizing with Golden and his hoodlums.

I should not waste precious time and paper on such matters — but my blood pressure is up over his nasty attitude. He is just the worst ingrate I have heard of with no exceptions. You will understand better than anyone else that I was not keen about running and much preferred not to do so.

Do not get upset over this McMahon business — but give me your good advice on how to handle it.

Please take good care of your precious self. Kiss the children for me and I send you all of my love and devotion, as ever.

Tom

1. Lippmann was a widely known author, journalist and political commentator. He was a founding editor of the *New Republic* magazine. In his coverage from the trials, he wrote that Nuremberg would be recognized as the equivalent to the Magna Carta.

Nürnberg, Germany
March 31, 1946

Grace, my dearest one,

This is a lovely Sunday morning and March is really going out like a lamb over here. Tomorrow is another month and my heart sinks at the prospect of not being with you for some time in April. I am thinking too of the garden and the planting and how much we have enjoyed getting things started.

From what you write the prospect of a place at the shore is very poor. I suppose everyone has the same idea. What about Coventry Lake, for a time anyway? The children could be at camp and they would be happy there. When I get home maybe we can all go to Maine or Vermont. Of course we will be on our trip to Dakota for much of the summer. I would like to take the children — at least the three oldest ones, maybe even Martha. We can do it easily enough — just take our time and enjoy things.

I wonder what the fall will bring. I am not very much concerned as I feel that this work has given me a solid background that should stand me in good stead. As far as politics are concerned I have not changed my view but I do want to see McMahon and Golden destroyed. It can easily be done with any kind of leadership. Please see Louis Johnson[2] and tell him that McMahon is what he is. Louis can have much influence on the Middletown people and I want to have people know [about] McMahon. You might invite Louis and his wife over for tea — then casually bring up the subject and tell him that people have written to me about McMahon and his tactics. Feel him out and try to find out what the situation is — then casually say that some people are suggesting that a group line up behind a Bowles–Dodd combination just to preserve a decent element in the party — and that these people feel that a fight must be made now against McMahon and Golden if the party is to be saved from that gang of hoodlums. Don't

2. Johnson was a family friend from Middletown, Connecticut.

be too strong about it — rather tell him in a tone that indicates you are not keen about me running but if McMahon and Golden are to be in control then someone must lead a fight to stop them and if I have to do it then that is a high price but a worthwhile one. Let him know that McMahon started this by his lies and that I am very angry about it.

(Interruption)

This afternoon I had to meet Walter Lippmann and his wife at the airport. We showed them Nürnberg, then had dinner at Jackson's. Lippmann is a remarkable person — he sat beside me at dinner. After dinner I had a long chat with his wife. So it is the end of the day.

This is a terrible hodgepodge of writing — but I am doing it as I can.

If I have to be here very long I will bring you and the children over. I think that is most remote. However, I do plan to have you come over for the last week or two of the trial. Now don't mention this — do not plan on it — do not say "No." But let us see.

I love you more than anything in this world — I send you all of my love and devotion.

Tom

Nürnberg, Germany
April 1, 1946

Grace, my dearest one,

You will understand if this letter is choppy and badly put together for I am writing in the courtroom. This notebook is a grand shield as I use it for the making of notes [here]. Thus when in a dull period I am able to sit and industriously write in this book — thereby creating or maintaining the appearances of attention while I write you a letter.

Sir David Maxwell-Fyfe is cross-examining Ribbentrop. He did quite well this morning, but now it is dull — too detailed, quite repetitive. So I have a few minutes with you.

I received two nice letters from you this noon. I also had a letter [from a friend] telling me that he and Joe Blumenfeld were trying to get the bar rules changed. He is not very hopeful—and I am very certain it will not be done—and really I somehow do not care. I shall not waste my substance on those little people. Also I fear I have let myself get too upset about the jealousy and treachery of McMahon. He isn't worth it—and he will get his comeuppance—mark that down in your book. He will reach a bad end.

So do not consider that I have made any decision about politics for the future—or indeed about law practice. My situation is very fluid—I want it to remain that way until I get home and until I can weigh all the angles of every situation. So for now I follow the policy of doing my job here and letting the future alone. I cannot do much from here anyway. I find that patience and calmness are my best allies—I shall continue to follow that line.

(Interruption)

These letters must be impossible from the standpoint of sequence and construction. Things began to happen in the courtroom and so I had to quit. We recessed and I worked in the office until six thirty then had a massage and dinner with the two Russian judges. Martin Popper of the Lawyer's Guild was here and he had them to dinner—a private one—as he is going to Moscow on Wednesday—(He is a very liberal NY lawyer). It was really a most pleasant dinner party—the four of us and two interpreters. They have invited me to Moscow when the trial is over and if you are here we will go together. They are grand fellows—as individuals all these Russians are really very likeable.

Two letters today—one with sand in it. I couldn't imagine how it got into the envelope and I had dark thoughts about tampering with the mail. Then the second letter told of the Groton Long Point sand. I am so pleased because you are going with Helen to her reunion—by all means do it. How I wish you could get some help—there must be someone somewhere. If only I could ship over a German girl—they would sign up for five years just to get there and they are good workers.

We are about through with Ribbentrop — should finish him up by tomorrow and then move on to Keitel and the others. I do think I am making progress at speeding things up — maybe the press has carried it — I don't know. Call Joe Blumenfeld and tell the reference that was written about me as to the number of defendants that I am to cross-examine should come out — I do not want that printed because it will come back here and may cause bad feeling. Also there is an awful lot of corny stuff — too much Horatio Alger, etc. I want that all toned down or eliminated. Finally will you ask Joe to let you read it before it is published anywhere. Also call him as soon as you get this letter as I am afraid it will be published soon. This is very important — I suggest that it be published in the *Norwich Sunday Record*, the *Hartford Times*, the *Bridgeport Post* and one of the New Haven or Waterbury papers. If it is properly edited it can be a useful story — and it is acceptable that way as a special job by this reporter over here. Please follow it closely and read it yourself and say what you think about it and use your red pencil where you think you should — then return it to Joe.

Well, dearest, I love you with all my heart and devotion. You know how often I tell you the same story — because I like to tell you. And I never tire of reading of your love for me.

Tom

Nürnberg, Germany
April 3, 1946

Grace, my dearest one,

Ribbentrop down — Keitel to go. And 17 to go for a touchdown. Yesterday saw the end of Rib but not until Amen made a mess of the cross-exam for us. He is impossible and a real faker, and this myth of the great prosecutor is just about exploded. The court was fed up and so were all the people in the courtroom. It should end his part in the case but the next defendant after Keitel has been assigned to him and it is too late to change and anyway the proof is so strong against him that Amen cannot do too much harm. However, the court called all the chief prosecutors in [today] and said they wanted the cross-exam cut down. I of course represented the Justice as he is in Paris. As a result the four of us met this morning and agreed on a strict division of the remaining defendants. I talked with the Justice on the phone in Paris this morning and he told me to make any arrangements I saw fit, and he agreed with me that we could not permit the judges to preclude any prosecutor from asking any proper questions. I so told the judges tonight. The judges did not press it mostly because of our opposition and also because of the arrangement we made among ourselves this morning. It looks as if I will do all the cross-examining for us after Kaltenbrunner — maybe with one or two exceptions. At least I will be in a position to hurry it along.

Keitel came on the stand this morning and I must say he made the best appearance so far. Somehow I have a feeling for him. I was glad he looked like an honest soldier. Of course he is guilty but to a lesser degree in my own opinion. He will be on the stand another day or two.

Tonight I went out to see General Gill who is laid up with a bad leg — I had some matters to discuss with him. He is the same old goat and he went out of his way again to knock Gordon Dean.

No letter from you today but I cannot object as the mail has been much better lately. I had a letter from Eliot Janeway telling me that plenty of people are fed up with McMahon and that McMahon has been trying to stop Bowles and Dodd and is for Tone. Well we know that.

It is spring here now — I have been without a top coat for two days — and this weather makes me so lonesome and so homesick and so anxious to get back to you. For now I say goodnight to the dearest girl in the world.

Tom

Nürnberg, Germany
April 5, 1946

Grace, my dearest one,

Yesterday was another trial day. They run on so and surely this case has already set a record for me and for most lawyers. Keitel was on direct examination all day—he continues to be a most frank witness and to make the best impression so far. Justice Jackson arrived from Paris late in the afternoon and he called me from the airport. He is really a grand person. He thanked me for the way I have handled the case in his absence. He is still suffering mentally I think over his cross-exam of Göring and some of the press accounts have been most unkind. He really did a fairly good job and in many places an excellent one. I did not leave the office until well after six and then I had dinner with Fr. Walsh and Albrecht but beforehand I had a good massage and sweating out. After dinner Walsh and I retired to my room and we discussed the examination of Rosenberg which I am slated to do. Walsh has much knowledge of Rosenberg's ideological influence and teaching. We sat very late and finally Albrecht joined us. So went another day in Nürnberg and no letter from you to brighten me or the day.

This morning I was up early and had breakfast before eight then I went to the barber shop and got fixed up, including my first manicure! (God help me.) I was in court all day—Keitel still on the stand. At noontime I had lunch with the Justice in his office—we had a long talk about the case, about Biddle, about the law business, about children. He told me that when he was Attorney General his son Bill, who was at Yale, was arrested by the New Haven police for taking a bus sign to his room. It was during the presidential campaign and the papers played it up. That morning in Washington, Jackson was feeling rather low about the press reports when he attended a cabinet session at the White House. Jim Farley[3] met him going in and rushed up

---

3. James Farley was postmaster general and was one of FDR's closest advisers.

and said, "Well, that boy is no sissy." Then the President came into the cabinet meeting holding the morning paper and said with a sly grin, "Well, I see I am not the only one who has boys." We chatted after lunch for another half hour. I really like this man — he has brains and character.

This afternoon Rudenko began the cross-exam of Keitel — it was poor. After court I attended a meeting of the chief prosecutors. The British are becoming very concerned about the length of the case. We discussed ways and means to cut it down and we all agreed the court is mostly to blame (just like lawyers). We discussed summation — the British wanted to make the last argument, but it was agreed that all should be heard. After this session I met with Schacht's lawyer and went over his proposed list of documentary evidence in an attempt to cut it by agreement.

I had two grand letters from you today and one had the clipping — the picture from the Hartford paper. I am sending a letter Joe Blumenfeld wrote to me — I doubt that anything will come of it — but I cannot get over his wonderful friendship. He is a wonderful person and I am forever in his debt. After you read it call him up and tell him how much we appreciate it.

I love you, dearest, with all my heart and soul — you will understand if my letters are short. I am so pressed for time. You know I really adore you — always have and always will.

Tom

Nürnberg, Germany
April 8, 1946

Grace, my dearest one,

As you can see I am cheating again in the courtroom. I take advantage of dull spells to dream of you and the children — and now and then I find I can even write you a few lines.

Friday was another trial day. Keitel still on the stand and he practically admitted his guilt.[4] Late in the afternoon, General Rudenko started the cross-exam. It was fair—much better than his first effort. I worked very late—right after court we had a chief prosecutors meeting. Then I had a long session with Dr. Dix who represents Schacht. Saturday the court sat until noontime—Sir David examined Keitel in far, far too much detail.

Yesterday was a beautiful day—as most of the days are now. [Last night] I went to a small cocktail party given by Raymond and Tanya Daniell of the *New York Times*. After the party I rode to Jackson's home with the Justice—having been invited for supper. It was a pleasant evening and I enjoyed every minute of it. We sat and talked for a long time. He told me (out of ink) some really interesting stories about Roosevelt. For example, Roosevelt wanted Jackson to run as vice presidential candidate in 1940—it didn't work out. Then Roosevelt wanted Cordell Hull to run and intended to name Jackson as Secretary of State. He told me that Roosevelt wanted him to run for the governorship of New York. This did not work because Roosevelt failed to take the matter up with Jim Farley. Well, all in all, it was a very pleasant evening.

Today we were in court all day and Keitel is still on the stand. As you may know I crossed him up pretty well and got what amounted to a confession from him.

I am very lonesome tonight—homesick and heartsick, too. This is one of the times when I feel like walking out. I miss you terribly and I miss the children so too. I would give almost anything to be in Lebanon tonight just to sit by that fireplace—a little gin rummy. I would even let you win.

Tom

---

4. Dodd asked him if he understood that as a professional soldier he was not obligated to carry out any act he considered criminal. Keitel agreed. Then he asked Keitel if he carried out criminal orders. "Yes," Keitel answered.

Nürnberg, Germany
April 9, 1946

Grace, dearest one,

Another two days have passed over my head and I am struggling
to have a few minutes with the only girl I have ever loved. Really I am
actually busier than I have ever been in my life. The whole burden of
this case is very much on my shoulders — that is, the actual courtroom
part of it. I have to be in court every minute and there are so many
problems and so much by way of preparation. No mail from you now
in some days — but I know it is the mail delay — yet I do so look for
your letters.

Amen did some poor cross-examination of Ribbentrop and he will
do Kaltenbrunner but after that nothing more. Somehow he gets on
my nerves and he is so incompetent. The Justice raised Cain about the
defendants and their attempt to put out a lot of anti-Jewish propaganda
yesterday. He has his "dander" up and in many ways I do not blame
him. This court has been very careless and at times silly in its administration of this trial. Biddle doesn't know enough to act as bailiff. The
Lord Justice is too old and too easy to really keep these mugs in place.
But we will keep on and see it through.

Today we heard a long reading of a lot of matter that is already
before the court. I objected to having it read, but got nowhere. It took
two hours. I had a good talk with the Justice and we both decided that
we will not let this case get us down — or get our blood pressure up. We
will just keep on trying it to the best of our ability and keep trying to
move it along. He is going to Czechoslovakia tomorrow — and while he
wanted me to go along, that is out of the question. For we cannot both
be away at one time. The Kaltenbrunner case began today and it
should be over in two days. So we are moving on but o! so slowly.

I am enclosing a letter I have written to McMahon. If you are not
in agreement, do not send it. I am not at all sure about it. Somehow
I am not too keen about it. Of course I admit that this attitude of

McMahon makes me very angry. However, remember that I am not able to size up the situation from here. All of the supporters are of course anxious — but they have little to lose. Perhaps it is better to bide my time and just sit tight. I really have a very open mind. And I do want you to think it out carefully. I have great confidence in your judgment.

I love you with all my heart — sometimes I do not see how I can go on another day without you. You are always in my mind and in my heart.

Tom

Nürnberg, Germany
April 12, 1946

Grace, my dearest one,

This morning the Kaltenbrunner case continued with K on direct examination by his own lawyer. He is a crummy-looking creature, really an evil-looking man. He was Himmler's chief assistant and he participated in all of the horrible crimes that were committed — we have witnesses who saw him watching the operation of the gas chambers where all the unfortunates were executed by the thousands. He had the various types of executions put on as a demonstration for him — shooting, hanging and gassing. Three human beings were used to show him how it worked!

Yesterday we finished up with Ribbentrop at long last — it certainly took much more time than was really necessary. The Justice left for Prague and he and I had a chat Wednesday before he left.

Last night I worked in the office and later went to the hotel for dinner. I am sick of this hotel and with the good weather coming on I must move out to a decent house. The hotel is noisy — and hotelish.

I started this letter in the office — forgot — and started anew. But here it is — my unfinished symphony.

Tom

Nürnberg, Germany
April 14, 1946

Grace, my dearest one,

It is Sunday night and for the first time in three days I have time
to sit down at this machine.

Friday, Kaltenbrunner was on direct exam in the morning and on
cross in the afternoon. Amen did a miserable job — but the very attitude of K made him look much better than he was. I was very much
disgusted with Amen and I have made up my mind that he will do no
more in this case. He is a gross individual and utterly incapable. The
public of course will not see it too clearly but to lawyers his performance was very shabby.

I had a letter from Helen telling me that Rosemary McMahon
asked in a friendly way if I was "really interested." Well, you and I know
that she did not ask that question innocently. I still am not too keen
about it. Somehow I have a feeling I should not get involved. Why, I
know not. I just am not anxious for it. I am sure I would be even less
interested except for his nasty attitude. Maybe I should play a cautious
game and nail him when he cannot get away or bite. The Yankee way
may be the best way.

Yesterday, we had a session of court until 1 p.m. I worked all afternoon getting ready for the Rosenberg cross-exam. Just before recess I
argued the question of admissibility of Rosenberg's documents.

There is so much to do to get ready for Rosenberg. He was the Nazi
philosopher [as well as minister for the occupied territories] and not an
easy one to examine. Somehow I never get any easy task in this case —
but I really have no very serious complaint.

From your letters I gather that my son Chris is really some boy and
he must be all colors of the rainbow. The last three letters tell of him
spilling red and blue ink and nail polish on himself. It makes me
"blue" — not the same blue — to think of him and the other children
and of you. How I would like to be with you right now.

So, my dearest Grace, I close another letter from this wrecked city of Germany. I send you again my tender love and my constant and never ending devotion. To the children, my affection.

Tom

Nürnberg, Germany
April 15, 1946

Grace, my dearest one,

This will be a short note. I want to get back on my one day schedule. I will try to write, even a short note, each day.

We didn't move much today. Amen wasted the morning — over another witness who confessed to 2½ to 3 million murders.[5] Actually! He put that many deaths at Auschwitz. I suppose it shocks you — it does me to some extent — but we have had so much of it my mind is numbed by so much of it. Anyway it took the best part of the day before we got through — and it was a waste of time as we have plenty of proof of that character. The Rosenberg case started about 4 p.m. After work I came to the hotel and attended a dinner party given by the Justice for a group of American publishers. Present were Henry Luce (Clare's husband), Adler of the *NY Times*, Cowles of *Look*, etc., etc. I had a chat with Luce and a long talk with Adler and with Owen of the *Baltimore Sun*. Now I am ready to say good night — to the one girl in the world whom I love with my whole heart and soul.

Tom

---

5. Colonel Amen's questioning of Rudolf Höss, commandant of Auschwitz, revealed startling numerical evidence of genocide previously only estimated. Höss said, "I commanded Auschwitz until 1 December 1943, and estimate that at least 2,500,000 victims were executed and exterminated there by gassing and burning, and at least another half million succumbed to starvation and disease making a total dead of about 3,000,000. This figure represents about 70 or 80 percent of all persons sent to Auschwitz as prisoners."

Nürnberg, Germany
April 17, 1946

Grace, my dearest one,

Two more days are gone. I cross-examined Alfred Rosenberg this morning and think I did an adequate job — everyone seemed highly pleased with it. I had many compliments from all sides. I did it in about two hours and thereby set a new record here — and I trust a new pattern for the rest of the case. He was most difficult to examine — an evasive lying rogue, if ever I saw one. I actually dislike him — he is such a faker, such a complete hypocrite. The Russians took him on afterwards and did very poorly. They will insist on cross-examining — even where it has been thoroughly done by someone else. They, of course, do not know cross-examination — it is unknown in their practice. They have learned something about it from observation, but they have no sense of timing or restraint — or of the real purposes of the practice. We also finished the whole Rosenberg case today — which is again a new record — only two days for the whole Rosenberg defense. I tell you, Grace, if I had command of each defense case I could cut this trial in half.

Thus, my dear, I recount two more days of my Nürnberg saga. Two more days over my head — two more days nearer to you. Two more days without you.

Tom

CHAPTER 13

Perjury High, Wide and Handsome

JACKSON WRITES TO TRUMAN praising Dodd's work. Dodd cross-examines Funk, who took human deposits for the Reichsbank. The *New York Times* reported that Dodd "brought out that the Reichsbank's gold supply was augmented by fillings from the teeth of concentration camp victims." During a break in the trial, Dodd travels to Czechoslovakia where he tours the site of what was once the town of Lidice — the community of thousands that the Nazis obliterated. He tells Grace, "The women of Lidice are searching Europe for their little ones." Dodd and Jackson continue their obligatory entertaining in the evenings, and Dodd welcomes Walter Cronkite and his wife, Betsy. It seems Dodd has many admirers, including defendant von Ribbentrop, who calls him "the most attractive personality of the prosecution."

Garmisch, Germany
April 19, 1946

Grace, my dearest one,

Somehow it has not been much like the Good Friday we know. The court recessed yesterday at 4:30 p.m. after a day which saw Hans Frank take the witness stand and make the most dramatic admissions of the trial. He has become a Catholic and I guess it took. We expected him to be a most ornery defendant — his record in Poland was wicked. Well, you no doubt know from the press that he practically admitted his guilt. We saw little need for any cross-examination. I asked him only a few questions hoping to get even more admissions from him. I got only one. He stung Göring on his theft of art treasures. We also finished two of his witnesses and as a result we moved much nearer to the end.

This morning I left with Justice Jackson, in his car to come here to the Alps for this weekend. We are in the Duisburg House here in Garmisch. It is a beautiful place in the Alps — where all the famous winter sports are played. We stopped on the way at Dachau for lunch — attended the trial of the 61 defendants who ran Mauthausen concentration camp. We saw the Dachau camp — the gas chambers and crematory where thousands were executed and disposed of by the Nazis.

You are in my thoughts this weekend — and I know we will never be apart for so long again. I hope all of this effort in this case will be worthwhile. It should be. Jim Murphy wrote that I was not getting any public credit — well, maybe not. Perhaps some credit will come, if deserved, a little later. Right now I want to get the job well done. And all I ask is that I get home to you. Do take good care of your precious self.

Tom

Garmisch-Partenkirchen, Germany
April 21, 1946

Grace, my dearest one,

Easter Sunday — and it has been a memorable one. Yesterday, as well as today, was a bright and glorious day in this wonderful part of the world. I awoke to find the sun streaming in and I looked out on the most beautiful snow-capped peaks of the Alps.

After breakfast, Justice Jackson and others in the party rode the Bavarian-Zugspitze mountain railroad to Schneefemerhaus, almost at the summit of the Zugspitze. Such scenery I have never known before. It was a steep ascent and it took two hours before we were up over 9,000 feet. The hotel stands on a glacier — and as we looked out it was like a scene from another world — the skiers were small black moving objects on this tremendous slope of snow and ice. The trip down revealed new scenic wonders and we were back at Garmisch at 6 p.m. After supper we went to the ice arena and saw an ice show that makes Sonja Henie look amateurish.[1] We were special guests — and painted on the ice were the symbols of the International Military Tribunal.

This Easter Sunday morning, I drove to Oberammergau, scene of the Passion Play and attended mass in the beautiful village church. Oberammergau is a lovely Bavarian community. This Easter the men were all in Tyrolean dress — also the women. I stopped at the Benedictine monastery and was shown through by a monk. The church is beyond description — it was 200 years old when Columbus discovered America!

I returned to Duisberg for a sunbath on the terrace. After lunch we drove through the Alps to Innsbruck. We drove on for another two hours to the Brenner Pass — scene of the now infamous meetings between Hitler and Mussolini.[2] We crossed the Austrian-Italian border and rode into Italian territory for a few miles. The return trip was as breathtaking — along a mountain highway, with drops of thousands of feet at its edge. I rode in an open jeep — and I could look down the precipices as we rode along. Really Grace, we must do all of this with the children someday. It is so beautiful, so historical. There is something in the air. I will not be content until we see all of this together.

You will have received by now my wire about the letter to

1. Sonja Henie, of Norway, won three Olympic gold medals in skating and became a movie actress.
2. On March 18, 1940, Hitler and Mussolini met there to celebrate the pact between Germany and Italy.

McMahon. My mind is made up. I will not run. I am tired. I want to have some time with you and the children. I want time in the future. I will practice and we will have summers and other vacation times together. That is what I want more than anything else in the world.

My dearest, I send you all of my love and devotion at this Easter time — and ask that you give our little ones my love and affection.

Tom

Nürnberg, Germany
April 23, 1946

Grace, my dearest,

We are back in harness again after a very pleasant weekend in Tyrolean country. We left about 10:30 for the return trip. Lt. Whitney Harris and I rode in the open jeep. We arrived in Munich at noon and joined Justice Jackson for lunch at the Excelsior Hotel. Right after lunch we started out and arrived in Nürnberg about 5:15 p.m. Harris, Willis Smith, Albrecht and I had dinner together and sat talking for a long time.

This morning the court reconvened. We continued the Frank case all day. Of course we heard of the death of Chief Justice Stone.[3] We are hoping Justice Jackson will take his place. He would, in my opinion, make a great Chief Justice. We held a short memorial service just after the noon recess today. The Lord Justice made some appropriate remarks and Justice Jackson responded with great good taste and with impressive dignity. The defendants were present in the dock — I watched their faces. If there was any noticeable reaction — it was a kind of confusion, a lack of understanding.

3. Stone died after suffering a cerebral hemorrhage on the bench while reading his dissent in the case of *Girouard v. United States*.

Martin Popper of the National Lawyers Guild returned today from Moscow. He wasn't there long. It was all very easy for him — no red tape, no objections, no delays. I have no facts but I do have my own thoughts about a young lawyer who so easily gets to Russia these days — he stayed 16 days. He must carry a card — or have a password if you know what I mean. The Lawyer's Guild is very "liberal" — O! very.[4]

Chuck Alexander brought back a dark report on the USA. All the travelers do — that is, those who go over for a trip after having been here for some time. I try to balance the reasons. But I am inclined to believe that our people are too selfish, too shallow, too greedy and too irresponsible. It is, I fear, something that must be changed if we are to prosper and play our proper part in the world.

I am so anxious for you to see Europe — a few weeks will be enough to show you the differences between the continents. I was so impressed with the beautiful scenery in Bavaria — and suddenly I realized that the American billboard and all of the ugly roadside signs were missing. It makes quite a difference really. And the absence of silly radio advertising is so refreshing. I must admit that these Europeans are, in so many ways, much more advanced than we are. I never thought so — you know how we have been taught. Now, I am not "going continental" but I am sure you will agree when you see this part of the world. And by the way, do not brush off my plans to have you over here at the close of the trial. You have always been a doubter about these things — and I have been almost always right.

I trust you have not mailed the letter to McMahon. Do not say anything about it. Let matters take their own course. I will prefer not to move a hand — things will work out for the best that way.

Now dearest, I feel you owe me a nice long letter. Why not take a few hours some evening and really write me a long one. I love you

---

4. Popper later defended Hollywood figures who were blacklisted.

with my heart and soul — and as ever I send you all of my love and devotion.

Tom

Nürnberg, Germany
April 25, 1946

Grace, my dearest one,

This has been a very interesting day. The defense witness, Gisevius,[5] has been on the stand and as you may have read in the press he completely destroyed the defendants — man by man, with the exception of Schacht, for whom he was a good witness — but not good enough in my opinion to exculpate Schacht or to save him from punishment. Justice Jackson cross-examined him and brought out amazing and indeed shocking information about these Nazis. The defendants looked very glum — and disconsolate and indeed they might. They are a group of evil, wicked men. This is perfectly clear to me — and I have been in a position to know. Gisevius did not complete his testimony when the court adjourned for the day. He will be on again in the morning.

I had another letter today from Howard Brundage enclosing a clipping from the Chicago paper about the cross-examination of Rosenberg. I guess it was rather well received. Howard still suggests that I go to Chicago to practice with him. On our way to South Dakota [this summer], we will see him and talk it over. I will make no decisions over here, except those about politics this year.

The death of Chief Justice Stone has of course shocked all the American lawyers here. Of course there is much speculation as to whether Justice Jackson will become the new Chief Justice. Confidentially he

5. Hans Gisevius, a lawyer, compiled dossiers on Nazis and was part of the bomb plot against Hitler, after which he fled to Britain.

showed me a letter he had written to President Truman. In it Jackson said if the President wished him to return to the court he would do so. It went on to say I should be placed in charge and it certainly praised me to the sky. In closing the part about me Jackson said the President should keep me in mind for any important legal work he might have or need done. It really was a most generous compliment and to the President of the United States. Of course I feel very proud of such a compliment from a man like the Justice. If he is named Chief Justice he can and will continue as Chief Prosecutor. This case needs him until it is over — entirely. I will serve him if he has to go back to the U.S. for a while — but no man is big enough to fill his shoes on behalf of our country. It will all work out for the best. I am content to continue to do my very best for Jackson and in the interest of the United States — in whatever capacity.

Yesterday and the day before we finished up the Frank case. We are moving ahead and will finish Streicher in another few days, after the Justice cross-examines Gisevius.

Dearest, I know how hard it is for you — all alone with so much responsibility. I worry about you — and I long to be home with you. Soon it will be so. My longing is intense — and more often than you know I am sick at heart because we are separated. I love you with every pulse beat — so deeply and so consistently. Do have heart. You are part of my effort here. Without the knowledge of your faithful heart all of this is in vain. Without the encouragement of your lovely spirit I could not go on. I send you again, as always, my full measure of my love and devotion.

Tom

Nürnberg, Germany
April 28, 1946

Grace, my dearest one,

Friday, the 26th, saw the end of the defense of Frick and the beginning of Streicher's defense. The Justice did a good job at examining Gisevius — as you no doubt saw in the press. You are aware, too, I assume, of Göring's attempt to intimidate the witness. It created a furor in the courtroom.

Yesterday, there was no open session of the court, but I attended a closed session at 10 a.m. The Justice asked me to represent the U.S. The judges want us to cut down on the cross-examination and I thoroughly agree. I spoke up and said the U.S. would not examine any witnesses except those for whom we have primary responsibility. I also chided General Rudenko for wanting to examine Streicher after the British. I asked why he didn't turn over any questions he wanted asked to Griffith-Jones. It ended with the judges asking that we agree among ourselves to cut down the examinations.

[Later] Albrecht and I went out to look over our new house. It is a very nice one in the suburb of Dambach and it will be much more pleasant and more comfortable than the hotel.

Today Streicher finished his testimony — was cross-examined and then we finished two of his witnesses before the end of the day. After court I attended a chief prosecutors meeting with the Justice. It was a bit hot — as the Justice let Rudenko know we did not like the Russian insistence on so much cross-examination by their people. It ended all right — Rudenko took it — and backed down.

We had dinner at the house tonight — and it was well prepared and well served. I had a letter from Charlotte Opper today — telling me about Easter Sunday in Lebanon. Also a short note from Eliot Janeway — asking if I could "escape" from here. But no letter from you — so the day was not too bright.

It seems years ago since I said goodbye on the pier in New York. If only we could end this trial soon. But, dearest, we must be patient — I think it is worthwhile and like most worthwhile things we have to put up some sacrifices for it. I am quietly at ease now that I am sure I will not become involved politically this fall. Howard Brundage has written again about Chicago. We will think it over and perhaps look it over together.

With this letter, as ever, I send you all of my love and devotion.

Tom

Nürnberg, Germany
May 1, 1946

Grace, my dearest one,

I think of our annual May breakfast and how pleasant and happy we have been. This year we will not have one together — but next year we will have a grand one.

I am nursing a lame back, neck and shoulder. Apparently, I caught a cold somehow. It is painful and uncomfortable, but nothing more.

For the past three days, we have moved inexorably — but slowly — on. Streicher is down — and out. The British finished him off last Monday afternoon. Nothing much happened — we took no part in the cross-examination. After court on Monday I worked all evening on some preparation for the defendant Funk. Yesterday Schacht was on the stand all day. He is an old hypocrite — a typical banker, full of righteous phrases and evil designs and working both sides of the street. The Justice held him to a fairly direct line of testimony, but it is difficult to do much when the court is so weak. Today Schacht was on the stand all day — he will finish his direct testimony tomorrow. The Justice will cross-examine him and then comes Funk and I will cross-examine him.

No mail, dearest, from you so far this week. I worry after two days — I fear you may be ill, or that one of the children is ill. I know it is the mail, but I will be relieved to get a letter from you. And besides I do so need your letters.

When this is over I will feel that I have done my part and I want to be "Lawyer Dodd" — no more, and I hope no less.

Tonight after court Colonel Kimball and I played one set of tennis. Yes, I am rather bad at it — but it is good exercise and I want to go back to you in good shape. I must not arrive obese and soft — you might find me altogether uninteresting. After all, those country boys are good physical specimens.

Give my little ones my love and affection and take my love and devotion to you.

Tom

Nürnberg, Germany
May 2, 1946

Grace, my dearest one,

Lt. Whitney Harris is carrying this letter to the States. He leaves in the morning so I am writing this just before retiring tonight. He is also bringing you a wedding anniversary gift. It is a gold Swiss watch which I hope you will like. It is a good one, Grace — a very good one — but not anywhere near as much as I would like to give you. I put a note in the case with it — but I want you to know that this year on May 19th — you are as always close to my heart.[6] You have been my inspiration and my consolation. If I have done anything worthwhile I owe much of it to you — and all of the motivation for it. Looking back is a refreshing recollection of joyous days. Looking ahead across the years, with you at my side, is the fair and happy prospect of a grand life. I am lonesome tonight — lonesome for you. Yet I know that when this task is done I will return to find you waiting in loveliness. Until then, you and I will keep our faith and our love together.

The Schacht case is nearly over.[7] The Justice opened his cross-examination this afternoon and he is doing it very well. After court he asked me to go into his office. A battery of movie camera men took pictures of us — so you will see them, I suppose, in the news reels. Schacht

6. A reference to a wedding anniversary.
7. As Jackson cross-examined him, Schacht responded, "I was only a minister without portfolio." Though he admitted support for Hitler in economic measures against the Jews, his responses to Jackson registered with the court, which ultimately acquitted the former Reichsbank president.

should be through with his case tomorrow. Then comes Funk whom I will cross-examine — I hope it goes well. I will do my best.

So my sweet, good night. I miss you very much tonight — I long to hold you in my arms. Whenever you look at your wrist for the time — think of how much I love you.

                                                                    Tom

_____

                                                    Nürnberg, Germany
                                                        May 5, 1946

Grace, my dearest one,

We finished the Schacht case yesterday — I thought the Justice did very well in his cross-examination. What did the press say? Funk started his defense late yesterday and we had court all this (Saturday) morning. I will cross-examine him on Monday. We have ten defendants left — but now the end is really in sight. I do not want to raise any false hopes but maybe I will be home sooner than we expect.

Last night I worked quite late here at the house preparing for Funk. I want to do a good job on him. I have Schirach and Speer to cross-examine also. We have only those two remaining — the other eight are divided between the British, Russians and French. Thus I will have cross-examined four defendants and besides participated with the British in cross-examining Keitel. The Justice did two — Göring and Schacht — and Amen did one — Kaltenbrunner. Two of ours — Hess and Frick — did not take the stand. So out of seven who did take the stand I did four — which is a good part of it.

Tomorrow night I am having dinner with Justice Jackson at his house. He is a grand man, Grace — and I am very proud of my association with him — and even more proud of his friendship. You will like him — and you will meet him.

You wrote yesterday that you were perplexed about my cable concerning the McMahon letter. I simply have no desire to run — I cannot say why. The reasons are many. I only know something tells me "no." The possible appointment of Justice Jackson has nothing to do with it. He will finish this case in any event — no one can fill his shoes here. A little later I will publicly say I will not run. For now — for special reasons — I prefer to let things go as they are. In good time I will make my declaration. My love and devotion go with this letter.

Tom

Nürnberg, Germany
May 6, 1946

Grace, my dearest one,

Today I cross-examined Funk — and feel it went very well — everyone here seemed very pleased about it. I am told the American press was quite enthusiastic. We will see what the reaction is. At closing time today I had not finished so I will wind it up tomorrow morning. I do enjoy cross-examination and I had Mr. Funk pretty well carved up at closing time. (I guess that sounds a little boastful.)

Last night, I had supper at Jackson's. General Taylor and his wife were guests. I am almost afraid to tell you — but the Justice talked about returning to the U.S. at the end of June — and suggested I should go with him. Taylor can finish up the case against the criminal organizations. We would complete the case against the defendants before we leave. Well, don't plan on it. Something may interfere. It may not work out but how I hope it does. Off we go to South Dakota and Yellowstone!

I had a letter from Matt Moriarty[8] today. He said Bill McCue talked to him recently and when Matt suggested my name for the governorship — Bill said he did not think I was "ready" — O! but good friends and grateful ones are rare. Well, ready or not I am not running.

I dreamed about Carolyn Saturday night — I thought she was on a horse, or driving one, and in danger. It was so real it frightened me.

8. **Moriarty was a close friend of Tom Dodd's.**

Then I dreamed about my mother — very realistically. You know these darn dreams give an Irishman the quivers. I wish I would dream about you tonight. It's been a long, long time.

Tom

Nürnberg, Germany
May 8, 1946

Grace, my dearest one,

Well, this is the first anniversary of V-E Day. It was not observed by us excepting for a luncheon this noon. Present were all of the Judges, the Justice, Sir David, members of the Prosecution staff of all countries here — altogether about 25 of us. The Justice made, as usual, a few very appropriate remarks, General Nikitchenko, the Russian Judge, proposed a toast to Truman — it is his birthday. No American knew it — or if he did, he forgot it. It was quite amusing.

We turned the corner yesterday. We are now actually in the second row of defendants as they sit in the dock. The case of Admiral Doenitz began about 3:30 yesterday and he is on the witness stand as I write these few lines in the courtroom. I finished cross-examining Funk yesterday morning. I feel it was successful and I am pleased because the British and American judges complimented me. Sir Norman Birkett, the British alternate Judge and a great trial lawyer in Britain, told me it was "one of the very best of the trial." He told others the same. Justice Jackson was very kind and generous in his praise, and so was Mr. Biddle. All in all everyone seemed to think it was very successful. I of course was glad of that. I am wondering if it was carried in the press at home. If so you know of it now.

Ralph Albrecht is leaving here one week from today. Sidney Alderman in two weeks — a number are leaving every week now. All of which makes it difficult for me to keep my chin up. Of course it is proper that they should go — for there is no doubt about the fact that the need for personnel decreases every day. We are moving to the end — even if it is very slow. But I suppose it seems slower to us.

I have had no mail in four days now and I am most anxious to get a letter from you. Do take good care of your precious self.

Tom

Nürnberg, Germany
May 12, 1946

Grace, my dearest one,

This is Mother's Day and I did not forget you. At Mass this morning I thought of you and of my mother and of your mother. It was inspiring to see hundreds of soldiers at Mass and at communion. After Mass there was a largely attended communion breakfast and I spoke and so did General Cleft Andrus, the commander of the First Division. It was a splendid affair and it was one breakfast I shall not forget. This afternoon I played four sets of tennis and won three! Afterwards I went to Jackson's for a cocktail party for Mr. and Mrs. Ogden Reid of the *New York Herald Tribune.* We came back here for a light supper — asparagus on toast — it reminded me of you. It is now after nine p.m. and in the time between supper and this hour I have been sitting out on the terrace.

Friday was another court day with Admiral Doenitz on the stand and under cross-examination by Sir David. It ended late in the afternoon. I left about three thirty and flew to Prague. We had a fine trip down and arrived about five p.m. We went to the Ancron Hotel where I stayed last January. Yesterday morning we all breakfasted early and at nine thirty were taken to the War office and there we were decorated with much ceremony. I was awarded the highest award that can be given to a civilian foreigner — the Order of the White Lion 3rd Class! It is a magnificent medal and it is on its way to you. General Gill got the same decoration; Amen and Colonel Kimball got 4th class and

Major Nimtz and Major Vonetes got 5th class while Bill Jackson got a medal of another grade. It was of course something I can never forget. I had known about it for a few weeks but I didn't want to mention it until it was actually given to me. The Order of the White Lion is an old decoration. Those of the 1st class can be given only to the President of the US or the head of state. The 2nd class only to Ambassadors or ministers. After the ceremony we were received by President Beneš. I was delighted when Beneš greeted me warmly and called me by name before I could be introduced. He immediately referred to our long talk of last January and said some very complimentary things about my work in the trial. All my fellow travelers were quite impressed and of course kidded me about it since.

As we left the Presidential Palace there came marching into the courtyard two groups of young people in native costume. With us at the time was General Ecer of Czechoslovakia — they spotted him and lifted him on their shoulders while they sang songs and then handed him a decanter of wine which he drank from while in the air. Before I knew what was happening General Ecer told them who I was — up I went on their shoulders and they paraded about the courtyard singing and cheering. Then up came the festive bottle and I took a good swig as they cheered some more. President Beneš was in the window of this office waving and smiling. It was all very thrilling.

The Czechoslovakian Youth Congress was convening in Prague and twenty thousand young people from all over the country were there in costume and that is how this group happened to be in the courtyard.

[Afterward] we had a magnificent lunch at the hotel and then were driven to Lidice — the community of thousands that the Nazis obliterated. Grace, it is almost impossible to describe my feelings. We were shown pictures of the town before it was destroyed — churches, schools, shops, homes, farms, etc. Today there is absolutely no trace of it — not even a stone — only fields, with crops growing.

The place is set off now as a shrine. In the center of what was the town stands a great crucifix, and below it a simple monument. The Nazis killed every male in the town, sent every woman to a concentration camp, and scattered the children all over central Europe. Then they actually obliterated the place — they built a special railroad into it to carry off every bit of rubble after they had burned and blasted everything and then they graded the whole area and planted grass and crops so there is no sign of any kind to show that there was any such place as Lidice. It is one of the most awful crimes in the history of the world. The children are mostly all missing. Some few have been found. You see the very little ones cannot remember — it happened in 1942 and of course that was four years ago. The women of Lidice are searching Europe for their little ones. The parish priest was killed first — then everyone else was done away with, all because of Nazi fury over the assassination of that monster Heydrich and yet the people of Lidice had nothing to do with it. I will send you pictures of what is left.

We left Prague by plane at 5:30 and were back in Nürnberg at 6:30. So ended a most memorable trip. I never thought I would be decorated by a foreign government. It is something for the children. Justice Jackson was to get the same honor but he feels that he cannot accept as a Supreme Court justice. I suppose by now it has been reported in the press but I did want to give you my own account of it all.

Tomorrow I will be back at work at the trial. We will, I am sure, finish the case against all these defendants by the end of June. Every day brings me nearer to you and how I long for the day when we are reunited.

We are all still wondering about the appointment to fill the place of Chief Justice Stone. We hear nothing and of course the Justice says nothing — I do hope he get, it. He is such a fine lawyer and judge.

For now I close sending you all of my love and devotion. Give my affection to the children.

Tom

Nürnberg, Germany
May 14, 1946

Grace my dearest one,

Yesterday I had four letters from you and read and reread them many times. I am so pleased with my birthday present — a lovely tree. Somehow that strikes me as just about a perfect present. What kind of tree is it?

Yesterday was taken up with the Doenitz testimony — direct and cross. On Saturday night, two young soldiers were killed. They were riding in a jeep with some other young people and were shot at by hidden assailants. One of them was young Bill Timmons of New Haven. I know his father and mother. The boy was due to go home today. He had sent a message to me last Thursday saying he would call on me before he left for home. I would have gone to the funeral but I had to be in court today. He is to be buried in France. It is a stiff blow for his family. We are all careful here, but there have been some ten or fifteen soldiers murdered since last summer. Our house is under 24-hour guard and I, of course, am always accompanied by a bodyguard. Actually, we are carefully protected — but these young soldiers are not — it is impossible to cover everyone.

I received your clippings from the *Bridgeport Herald*. I wish that speculation would end. I think I will put an end to it next month — by making a very definite statement from here. It appears that Tone is not so hot as a prospective candidate — well, Bowles will be worse. If the Democrats do not do better, they deserve no better. I agree that now is the time for me to practice law — and now is also the time for us to have time for ourselves. I have so many plans for the future. If even one third of them work out we will have much fun and pleasure together and with the children. I have some high resolutions about time with the boys and things I want to do with them. Time for the girls, too — and I mean for three girls — you, Carolyn and Martha.

Tomorrow is May 15th — and another year has gone over my head. Grace, dearest, I am at middle age, for forty is the turning point. My only wish is that I have the next thirty-nine years with you — that is heaven on earth as a prospect for me.

Tom

Nürnberg, Germany
May 19, 1946

Grace, my dearest one,

It is very lonesome for me all alone in this rather large house. I am under heavy guard at all times. Two sentries on the grounds twenty-four hours a day — and at night the whole place is flood lighted. Tomorrow a bodyguard moves in — so far he has not remained at nighttime. I suppose I should be grateful and feel very important. I have no such reaction. I doubt that any German would make any attempt to do me violence — and the "important" feature leaves me cold.

This past week was a busy one as the Justice was in London and Paris. I examined, or rather cross-examined, two witnesses related to the Funk defense and it went very well, I thought. Thursday Raeder was on the stand all day. Friday, Raeder continued his direct testimony. Yesterday, I argued the admissibility of certain documents offered by Schirach. Raeder then continued and finished his direct testimony at one thirty p.m. when we recessed until Monday. I worked in the office until late in the afternoon — then to the barber shop, to the house for dinner, some work after dinner then bed by ten o'clock. Thus as you see, my dearest, how my days go by.

I am so glad the watch arrived safely and that you like it. As I wrote — it is a good one. Omega is one of the three of the best made Swiss watches. Your letter about it made me very happy. Now and always I send you my deep and constant love and devotion.

Tom

Nürnberg, Germany
May 21, 1946

Grace, my dearest one,

Yesterday, Raeder continued his testimony — but under cross-examination. He followed the defense line — and committed perjury high, wide and handsome. Sir David did a good job I thought on the cross-exam. I am continually shocked at the appearance of former German admirals, generals, cabinet officers, bankers, etc., who get on the witness stand under oath and proceed to lie in the most shameful manner. Little wonder that catastrophe attended them.

Justice Jackson returned from London and Paris yesterday and looked more rested than when he left. This morning we continued with Raeder and finally got him off the stand a little after noontime. It has been much too long a defense — much of it irrelevant and of no value. I have the next defendant, Schirach, former youth leader under the Nazis and I intend to see that no time is wasted on a mass of irrelevancies. Strange — isn't it — that I should be cross-examining the Nazi youth leader? I, who devoted three years and more to the National Youth Administration in the U.S.A.

By the way, I am concerned about the McArees — I do wish he would get located. Can't John Farley help him? What about teaching at the State University? John Robinson might introduce him to some of the trustees. Some of them are friends of mine. If he will get busy on these possibilities something may turn up.

Don't try to do too much in the garden — or about the place. It is really too bad that the boys do not have a few chickens — eggs are high, I imagine, but so is grain I suppose. For now just hold the line until this assignment is over — keep things in status quo, as nearly as possible, until I get back. So my dearest, I close another letter, loving you with all my heart.

Tom

Nürnberg, Germany
May 28, 1946

Grace, my dearest one,

I must confess that my correspondence has completely gotten away during the past few days. This noon we finished the Schirach case — and now we are on Sauckel. The French and the Russians have responsibility for him — so I have some time to sit back.

Schirach opened his defense Thursday and late Friday I had him under cross-examination and it went quite well except for the fact that I did not have enough time in which to finish. The Tribunal did not sit on Saturday. I stayed home all day — slept late, then lounged about, didn't even leave the premises.

Joe Guimond arrived Saturday night from Frankfurt. Joe has been reduced in grade to Lieutenant Colonel and he is very unhappy about the Army and wants to get out of it. He cannot go back to practice law in Cleveland because it doesn't pay him enough. He asked if I would have a place for him in Hartford, New York or Washington. He does expect Margie over here during the summer and he thinks he will stay in the Army another year or so anyway. He told me the baby was better. I felt badly for Joe. I recalled how sure of himself he was a few years ago in Washington — so confident — almost to the point of being offensive. I remember your wise and kind comment at that time. You said we should indulge him and realize that he was naturally feeling the importance of his rank. He stayed over yesterday and came to the trial. I brought him into the courtroom and sat him at the counsel table while I continued my cross-examination of Schirach — which took up most of the morning session. Joe and I had lunch together and then he returned to Frankfurt.

Yesterday afternoon Schirach left the stand. After court last night, I had supper at the house — and had two couples who are about to be married. Two Nürnberg romances! Chuck Alexander and Anne Keeshan.[9]

9. Later in 1946, Charles W. Alexander and Anne Keeshan published *Justice at Nuernberg*, a picture book of the trial.

And Flight Lt. Al Sutton of the Canadian Air Force and Patricia Geoffrey–St. Eler of France. I felt like an old man entertaining four young people. I have agreed to give Anne Keeshan away—that is a new role for me. My own secretary, Evelyn Low, a British girl, is marrying Lt. Dave Pitcher of New York, also next month. Dave is on the staff here.

The Schirach case was closed this morning. We have seven defendants left, and while we move slowly, we do move nonetheless. I never dreamed that I was leaving for a year's work when I took this assignment. Yet—I do feel it has been one of the high points of my life and as time goes on I firmly believe it will come to be recognized as one of the most important events in the history of the world. To have been second man for the United States in such an undertaking is no small experience.

I sent some photographs to Helen and John, Mary and Phil, Carol and Stuart, the Maddens, Oppers. Who did I leave out? Let me know and I will make amends.

Do not try to do too much. Have some boy cut the grass. Tom and Jerry can keep the place picked up and they can also help in the garden. Be sure to make them help. It is so much better for boys to be trained that way. They will thank you later in life.

I send you all of my love and devotion—and my affection to the children.

Tom

Nürnberg, Germany
May 30, 1946

Grace, my dearest one,

This is Memorial Day—and as I start this letter I think of other years and of the observances that we marked together. I am very lonely tonight—lonesome and homesick. Only you can cure me.

Yesterday Sauckel finished his testimony and the French began to cross-examine. We will not ask any questions, nor will the British. The Russians will.

Last night I had a group out here to meet Joe Alex Morris, editor of *Colliers Weekly*. He dropped in to see the trial. The Justice went to Brussels yesterday so I did the entertaining honors. I had the United Press reporters, Walter and Betsy Cronkite, also Sir David, Colonel Griffith-Jones, Colonel Fillimore, John Berrington, Geoffrey Roberts, Elway Jones — all British. And Klaus de Keyserling, Dr. Kaufman, Dan Margolies, Bob Brandt, Charlie Burdell, Whitney Harris and Charlie Malcolmson — all Americans. It was all very pleasant.

Whitney Harris arrived late yesterday and brought the summer suits with him — and I searched every pocket for a note from you but no luck, not even a few scribbled lines. I know you must have been in a great rush, so I forgive you. Whitney said that he talked with you on the phone and that all was well.

Sauckel was on the stand all day today under French and Russian cross-examination. It was dull and slow. Ribbentrop has been express-ing great admiration for me. Calls me "the most attractive personality of the prosecution." He asked about my "racial background" and sug-gested I looked Spanish! I get all this from the prison doctor who talks with the defendants.[10] It is interesting but hardly complimentary.

O! Grace but I do miss you so — and I miss the children and I so want to be home. You have no idea how heavy my heart is — and it seems to be chronic. How I wish I could leave here tomorrow. Whit-ney Harris says the American public has lost interest in the trial. Is that your view too?

Dearest, take good care of your precious self — and of my little ones. I send you my undying love and devotion.

Tom

10. Referring to either Leon Goldensohn, a psychiatrist who monitored the health of the defendants, or G. M. Gilbert, a psychologist who conducted extensive interviews with them.

Nürnberg, Germany
May 31, 1946

Grace, my dearest one,

It is a shame that Charlie McAree or someone will not give you a hand. It will be much better to pay someone well to keep the grass cut. A good power mower is best but do the best you can. If it is too high in the rear of the house get someone to cut it down with a scythe — thereafter you can have it cut regularly. But do not worry about it, dear — don't get upset and don't get tired out working. My sense of values is not the same as it was a few years ago — or even one year ago. Petty problems are not worthwhile. I know what counts in life — this year has taught me. Never again will I pay too much attention to lawns, etc. I know now that you and the children are important — your health and your happiness. So do not get upset about the grass or the callousness of relatives and neighbors.

Last night, in his sleep, Charlie Malcolmson died. He was the man who took Gordon Dean's place. He was in the Department of Justice for some years and I knew him quite well. The night before last he was at the house with other friends. Apparently, he died of a heart attack. He was 39 years old. He intended to stay here for the subsequent trials and was planning to bring his wife and children over in August. His death rather depressed all of us. You will understand that my frame of mind does not allow for much room for tall grass. So don't you worry about it either.

We didn't get very far with [Director of Labor Fritz] Sauckel — the French and Russians cross-examined him at great length. I put a very few questions to him, then Biddle wanted to show off and in a most injudicious manner proceeded to go over a lot of ground that was quite adequately covered. He is impossible! What an ass of a man he is. And to recall that he has been a Federal Judge, Solicitor General, and Attorney General! What hands in which to place high responsibility!

Tom

Nürnberg, Germany
June 1, 1946

Grace my dearest one,

The Tribunal sat until one p.m. today, the usual Saturday schedule. I had lunch with Justice Jackson in his office and we talked about
his trip to Belgium. He received a royal welcome and was given an
honorary LL.D. I told him all that happened since his departure on
Wednesday. I told him about the meeting with the judges after court
in which we discussed our motion to finish the case against the individual defendants even to the point of final argument before taking up
the organizations. This was opposed by most of the defense and they
filed a counter motion. At the same session we discussed the amount
of time that would be allowed for final argument. Thursday night at
the request of General Rudenko, Sir David, DuBost, Rudenko and I
met in Sir David's office and Rudenko said he wanted to have our
views on the Katyn forest proof. (You will remember that the Germans
claimed the Russians murdered 11,000 Polish officers there and the
Russians claimed the Germans did it.) The Russians put in evidence,
here, the findings of their investigating commission and now Göring
wants to call some German officers to prove the Germans did not do
it but that the Russians did. Rudenko thought that under the charter
the defendants were not allowed to challenge such proof. I said I
thought they surely were. Sir David joined me. Rudenko was quite
reasonable about it. However, he said he was getting tired of attacks
against Russia by the defense and thought the defense was trying to
create discord among the prosecuting powers. He cited a recent application to prove the secret agreement between Russia and Germany
before and during the attack on Poland. In this application, Seidel,
the attorney for Hess, says he received a copy of this secret agreement
from an American Army man. This, says Rudenko, is an attempt to
cause trouble. I assured him that if any American gave the defense
what purports to be a secret Russo-German pact he did so without any

official sanction.[11] I agreed that it was an attempt to cause trouble between us, and I said I intended to demand that Seidel make known the name of the American. (My only fear is that Seidel will do so and the American will prove very embarrassing because I am sure there was such a pact and because he may be someone of sufficient rank to cause the Russians to believe we inspired it.) Finally, Rudenko asked if we would all join in a common protest to the court and he agreed to draft a proposed protest. I agreed as did Sir David and DuBost. I told the Justice that I thought Rudenko had something to complain about and that we should stand together and resist this sort of business. The defense is hoping to see a split between the Russians and Americans and British. They hope to go free in such an event. I then told the Justice how the trial had gone in the last few days and we both agreed it was moving along very well and that we could not push it any faster. We got talking about secret police systems and somehow the FBI came up. Jackson said he never had any control over Hoover and that when it was suggested that all the investigating agencies of the US be coordinated he, Jackson, went to Roosevelt and opposed it on the ground that it was a dangerous thing to put so much power in one place and that our safety lay in many investigative agencies. In this way, they were all checks on each other. We also talked about the ambassadors and Jackson said he did not believe in putting Army and Navy men in these places. We now have General Smith in Russia, General Marshall in China, Admiral Kirk in Belgium — none of them is really qualified by training for diplomacy — quite the contrary. [The Justice and I] chatted for another half hour and I left and did some odds and ends in the office.

It is now about 9 p.m. and I am here with you. I prefer to pass my time with you rather than reading or doing anything. You are so much on my mind at all times.

11. Von Ribbentrop went to Moscow to sign this eight days before the invasion of Poland. A secret protocol attached to the pact provided for the partition of Poland, while Finland, Estonia, and Latvia were assigned to the Soviet sphere of influence.

I had a nice letter from Judge Wynne thanking me for a picture I sent to him. He said he showed it to Judge Jennings who showed "interest" but made no comment. Wynne said this is the greatest trial in history and that while it seemed long to me now in a few years I would look back on it with great satisfaction. By the way, be sure to read Walter Lippmann's article in the *Ladies' Home Journal* for June — it is really good, I think, and it gives you some idea of how important this proceeding is. There is a great satisfaction of doing one's job, particularly a job like this. It really is of great importance to everyone and as Lippmann says some day it will be recognized as a great landmark in the struggle of mankind for peace. It is the highest calling of the legal profession and I am already proud of my part in it and because it has meant and continues to mean sacrifice and struggle I feel even better about it. And you, dearest, share very much of this sacrifice and struggle — you have made it possible for me to keep on over here. I will never do anything as worthwhile again — nothing will ever really be as important. Someday the boys will point to it, I hope, and be proud and inspired by it. Perhaps they will be at the bar themselves and perhaps they will invoke this precedent and call upon the law we make here. That is reward enough for any lawyer. I feel that we are doing something so important that it is awesome — it is almost purifying. It has a deep religious meaning, of that I feel certain. Surely it is God's wish that men not wage wars of aggression. The proof here is absolutely overwhelming. I would never have believed that men could be so evil, so determined on a course of war; of murder; of slavery; of dreadful tyranny. Never before has such a record been written and men will read it for a thousand years in amazement and wonder how it ever happened.

It will be a long, long time before the shame of Germany is forgiven and it will never be forgotten. And it is my belief that the German people are to blame for it — all of them in some degree. I have tried to understand the cause of it. I am nowhere near a conviction about it. But this I do know: there is something wrong with the race — and that something wrong seems to be partly geographical. Or perhaps it is something that shows itself only when they are separated from other influences and are by themselves. The same symptoms show through in German settlements — i.e. — the Bund[12] at home.

Well, dearest, I have been talking to you for more than an hour and it seems like only a few minutes. A good game of rummy would just set off the evening — then some cola and some smelly cheese.

I suppose the children are growing and I will notice great changes in them when I get home. Christopher will be quite a citizen — he was only an infant when I left. It tickles me to read of him raiding the refrigerator — chip off the old block I guess.

How did Carolyn do in school this year? She is so bright and so cute I know she will do all right. Tom seems to have become quite a dancer — it will give him lots of poise and confidence. Your tales of Jeremy and his turtles and pollywogs made me laugh. Martha and her vaccination brightened my day — she is so sweet and it doesn't seem possible that "Miss Butter" will be a schoolgirl in the fall. And, dearest, I am in my fortieth year! And you will be soon! Your "baby days," I suppose, are now really numbered, and I guess we can hang up our "family clothes" and settle down to raising this grand crowd we have. The best years are ahead, years of happiness and enjoyment and comfort with each other and the children. Just a little while now and I will be back to start them with you. This June night we are far apart as distance goes yet ever close in our love and affection.

Tom

Nürnberg, Germany
June 3, 1946

Grace, my dearest one,

Just a short note tonight — I fear I wrote a book last night. It has been a rainy Sunday. I stayed in bed until nine thirty and after a quick

12. This American Nazi organization, also called the German American Federation, was founded in the 1930s. Hitler personally placed Fritz Kuhn at the head of the group, hoping he could persuade Americans that Nazi policies were enlightened.

breakfast attended ten thirty Mass. Then I went to the office and did some work until about twelve. Lunch at the house at one and then to the ball field — but there was no game because of the weather, so I walked for an hour. I got back to the house about four — took a bath, then read awhile, then took a fitful nap. Dressed about six and had dinner at seven and after dinner walked about the lawn. It is now nine thirty and here I am. Whitney Harris has been away all weekend. He is a nice chap but not much company. He sings all the time — and is generally too young for me. I have been listening to the radio for a time tonight. Frank Morgan was on and was really funny.[13] I must confess I am again very lonesome tonight. It seems to be getting chronic. I turned down a cocktail party last night — I am tired of these affairs — and the same faces get monotonous. There is only one fact I want to see and it is always in my mind's eye — can you guess?

I have all kinds of plans for my return home. And while some of them may not work out, many of them will. First of all I hope to take at least a two-month rest — maybe three. During that time I expect to make new arrangements for practice. I definitely do not want to go back to my former place. While the Solicitor's job would be attractive for a short time — that or something of equal rank — I much prefer to try my own hand. I have a hard resolution not to accept speaking dates such as I have in the past. By that I do not mean I will turn all invitations down — but I will only accept worthwhile ones. After all this is a trial and it is too much to explain to people who cannot understand it — and who are looking for some new entertainment. I may at some time do some writing about this whole experience but even as to that I feel I want some time to elapse before I try it. There will be much writing done about this case — every lawyer who was here for even the briefest time will be telling all about it. Few will know the whole and the real story. Of course the Justice I feel sure will do some writing and he is the first authority. I will have had the next most complete understanding of

13. Morgan was a comedian who appeared on a variety of network radio shows. He was also a film actor.

the case — and from a trial standpoint I know the day to day situation better than the Justice does.

Now, dearest, it is near ten p.m. and time for good citizens to be abed. It is about 4 p.m. in Lebanon. I wonder what you are doing now? Are you out somewhere — are you busy in the house? Are you beginning to get supper ready? I can hear your lovely voice and see you as I remember you so well. How I will enjoy Sunday at home — we will have no guests — just the day to ourselves. I send you all my love and devotion and my affection to the children.

Tom

P.S. The radio is playing "When Irish Eyes Are Smiling" — it reminds me of you.

Nürnberg, Germany
June 5, 1946

Grace, my dearest one,

This day started well with two letters from you, and about four others. It made me feel better to know that Boyd Geer will keep the grass cut for you — thus you will be under no obligation to anyone. Generally your letters sounded more cheerful and that too is pleasing.

Leo Gaffney writes that Charlie had been in to see him and Leo thinks he can put over the job for him. It is strictly a political question and of course Leo let me know that he and the Democrats in New Britain were doing me a favor. Now please let both Charlie and Margaret know this at once. I think Charlie should have written to me first — and anyway I am not too keen about the way he has been acting.

Leo told me that my chances politically are not good at all. Bobby Hurley[14] told him I was a very unpopular young man and that he and

14. Hurley was administrator of the Works Progress Administration in Connecticut.

Golden and Murphy would oppose me! It made me smile. Surely that is no news from Hurley and I could tell Leo some really interesting comments on his own chances. Anyway Leo thinks he has a chance — not much of a chance — but a chance, etc. Poor Leo. The letter must have been very difficult for him. He doesn't know that I wouldn't take the nomination on a platter. But in letting me know of his own ambition he really made quite a story about what he was doing for my brother-in-law, Charlie McAree. So it goes.

The last two days have been regular trial days. We finished Sauckel and started [Wehrmacht chief Alfred] Jodl. Two nights ago, Lawrence Steinhardt and his wife and daughter were guests of the Justice at a buffet supper. I attended, too. He is our ambassador in Prague — was formerly in Turkey and Moscow and in my judgment is a very able man. I had a long chat with him and he told me some interesting facts about Czechoslovakia. He thinks it is NOT going "red." So do I.

I received a letter notifying me — or better asking me — if I would serve as vice president of the international Penal Law society. It is considered quite an honor. I have accepted. Maybe you and I can attend some meetings in Europe. It meets twice each year.

After Jodl we have only five defendants left — the end is really in sight now. It will come in another few weeks. Please keep up your courage. Keep happy. Keep healthy and soon all will be well.

                                                                    Tom

CHAPTER 14

Final Arguments

THE TRIAL BUILDS TO ITS CLIMAX—the last defendants cross-examined. After all his achievement, Dodd confesses to Grace that he has doubts about Nuremberg. "Sometimes I get so discouraged I wonder if any of this is worthwhile. Was I a fool to take on this long and difficult task while others remain at home and criticize us because we try to make the waging of war not worth the risk?" Then the news arrives that Dodd is to be awarded the Medal of Freedom by Truman for his Nuremberg work. The final arguments begin. Dodd sees a big change in Göring's demeanor. He "has been positively impish up to very recently, now gray and crest-fallen. Keitel wears the mask of the doomed already. And so it goes through the entire dock." Dodd's worry shifts to outside the courtroom—the Soviet threat intensifies. Dodd makes his final argument. He tells Grace, "The Associated Press man asked for an autographed copy!" Jackson flies home, and Dodd stays in Europe to await the verdicts.

Nürnberg, Germany
June 7, 1946

Grace, my dearest one,

It is a dark Friday. First of all the Justice failed to be appointed Chief Justice of the Supreme Court. We were all hoping for him.

Secondly, Bob Kenny, the Attorney General in California, was beaten for the governorship nomination by [Earl] Warren. So it goes. But I shall not call it a "black" Friday. Just a little "dark." I do not take these disappointments too much to heart. In my thirty-nine years I have been greatly disappointed on occasions. In most if not all instances matters have worked out all right—and as a matter of recorded fact matters have turned out better in all situations as far as I can remember.

You will recall how bitterly I felt in 1936 when by all the rules of life I was entitled to succeed M. A. Daly as Administrator of the WPA in Connecticut. Instead Hurley was appointed. Not long afterwards I was genuinely grateful for that disappointment. The debacle of last summer—the cheap dishonor of the Supreme Court decision—left me with a hard feeling of pain at the time. This opportunity would never have come except for Shields, Brown and two or three weak judges.

There are other instances—too numerous to recount. What I mean to say is I am not depressed by the disappointments of this day— or of this life. I have learned too much about the smallness—pettiness, the dishonor, the falsehood, the lies of men to expect too much—thus I am not too much disappointed. And where greed, ambition and politics are mixed, I am ready for almost any conclusion.

Yesterday and today were usual trial days. Jodl is still on the stand—nearing the end we all hope.

This morning a nice letter from you—one from Catherine, one from Dick Barrett who said he is working in the Labor Department in Washington. McMahon gave him the ice water treatment—Dick got this job through old [National Youth Administration] connections. McMahon is really bad news. He is now allegedly for Bowles for either the Senate or Governorship. It makes no difference. Unless the unheard of happens, the Democrats will be swamped.

Leo Gaffney really makes me smile. If I wanted the spot he should be out working his head off. As far as he knows I do want it. But he is writing to me to advise how hopeless my situation is and how strong he is. Or rather that he may have a "chance." He suggested that I could go into the law business with him while he is the governor — and it would be very profitable for me! He really hasn't much sense — else he would never write such a letter. I really think he means well — and is fundamentally decent. Just no balance, no deep attitudes. Bill McCue — also. His statement [that] "Tom isn't quite ready yet" is certainly farcical and reflects an absence of the very qualities deficient in Gaffney. You see it is the same old story. In politics a man has no friends. As I grow older I dislike political people more and more. They are a poor lot as a class — honor, decency and truth are usually not in them and gratitude is unknown. Before a nomination these politicians do not seek the best candidate — only the one likely to fatten their purses. After nomination they judge a man solely on the basis of what he does for them. The public interest comes at the very last — if at all.

The Justice is a really great man — he did not flicker an eyelash when he heard that Vinson was appointed. I was with him when he received the news. He said, "Vinson is a grand man and he will make a fine Chief Justice." Had Jackson been at home — had Roosevelt lived — well, all would be different today. Black and Murphy and Douglas — I am told — all worked strenuously to prevent his appointment. The Justice has told me that Black, the former Klansman, has not changed his bigoted mind, but to the public he makes it appear that he has. In the private sessions of the judges he shows it.[1] Murphy is woman crazy and actually emotionally unstable to put it mildly. Douglas is an opportunist — a trickster. Fine people for the highest court in the land. Little wonder that we get Browns and Maltbies and Jennings, etc., in Connecticut. I fear that as time goes on, as democracy tries to be more and more effective, the status of the judiciary will

1. Hugo Black became a member of the Klan in the early 1920s after successfully defending a Klansman accused of murdering the leader of the Catholic community in Birmingham, Alabama. Black resigned after a few years and then was critical of the organization. His tenure on the Supreme Court was the fourth longest in history, and his record includes strong support of civil rights.

radically change — mostly because, like all other powerful institutions, it has become too rigid, too tyrannical, too anxious to retain powers, and unwilling to move with the times.

My this is a long letter, and how I have declaimed in it. Are you still reading? Or did you give up three pages back? It is good to talk with you this way.

I am glad you are going to Groton Long Point for a few days. I hope the Bender girl takes good care of Tom, Carolyn and Jeremy. Is she competent? How old is she?

My dear, do take care of yourself and of the children. I send you all of my love and devotion.

Tom

Nürnberg, Germany
June 9, 1946

Grace my dearest one,

If you have time would you send me another bottle of the same vitamins — please. I think they help over here. As you know the diet is not too good. Also would you when you have time get me some black silk socks — size eleven — and some neckwear — only solid colors, not stripes or figures. Blue, dark red, brown and so on — you have good taste. Also black.

Asking for vitamins brings to mind the food situation here and at home. It makes my blood boil to read your letters about the food problem. There is no need for that at all. Our country can feed all of our people and some others besides. Between Bowles and his insane desire to run every last detail of life and the side which wants to turn to wild and open competition the country is in a mess. Maybe there are people starving in Europe — they are not in this part of Germany and everyone I know who has traveled over here says the same thing. In London you can buy all the good roast beef you want and get it at a reasonable price. In the restaurants a good dinner costs a dollar. France, too, is in very good shape.[2] England has been making and exporting — yes exporting — automobiles since last December. From what I hear the U.S. hasn't made them yet. At this point and from here I think Truman should be thrown out of the presidency. The Democrats have gone to seed. No really good man of middle age is known in the party — we are run by a lot of broken down political hacks and near-crooks. The world is not much better off one year after the war. We are living in turmoil — like an armed camp — under constant threat of war on a new and more horrible scale, torn by strife and dispute and utterly without leadership.

You asked what the true story is on the Russian who shot himself while cleaning his gun. I do not know — but no one here thinks it was an accident. The OGPU[3] is here of course. We have some of them spotted. The Russian was the most pleasant of their crowd. Some think he was getting too friendly with us and with the British so they just removed him. Life is cheap in Europe and dirt cheap in Russia and the farther you go east the cheaper it gets.

Sometimes I get so discouraged I wonder if any of this is worthwhile. Was I a fool to take on this long and difficult task while others remain at home and criticize us because we try to make the waging of war not worth the risk? Is the world so cynical, so deeply cynical as it sometimes seems to be? I must not let myself think so. And anyway I do not think so. Sometime the real value of this case will be known and understood. I have put a lot into this trial, Grace dear, more than I know myself — but the signs of the effort sometimes begin to show. I am tired, very tired, mentally. The grind of a five and one half day trial week — for months on end — preceded by months of preparation is

2. There was talk in Washington of a worldwide "food panic." President Truman sent former president Herbert Hoover on a fact-finding mission around the world, and as a result, a plan was developed to send any U.S. surpluses abroad. In Great Britain, a victorious nation in the war, rationing lasted until 1954.
3. Dodd was referring to the former name of the Soviet secret police.

more than I had really bargained for. Even the judges are beginning to show the strain, and that is as true of the defense.

However, I will see it through and in good style. I am taking good care of myself — better than I ever did in my life, so do not worry about me. Just take good care of yourself and the children and soon we will all be together again. Be careful of the children in the water — Jerry is so daring. I sometimes worry about that brook swimming, so watch them. I must get at my work and so I end this hectic note by sending you again all of my love and devotion.

Tom

P.S. Reading this over, I realize that is sounds very black. Things are not that bad. I guess I just miss you too much, dear.

Nürnberg, Germany
June 11, 1946

Grace, my dearest one,

Well, I assume that by this time the newspapers are headlining Jackson's message to the Judiciary Committee.[4] I knew nothing of it until about ten thirty this morning. I was in court — Seyss-Inquart was on the witness stand. The Justice walked in and smilingly handed me a copy of his statement. I was amazed. Then he told me much more. He said Black is a hypocrite and nothing else and he cited Black's Ku Klux Klan activity. Of course Black, Douglas and Murphy stabbed the Justice in the back on the Chief Justice appointment and some columnists have been trying to make it appear that Black threatened to resign

4. Jackson's letter to the Senate and House Judiciary Committees accused Black of a conflict of interest for participating in a labor decision argued by a former law partner of his. The two justices had an antagonistic relationship. In his letter, Jackson objected to being characterized during the campaigning for chief justice as causing discord in the court. It was his view that Black was the culprit.

if Jackson was appointed because of something shady about Jackson. These articles were inspired by Black and his associates — so the Justice decided to clear the air. I am delighted to put it mildly. You know my bitter experience with judges who were not above petty yet wicked influences. It is about time such conditions were openly aired. Jackson is fearless because he is honest and able. Where this will end I do not know — but it can only have a good result. The Justice has cabled Truman offering to resign his place here (not his Supreme Court place) if the President feels he is embarrassed. If Truman is ass enough to say "yes" then this case is gone. I would not stay under anyone else and of course I would not be named — and I would not want to be.

I am for Jackson — first and last. I know the man now — and he is a great American and a truly great advocate. He is right and honest and all the hypocrites and fakers are against him — Biddle, Murphy, Ku Klux Black, Douglas, etc. His enemies make me sure he is right.

Your letter about the change in the rules in Connecticut came yesterday.[5] Grace, dear — do you know I cannot get excited about it? That whole episode was so dishonest, so cheap, so corrupt it has left me with a feeling of disdain for that court. Somehow I do not care very much. Of course I am so grateful to Joe Blumenfeld — he is a wonderful friend. I can never really repay him for his faith.

I sent you a letter from Howard Brundage. I really feel more interested in that possibility — I at least want to talk to Howard and you and I will go out there when I get home.

I have no invitation to any Democratic meeting in Saybrook. I would not answer if I got it. Let McMahon and his forty thieves have their fun unmolested. I have made my decision about that business.

The Justice told me that Roosevelt deeply regretted his appointment of Black. Of course that was Roosevelt's greatest weakness — his judicial appointments, with some exceptions.

Seyss-Inquart took the stand yesterday. He is now under cross-examination by the French (very sticky) — then I will take him on.

---

5. Bar eligibility rules were altered to allow credit for federal service.

After him, four to go. We should finish the individuals about the end of this month.

June 14

So much has happened since I started this letter as to make it difficult for me to find time to finish it.

The Justice left Tuesday for Oslo and Stockholm. We have no direct news as to what the reaction has been to the Jackson statement. Many cables have arrived — all favorable. I am getting all of them.

The Seyss-Inquart case continues. I cross-examined him and four witnesses and it went all right. Sir Norman Birkett, the British alternate judge, stopped me in the corridor and was most complimentary about my cross-examinations. Anyway it made me feel good.

Tomorrow is the wedding day for Evelyn Low and Dave Pitcher. I am enclosing the invitation I sent out. I feel rather sorry for Evelyn. She is a nice girl and I get a kick out of giving her a nice send off. I will send you a full report.

As yet no word from Joe Blumenfeld on the change in the court rules. Was there a mistake? Of course Leo Gaffney's letter confirms yours — but it seems strange that Joe has not written to me. I haven't written to him as I want to be sure we have the right information.

We finished Seyss-Inquart at noon today[6] — and started at once on von Papen. We have three to go now — slowly but surely we move towards the end.

I had a note from McMahon today — thanking me for a picture which I very recently sent to him. He was very cordial and indeed complimentary about my efforts here. Very unctuous.

6. Here, Dodd sprung one of his traps. He asked Seyss-Inquart if he accepted responsibility for the atrocities committed in Poland while he was deputy to Frank there. The defendant tried to dodge the question, saying in effect that he wasn't responsible. Then Dodd confronted Seyss-Inquart with the defendant's own directive giving great power to the security police.

Your letter of today again mentions the change in the rules — it must be so. You also write that you haven't heard from me in a week. That is strange — I write regularly. Sometimes, perhaps, missing a day or two, but never more than that. No dear, I am not becoming "bachelorized." On the contrary — I miss my home, my dearest Grace and the children. Many and many and many an evening I have longed for some confusion, some children's quarrels, some little peoples' mistakes, some good old Dodd household mix ups.

Here is a special — top secret! I have been awarded the Medal of Freedom by Truman for my work here. It will be bestowed in the next few weeks by Justice Jackson. I have seen the citation and I thought you should know it too. It is a great honor and something we will always cherish. Please do not say anything about it until it is actually given to me.

Strange what changes can occur in one year. When the Supreme Court ruled last July, I little thought that within a year the President of the U.S. would give me a medal for my work as a lawyer. Even less did I expect that the judges would change the rules. Well, it has not been all easy sailing. It took this hard year of separation from you, and this year of living and working under difficult circumstances. Nothing really worthwhile ever comes easily — for me.

Be sure to let me know what the Democrats are doing. I hear that Truman has put pressure on McMahon for Bowles. I really think he will be defeated, but on the other hand he may get great support from people who believe in price controls, etc. With the bad situation developing, he may make it appear that failure to follow his advice is the cause of the trouble. This I do not believe. Anyway I dislike Mrs. Woodhouse,[7] Alfred Bingham, Snow and Bowles running the party in Connecticut. They are all carpetbaggers and opportunists. However, only time will tell the story. If the Republicans are half smart they will run a good Catholic candidate against him, and the rest will be easy for them.

7. **Representative Chase Going Woodhouse.**

Well, this letter is far beyond the bounds of good letter writing form. Please do take good care of yourself and of the children. I am very proud of Jerry and his first communion, and really, Tom wrote two very intelligent and interesting letters. Why doesn't Carolyn write a few lines? Martha has written me some very nice ones. Tell Chris to make his mark (X). For you, as ever and always I send all of my love and devotion.

Tom

Nürnberg, Germany
June 17, 1946

Grace, my dearest one,

The wedding went off very well. The ceremony performed by Fr. Lavelle took place in the living room before the fireplace. We had a splendid wedding cake made by the pastry cook at the Grand Hotel. About seventy-five people came and everyone seemed to think it was a nice wedding—we even threw rice!

The court did not sit on Saturday, so von Papen is still on the stand. He should finish up by Tuesday. Then comes Speer—he is the last defendant for whom we have responsibility. I will cross-examine him. Thereafter come Fritzsche and Neurath and that is the end of the dock.

I still have not heard from Joe Blumenfeld. I just wonder if there is some tie up in it—or if it's not what Joe first thought when he called you.

Justice Jackson returned from Norway and Sweden today. [There is] nothing new on the Black matter. It will be strange if Black does not make some reply. But what can he say? The facts are true, I am sure. Now that the Ku Klux Klan is reviving undoubtedly some case or cases will go to the Supreme Court involving the Klan. Will Black disqualify himself? It seems to me that it makes little difference. He and the court will be embarrassed if he does—and if he doesn't.

June 17

Von Papen continued his direct testimony this morning. Justice Jackson came into court about noontime and appeared to be in fine spirits. At noon recess he asked me to have lunch with him in his office, which I did. He said that he had talked to Washington on the phone and there was much discussion over his Black statement. He said he had expected as much — his only fear was that the Republicans would take his side! He also said, "I have hunted skunks before. I expect to have some scent thrown at me." Besides Justice Douglas wrote him a very cordial note the day the story broke in Washington — after it had been made public — but made no reference to it. Justice Frankfurter wrote to Jackson saying that Jackson had reported the situation exactly as it was. Justice Jackson told me that he might resign if this situation is not cleared up. I urged him not to do so and he seemed to agree with me. At any rate he will not do so unless further developments, after he is back on the court, make it seem that he must do so. Jackson again told me the story of the conflict between Owen Roberts and Black. Black was feeding inside confidential court information to Drew Pearson, the columnist. Roberts became very angry about it as did Stone and Jackson. When Roberts retired, the Chief Justice prepared the usual letter of commendation for all the Justices to sign. Among other things it said that Roberts always did his duty as he saw it, or words to that effect. Black refused to sign the letter with that statement in it. Consequently, Roberts, who served long and well as a Justice, is perhaps the only one who ever retired without a word of commendation from his colleagues. All because he refused to condone a violation of the confidential judicial conferences.

I said that I could not see how Black could make any reply to the statement of the Justice. To this, Jackson said, "Well, I suppose he might make the same answer the young man made who was asked to marry a certain girlfriend who was pregnant." I said, "What was that?" Jackson said, "His excuse was — 'she is only a little pregnant.'"

I always enjoy chatting with Jackson, because he has a very earthy yet very direct and impressive way of expressing himself.

Von Papen's still on the stand at the end of the day, but should be through tomorrow. For now, my dearest, I send you my unchanging love and devotion.

Tom

Nürnberg, Germany
June 22, 1946

Grace my dearest one,

I feel very guilty because I have not written for three days. But you know it is not neglect or intentional carelessness. The truth is that I have not had the opportunity this week. We finished von Papen and Speer and this morning we started von Neurath. Only Fritzsche remains in the dock. I did not cross-examine Speer — but I wish I had done so. I urged the Justice to do it. I felt he needed it as Speer was the last one for whom the U.S. had primary responsibility — and I thought too that Speer would be easy and Jackson would look good.[8] Well, he made a mess of it. That is, he did not do at all well. He just cannot cross-examine. Of that I am completely convinced. When the Göring case went so poorly I felt that Biddle had made Jackson's task very difficult — that Göring was himself a very difficult man to examine. That perhaps the Justice had a bad day — that on the record it wasn't as bad as it sounded.

With Schacht, I reasoned that Schacht was tough. We had a fairly weak case — and that Jackson was nervous because of his Göring situation and that all in all it wasn't too bad. But after yesterday — I know now — that the Justice simply does not have the ability to cross-examine.

8. According to historian Joseph E. Persico, Speer requested this change, arguing it would help the prosecution in its effort to get cooperation from the defendants. His real motive, as reported, was to avoid Dodd's "sharp" questioning.

It shocks me that he doesn't know it himself. He could have avoided all this by staying out of it entirely and by exercising only the duties of chief counsel in a case of this size. Speer was ripe for plucking — but it didn't work out. Of course he will not escape — we have far too much on him. But we could have destroyed him — as he really deserved. Well, anyway, we are moving along.

I had a letter from Eliot Janeway telling me that Clare Luce[9] would very likely run for the Senate — and Baldwin for re-election. The letter had an undertone I thought. He said McMahon was not for me — he was sure of that. He thought the strongest ticket for the Democrats would be O'Sullivan and Bowles. He wrote that I was handicapped because of my association with this case and with Jackson and he suggested that I wait at least two years.

Well, well — what does this mean? First of all I think the Luces put him up to part of it. You know it is an ugly thought — but I think Clare realized that the Catholics in Connecticut are very strong. I hope I am in error. She was flirting with Buddhism a few years ago — before she became interested in politics. As for McMahon's attitude, that is no news. He is already for Bowles. I know that and don't be fooled by Woodhouse. She is a poisonous old cat. If I wanted to run this year she would work tooth and nail against me. The rest of the story about O'Sullivan is interesting, but Janeway hates Jackson. You will recall how he tried to persuade me not to come over here. I am not worked up about his case or my part in it. I would welcome a battle on that level.

Joe Blumenfeld has written to me about the new rule. I gather it is not all that Joe asked for — and somehow I have my fingers crossed about it. When I see the actual text I will be able to tell better.

Grace, dearest, I am so very lonesome these days. I so long to be home. You just cannot know how I feel — how my heart aches. I doubt that I can stand it much longer. Weren't you sweet and thoughtful to

9. Clare Boothe Luce, wife of Henry Luce (founder of *Time* magazine), was a playwright, editor, politician, and social activist. She served in the House from 1943 to 1947, representing Connecticut.

put that plant on my mother's grave? I am sure she smiled at you. She would be so proud of you anyway.

My dearest, I send you all of my love and devotion — my affection to the children.

Tom

Nürnberg, Germany
June 24, 1946

Grace, my dearest one,

This noontime I had the Austrian delegation for lunch. The Minister of Justice, the Chief Justice, two of their assistants, etc. They told me that the Austrians are on a 1,200 calorie per day diet. That is starvation. LaGuardia, head of the UNRRA,[10] just will not send them enough food, while the Italians get more than they need. The Russians will not allow Hungary, Romania or Bulgaria to ship them food — as, of course, Austria is very anti-communist and heavily Catholic. What a mess this continent is in.

I haven't written anything about my departure date [for home] simply because I am not yet sure of it. As soon as I know you will hear from me. Just keep your spirits up, keep busy, and time will pass along. It is hard, I know.

Howard Brundage wrote to me and enclosed clippings from the Chicago papers about the Jackson–Black feud. He said it was a boomerang for Jackson — that most people thought he was peeved because he failed to get the Chief Justiceship. That it was bad taste, etc. Is that the opinion around home? Was it news in politics? Keep me advised. But most of all keep yourself and the children well and happy — that is the most important thing in this world for me.

Tom

10. **Fiorello H. LaGuardia, the former mayor of New York City, was named director general of the United Nations Relief and Rehabilitation Administration in 1946.**

P.S. Grace, dearest, if I am detained here until September could you come over for say a month or six weeks? How would you work it out with the children? I am not sure I can do it — but I think I may be able to have you brought over. Don't get too excited — just coolly figure out some plan for the children.

Nürnberg, Germany
June 25, 1946

Grace my dearest,

This is a "quickie" — I haven't the news to write a letter of decent length. Today von Neurath finished his own direct examination and the British finished their cross. The Russians will consume a few hours tomorrow (for no good reason except home consumption — they do it all the time and have very much delayed the trial).

Leo Gaffney wrote to me recently and said that McMahon has a special plane at his disposal from Sam Pryor, the Republican National Committeeman for Connecticut — and also the big booster of Clare Luce. Also McMahon double-crossed Leo and the New Britain boys on the radio station because the *Hartford Times* wanted it. Of course you and I are not surprised. I only wonder how long it will be before half the state is wise to him. The game is that Clare is to run for the Senate and beat Bowles — thus McMahon remains the only Democrat from Connecticut in the Senate. It's pretty dirty, isn't it?

June 26, 1946

I fell asleep last night before I finished this letter. Anyway nothing happened except sleep — Whitney came in to see me when he got home and we chatted for a while. This is a beautiful morning — the first one in many weeks — I do hope it continues fair. Most of all I hope I get some letters from you today. I continue to miss you terribly, and long to be home with you.

Tom

Nürnberg, Germany
July 1, 1946

Grace my dearest one,

Saturday, the court sat until one p.m. and we finished the last defendant! We all feel we passed a great milestone. However we are now bogged down again. You will recall that the Russians insisted on inserting in the indictment the charge that the Germans murdered 11,000 Polish officers who had surrendered in the Katyn forest near Smolensk. Of course the Germans have always claimed the Russians did it. Now we must hear three witnesses for each side. God knows how many days this will take. For my part I think it is a toss up — they are both capable of it. Both had motive for the crime. And in any event both share responsibility because the rape of Poland in 1939 was a joint venture between them. Only one thing — one "small" matter — is undisputed. Some eleven thousand Polish officers were mass murdered in cold blood. Also it is agreed that either the Germans or the Russians did it. I insist that the dispute between them is of little interest to the world — even less will it interest history.

Yesterday the testimony of the Russians and Germans continued. It sounded like a coroner's inquest — corpses, skulls, condition of bodies, vital organs, decomposition, etc. I still say a plague on both of them. They both plundered Poland — in the cause of which they jointly and severally murdered many people — including these officers. They are therefore both responsible.

The final arguments should certainly start tomorrow. The end cannot be too far away. Do keep your pretty little chin up. I know how difficult it is because of my own feelings over here. Try to get as much rest as you possibly can. I have become a great believer in rest. The body will do wonders if only it gets half an opportunity to rest up.

My love to you, dearest.

Tom

Nürnberg, Germany
July 4, 1946

Grace, my dearest one,

The Fourth of July in Germany passes quite unnoticed. The soldiers made it a holiday — there was a ballgame this afternoon, airplanes flew overhead this morning and tonight Judge Parker is giving a party. But the court went on as usual. The final arguments began this morning — a rather auspicious day perhaps. Yesterday both the defense and the prosecution offered various items of proof clearing up the record, etc. I cross-examined the last witness — Erich Kempka, Hitler's chauffeur. You have seen his statement about the last days in Berlin.[11] So closed the oral evidence against the individuals in the dock.

Tom wrote me a very good letter. Very well done indeed — his sentences are well constructed and his spelling is all right. Tell me if, by writing to him more often than to the others I am causing any sore hearts. I will of course write to the others, too. Jeremy is rather sensitive and I wouldn't hurt him for the world. Perhaps I should write to them all at the same time. What is your advice?

July 5

The party given by Judge Parker last night was something to remember. All the delegations here attended. There was some good natured barbs at the British — and they seemed to enjoy themselves. So passed Independence Day 1946 in Nürnberg. What did you and the children do? I worry a little bit about King's Brook — so many bathe in it — and the water runs low. Are you getting raw milk now? If so you should boil it — you know medical men now believe infantile[12]

11. Kempka first claimed that he was a witness to the suicides of Hitler and Eva Braun. He then admitted that he left Hitler's bunker in Berlin beforehand and came back when they were already dead.
12. Reference to infantile paralysis — poliomyelitis — later commonly referred to as polio.

is carried in milk — and they are almost certain that flies are the carriers. I know you are careful, dearest — but I did want to remind you, and to inform you because the Army medical research is really quite good.

Jackson may fly home about the first of August for a few weeks. The trial will not be over then. There will be about two or three weeks of proof involving the criminal organizations named in the indictment. Thereafter the case will end and a judgment will be rendered. I will not, of course, stay for the so-called Mass Trials — or subsequent proceedings as we call them. This case is enough. I yearn to be home with you and with the children. Do, please do, take very good care of your precious self and of them. You must all be healthy and happy when I get back. Again, I send you my love and my devotion.

Tom

Nürnberg, Germany
July 16, 1946

Grace my dearest one,

Well, I do feel very, very neglectful because I have not written a letter in three days and I do think that is the longest time since I left about one year ago. But, dearest, I have not been careless — or really negligent, or forgetful. On the contrary, you were as ever and always in my mind. But we have been working on the final speech of the Justice and it has been close work and tiring, too. As far as the trial goes there is really little new — the defense final arguments go on. Today we are through with more than ten of them and we may finish all by the end of this week.

I am glad that Father Walsh called you. However he should not say I will be here until mid-September. For that is something no one knows. The Justice will make his final argument and then return to the States for a few weeks. He has asked me to remain here, in charge, while he is away. During that time the Tribunal will hear testimony about the six organizations named in the indictment. (This is not to be confused with the so-called "Mass Trials.") After this evidence is in the tribunal will deliberate on the case — perhaps for two or three weeks. Then comes the final judgment and sentences. The Justice will fly back for this. So you see it is rather difficult to fix a date. Of course it will be some four to six weeks hence, maybe a bit less, maybe a little more, but that is as close as I can predict now. In any event, dearest, I will lose no time that I can save, and my yearning to return to you and the children is simply beyond my power to explain or express in words. I live for that day. You asked, "Will we find each other changed?" My answer is that I have changed. My love for you has changed. It is incredibly stronger than you can imagine. It was always tremendous, but now it flows so deeply — so completely in every vein and vessel of my being. Is that a change? Yes, I have changed too about the children. They were playthings — sometimes beloved little annoyances, sometimes even outrageous little barbarians. But now they are personalities with whom I hope to really exchange ideas — with whom I will enjoy recreation. I want their company more than before and I need it now too. Is that a change? Yes — I have changed about my ideas of living too. I want to be home — in our home. I want to stay there. I do not want to be away from it. I want to spend evenings there and with you reading a good book, the little citizens asleep upstairs. Not just a few nights a month but almost every night. Is that a change? You will have changed too. I am sure of it. I know you will be more beautiful, more lovely than ever.

The defendants reflect the ending of these proceedings. They seem to feel that the days are definitely numbered. Even Göring, who has been positively impish up to very recently, now is gray and crest-fallen. Keitel wears the mask of the doomed already. And so it goes through the entire dock. General Jodl and Seyss-Inquart being exceptions to some extent and mostly because they are more stable emotionally.

I try so hard to be fair in my own mind with Russia, but I am convinced that there can be no compromise with her, unless and until she drastically changes her ways. Everything — and I mean everything — that we have charged the Germans with in this case has been done, and worse, is being done by Russia. Four hundred thousand Tartars were recently moved by force from the Crimea where they have lived for centuries because during the war some of them joined the Germans. They are terrorizing all of Eastern Europe. In Hungary, a recent election gave the communists only 25 percent of the vote — but the freedom-loving Russians simply refused to permit the 75 percent majority to form the government. Romania, Bulgaria, Yugoslavia — all are in her clutch. Catholic Austria is being starved and stripped by Russian command. Italy is being punished too. And we sit by and permit it!

In an article, Arthur Krock of the *New York Times* lamented the present state of affairs between the U.S. and USSR. He argued that some of this was due to the fact that official Russian propaganda deceived the Russian people into believing that the U.S. was hostile to Russia. So, he concluded why not have a great national referendum taken in the U.S. to convince Russia that Americans are not hostile! My God! Can you imagine that situation? The people of the U.S. having fought this war, having saved Russia, having saved the world, desiring only to live in peace, reducing its armies and its navy and its air corps, loaning billions all over the globe, feeding millions everywhere, must on a certain day, like ancient public penitents, file to polling places to vote NO to the proposition, "Do you feel hostile to Russia?" In order to appease the Bear! I fear there is no common ground between us. Nor can there be. Roosevelt at Yalta and Truman and Byrnes[13] ever since have been thoroughly whipped by Russia — and until and unless we do better with our own affairs — at home and abroad — fate will be unkind to America. The Achilles heel of this great trial is the Russian participation in it. It isn't a pretty picture, dearest — for us who want only to raise our children to be good citizens who love their neighbors and their God.

I must stop all of this writing about Russia and affairs generally. I should be telling you how much I love you. It is so much better for me — for my spleen, for my blood pressure, for my soul.

13. **Secretary of State James F. Byrnes.**

I close vowing my undying love and devotion to you and sending, through you, my affection for the children.

Tom

Nürnberg, Germany
July 20, 1946

Grace, my dearest one,

My friend Jerry Kelleher—he is the colonel who took Corley's place—is leaving Monday, relieved of duty here and given a very poor assignment in Gegensburg, Germany. Father Lavalle also has been relieved as chaplain. He leaves on Monday too. This is all part of another story. The story of General Gill. I have discovered many things about his doings here—but the most important factor is, in my judgment, his bigotry. He shows it—but he is smooth and silky. Yet he quietly cuts the heads off of each Irish Catholic in town. I have pretty well blocked him insofar as my own affairs are concerned. He tried to get rid of Father Walsh last February—I blocked that. But when it comes to Army matters of course I am not effective. I have no say there, and must not interfere. I feel very badly for Kelleher—he has a brilliant war record, and he applied for a commission in the regular Army but didn't get it. This is incredible but true. Believe me dear this Army is a mess—it is rotten to the core. I will have much to say about it when I get home and when the opportunity presents itself. There are more over-aged, over-glandular generals and colonels mooching about than you have ever imagined. All drawing fat salaries, big liquor rations and contraceptives by the gross. You will recall how often I have said that I wished no son of mine to enter Annapolis or West Point. Now I know how right I am. It is a Valhalla for bums—with a few exceptions. The men who really fight our wars never survive in very large numbers, and they are privates, draftees, enlistees, and junior officers. When a senior officer gets hurt or killed it is usually a mistake. The little people, Grace dear, fight these wars at home and on the battlefield. Apropos of this whole subject the Army and Navy officers are constantly heckling us and criticizing this trial. I sometimes believe they do not want peace in this world. They value medals too much. God help mankind if they get the upper hand.

Now, let us see if we can't talk of more pleasant matters. The Justice has written a truly great final speech. Be sure to read it — all of it — for you will find it of the greatest interest. In my opinion it will rank high in literary and legal history.

My heart is heavy because I am not leaving next week. Of course only a few more weeks remain at the most.

The father of Major Watson who is involved in the gun theft came to see me recently. He offered me $25,000 to defend his son. I could not do it — as a matter of right conduct, or of decency. But Amen took the case after I refused it, and he is one of those over-age, over-glandular swine with a colonel's rank. I am not so sorry about the fee as I am angry at Amen. There goes my blood pressure again! This is my angry day, I guess. I must not permit these matters to disturb me — they are not very important as really important things go.

I will start to ship things home next week — clothing, books, papers, all kinds of odds and ends that have accumulated in a year. Let me know when these things arrive. Your package of ties and socks is lost I am sure now. I should tell you to insure and register them. I have ordered some suits from Rosenberg in New Haven. They are to be made according to the pattern of the ones they made for me last year. I intended to have them sent here but now I think I will have them sent to Lebanon and you can bring them with you when you meet me in New York. How I long for that day! It is more than a year now since I said goodbye to you at the Union Station in Washington. My heart was sad that day, but had I known it was goodbye for a year — with only a brief, so brief, reunion at Xmas time — I most surely would not have left. But now it is almost over. I will have you in my arms before the leaves fall — and never again will we be separated.

Tom

Nürnberg, Germany
July 28, 1946

Grace, my dearest one,

Jackson leaves this week — and with him Amen, Gill, Bill Jackson, and a few more. I suppose they will receive a lot of attention when they arrive. Well, I am not regretful. I really do not care about flying the Atlantic again — twice is enough for a while. And anyway in only a few more weeks I will be along.

The defense finished its final arguments on Thursday afternoon and none of them varied too much from one another. They were all quite abstract and rather filled with misty metaphysics. They did not discuss the evidence or the facts of the case as we know it in America. Of course they were hard put to make any decent arguments for their clients but I had expected something more than we got.

Justice Jackson started his speech Friday morning and he delivered it very well. I assume it was carried fully in the press, particularly in the *New York Times*, but if not, I will send you a complete copy of it as I think it is worth reading. He has a great style, notable for its clarity and simplicity. In my judgment, his argument will take its place among the great arguments that have been made in great cases. He finished at noontime on Friday and Sir Harley Shawcross began his summary for the British. It was a very long and detailed argument and a very good one, but it did not have the brilliant literary value that one finds in Jackson's speech. Shawcross concluded on Saturday a little after one o'clock. On Monday the French will start their argument, and the Russians will conclude. I expect that about Tuesday noon these, the main final arguments in the case, will be over. The organizations should not take more than two or three weeks and thereafter I will be on my way.

Last Thursday night I attended a dinner given by the Russian judges. Justice Jackson and a small group of Americans were present. They entertained very nicely with all kinds of vodka and plenty of it. It is a very strange thing that they insist on trying to get everybody intoxicated. I rather believe it is more of a yokel idea than any deep political intrigue for most of the time they get themselves pretty well plastered and are consequently in no condition to carefully elicit information from the drunken guests. Of course their secret police are always in attendance. They are here in the guise of interpreters, one or two as newspaper men. This of course is a surmise on my part but based on many months of observation. It seems perfectly clear to me from observing them that even the Russian judges and Russian prosecutors are under the control of these secret police officers. Whenever the Russians attend a party they arrive in a body and they leave in a body. If one of them is invited individually to an affair, he or she has to get permission before attending.

As I listened to the arguments of Jackson and Shawcross, I was thinking of the Russians and it was ever in my mind that all of the crimes which the Nazis have committed have been committed by the Russians, and from what I hear — may still be committed by the Russians. The Russian participation in this prosecution is the Achilles heel of the great trial. Some day we may have to explain it. Of course time changes many things and it may be that the Russians themselves by their very participation here will more completely realize the course of their own conduct. You will understand too that I had some rather somber reflections on British conduct not so many years ago. While Shawcross was talking — when he talked of the Nazis destroying educational facilities in Poland, of forbidding anything but the most elementary teaching, of the exile into a kind of serfdom of fathers and mothers, and the destruction of cultural institutions — of course I thought of what happened in Ireland not too many years ago, of what happened in other British colonies, and what is probably still happening in India. This does not mean that they should not participate in this trial. I am glad they have progressed far enough to denounce such measures, and I know too that our own skirts are not completely clean. But thank God they are cleaner than those of any other great nation on earth.

Tonight there is a party being given by Justice Jackson for all hands. I expect it is in the nature of a farewell affair as he intends to get away the day after tomorrow. The Justice presented me with a beautiful leather-bound book containing photographs of Nürnberg and he wrote a very generous inscription in it. I have sent it along to you and I know you will recognize it as a treasure and take good care of it.

Well, dearest, I so hate to remain here for even a few weeks. I did suggest to Jackson that I leave at once, but he asked me to make the argument for the organizations—except the High Command, which he wants Taylor to make because he is an Army general, even though synthetic. I think this is silly but I am so anxious to leave I do not care. I have done more than my share here, Grace. I am so anxious to see you my dearest—I simply count the days until I have you in my arms.

                                                                    Tom

---

                                                   Nürnberg, Germany
                                                   July 31, 1946

Grace, my dearest one,

This is a last-minute note which will be carried by Justice Jackson's plane to the U.S. The photograph is self-explanatory. I think it's worth framing, don't you? Here too is the official citation—I will have that framed. Do put them both away carefully. The medal is on its way—registered mail. I think the children will value it someday.

The Justice leaves today at two p.m. and he should be in Washington by Thursday night. There has been much confusion about his leaving—goodbyes, packing and parties. Somehow I have some doubt that he will return for the end of the case. It surely has cost him a great deal—principally the Chief Justiceship of the Supreme Court. But he has made a great contribution to mankind. Future generations will know it better than ours.

Now a few suggestions:

Have you done anything about your Persian lamb cap from

Prague? Isn't this the time to have it fixed for the fall? Go to a good furrier — for that is an expensive fur — really. I want to get you a coat to match it! The coffee set which you have is not the one I have been writing about. The one from Prague is not finished yet — I think you will like it. Also the china has not been shipped yet but will be soon. Boxes will be arriving soon. In them will be clothing and papers of all kinds. Don't try to carry them from the post office. Get the Geer boy or someone else to help you. Put them away for me, as someday I may do some writing.

For now, my dearest Grace, I send you again my undying love and devotion.

Tom

Nürnberg, Germany
August 6, 1946

Grace, my dearest one,

Somehow my correspondence is lagging these days — but surely my interest is not. I am absolutely burning with a desire to get home. Maybe the nearness of the end and the rush of things to do makes time more scarce than I realize. In any event, soon enough I can talk to you I hope — and letters will be a thing of the past.

Since Jackson left we have been continuing with the testimony concerning the organizations. We finished our part of it in jig time — but as usually the British have slowed things down. Anyway, we will finish about the seventeenth of August. I will make a final argument for the U.S. on the organizations — but after Jackson's speech on the defendants it will be anti-climactic, I fear.

I am wondering what the reaction was at home to Jackson's return. Be sure to send me the news. Also was there anything said about the Medal of Freedom?

A Mr. William Johnston, of Newtown, Connecticut, arrived here with the Red Cross yesterday with a letter of introduction from McMahon. I got him a seat in the courtroom and last night had him out to dinner. Right away he began to tell me how important and powerful McMahon is — and that he is Presidential. Yes dear, he said "Presidential" — that is what the man said. Then he said, "You know they are talking about you for governor in two years." I said, "Who is?" He answered, "The people in McMahon's office." Well it made me laugh. But I said, "Well, that is nice." Then he hurried to tell me that Snow would lose and it would be easy for me "the next time" and as to Clare Booth Luce — "Well, don't let anyone talk you into that," said my good Mr. Johnston. I kept changing the subject and he began to get uneasy. I talked about trivia — the weather over here, etc. — and I was exceedingly mellow about mankind in general. Every time Johnston mentioned a Connecticut name I waxed complimentary. I wish you were here — it was really amusing. Then I jolted him by saying, "O! yes, I will be home well before the convention." He was ready to send a cable at that point — but I detained him with boring small talk until about ten p.m. If ever the messenger boy got all mixed up this was the time. Ho! Hum!

I should be leaving here the 11th or 12th of September — at least that is how it looks now. I haven't any shipping reservation yet — and will send you all details when I know them. Anyway, dearest, the end is in sight. Do plan a few days with me in New York and Washington. I can clear up all odds and ends then have a long time at home without interruption.

Dearest, I love you with all my heart — do take good care of yourself and in a few weeks you will be in my arms. Kiss the children for me.

I send you all of my love.

Tom

Nürnberg, Germany
August 10, 1946

Grace, my dearest,

This will be a short note as mine go for I am busy getting a final argument ready on the organizations. It is a great chore and there is so much to cover. On the other hand it does mean the end and with four lawyers all making final arguments there will be much repetition. So I feel a little "ho hum" about it. I could leave here right after I argue I suppose but I would like to be here when the final judgment is given. Joe Blumenfeld thinks I should go right home but that is because he thinks I should be around when the Democratic convention takes place. I cabled him and asked what he thought after I received your letters of this week. Please tell me what you think I should do. You will understand that the verdict will come about two weeks after the argument — or around September 9th. Probably as late as the 16th, but no later. If I go home after my argument it would be silly to return with Jackson two weeks later. On the other hand it might be in my interest to be in Connecticut at convention time just to remind a few people that I am still around.

I have been reading a book on how to relax. It is very short — and really it is good. I must get you to try it with me. It has already made me feel rested. When we are on our vacation trip I will instruct you. It is a good book to read — "Release From Nervous Tension," by David Harold Fink, published by Simon and Schuster. Get it and let me know what you think. There are some wonderful ideas in it and I think we should try to get Tommie started — he is like me, always a bit tense, and it is not good for him. Churchill among many others follows the system.[14] It was suggested to me by a Frenchman who has tried it.

14. Advice from Fink included "You don't have to do anything you don't want to do," and "Successful people have cultivated the habit of never denying to themselves their true feelings and attitudes. There is no need for pretense."

I still haven't seen Joe Guimond and I must do so as soon as I can get a day of free time. I wonder if Margie has arrived yet. Lots of wives are coming in every day. They can have it. I do not want you or the children living here. Europe is a mess. I guess it always will be. The "peace" conference is really a farce[15] — the world is an armed camp, and this old continent is seething and I believe it will break out in another terrible conflict in the relatively near future. This war has settled nothing much except that Russia is more of a menace than ever. It is a pity that we didn't let the Germans and the Russians wipe each other out. The rest of the world cannot live in peace with them — there is no doubt in my mind about that. It is all very sad to contemplate. It has made me realize how fortunate we are dear — we must live our days out fully and enjoy every minute of them with each other and with the children. That is all there is except our work. I think I have changed many of my ideas about things. I know I have changed my values. I will chew your ears off when I get home — telling you all I have in mind.

I must close this as I have to get back to work — as ever I send you my never dying love and devotion.

Tom

Nürnberg, Germany
August 17, 1946

Grace, my dearest,

The past week has dragged. I had hoped to close the testimony by today but now it looks like another ten days or two weeks. But I believe the judgment will come down very quickly. I wrote to you about my cable to Joe Blumenfeld. Since then I have written to him.

15. Representatives of twenty-one nations gathered to discuss, among other things, the threat of Soviet domination.

It seems to me that I would be foolish to fly home and not wait ten days for the decision—after all this time and effort. Joe of course thinks I should get into the political fight. My own judgment is that I could not beat McMahon's gang even if I wanted to. He is too strong as a new Senator. Let him have two more years and his candidates defeated this year and it will be easier to take his measure. Of course this is most likely the right time for me—but I do not believe it can be done. Talk and interest are not enough for a nomination in Connecticut—the delegates make the decision. On the other hand, Bowles and Snow may beat Alcorn and Luce. Then McMahon will be riding high. What is your intelligence, and what do you think about the situation? I am almost completely without any real information and of course that makes it impossible for me to make an intelligent decision. Joe really doesn't have the political connections—else he would send me the news. I never hear from John Farley. John Robinson writes me one version today—a different one next week. Well, so it goes.

I have been up to my neck in work and besides I have been trying to write my final argument. All of this will explain the scarcity of my letters. Once I get the argument finished, all else should be easy sailing.

The summer is nearly over—a second summer away from you. How I miss that time in New England and how I wish I could be there just for this weekend. I simply refuse to fix my departure day—even for myself. I cannot tell yet. It cannot be too long. What about my suits, Grace? Did you call Rosenberg in New Haven? Have other packages arrived from me? Some with clothes, some with papers and documents. Please let me know. Also I sent home a specially bound volume of pictures of the trial which Jackson presented to me—has it arrived?

For now I send you my love and devotion.

Tom

Nürnberg, Germany
August 22, 1946

Grace my dearest one,

My time is completely occupied — I have been working every night. We are nearing the end — but very slowly. Göring and Funk went back on the stand over my strong objections. I know the defendants, some of them, are hoping to stall this trial. They believe that sooner or later we'll have trouble with Russia. Of course the Peace Conference in Paris encourages them. It is a mess, isn't it? My night work has been put in on my final argument. It is about done now. A copy should be in your hands in a few days. I feel that it is adequate. It is not easy to write a second "final" argument in any case.

Yesterday Tom Clark arrived.[16] He and his wife came directly to my office. I had him sit at the counsel table with me — then we held a press conference — we had a long talk. He said McMahon told him I might run for the governorship. I told him I would not.

I had some letters this week from Joe Blumenfeld, Joe Cooney and Leo Gaffney. Jo B. and Leo urged me to come home at once. But I am not going to do it. A long time ago I wrote and said I would not be a candidate for any office this year. I have not changed my mind. Now and then the idea has seemed appealing — but basically my judgment is unchanged. I am not interested. You can tell Joe Blumenfeld and any others that I have completely made up my mind and I will not change it. I am sure of the rightness of this decision. Something tells me "No."

Soon it will be September. A few weeks ago, when I talked with you on the phone, I thought I would be home by this time. That was a mistake so now I am back at my old position — I simply cannot fix a departure date yet. It cannot be too far off — and it cannot come soon enough. Summer is over with here — the leaves are falling and the

16. Clark, who worked with Dodd in the Justice Department, was U.S. attorney general from 1945 to 1949.

temperature is low. Fall comes early here — earlier than in Lebanon. It makes me lonesome. You know how I love the early fall months in New England. I haven't seen the season in almost two years now. I do hope and pray that I will see it this year. Perhaps you and I can take a trip into Vermont or New Hampshire when I return. I suppose the children are getting ready for school again. What grade is Tom in — and Jeremy — and Carolyn? I am rather mixed up about it. I do know that our new little school girl is Miss Martha. Somehow it does not seem possible that she is so grown up. Am I right in thinking that Tom is in the fifth grade, Jeremy in the third and Carolyn in the fourth? It seems silly that I am confused — but I always have to count back to be sure — even about their ages.

It now looks as if I will make my final argument next Wednesday afternoon or Thursday morning. If so the case should close August 31st or September 2nd. Somehow I think of nothing but when I will be able to leave here and return to you and the children. Grace, dearest, I am so very anxious to get home to you. I send you my love and devotion.

Tom

Frankfurt, Germany
September 1, 1946

Grace, my dearest one,

Your letters sound as if you feel I have been purposely neglecting you. If you only knew how much I enjoy writing to you and how I feel when I have to neglect you for a few days. Dearest, you are always in my mind and ever in my heart. These last few weeks have been very difficult for me with Jackson gone. I have had to carry on in court and take care of the many matters that he handled outside of court and the entertaining alone has been killing. Thursday night I attended a British party for Sir David; Friday I had a buffet supper and dance for the press; last night, Saturday, I attended a party given by the press. Tonight I simply could not go to Colonel Andrus's dinner party — I am too tired.

Tomorrow night the Russians are having a big dinner. And all week I have had to give luncheons for generals and prominent visitors. It really has been terrific. As you know yesterday was the last day — at long last! It was a very interesting session. The courtroom was crowded — every seat was taken. The defendants made their last speeches — some were good, others poor. I have the dubious distinction of being the one Göring named as having misquoted him — which of course I did not do, as he knows.[17] I felt that history was being written yesterday — and I felt the tragedy of it all too. I do not know what the judges will do and really I am not concerned about the sentences. I do feel they are guilty in some degree. They should be found guilty — but as to sentence that is not my job — thank God.

As you know I made my final argument on Thursday afternoon. I believe it went all right. Everyone was kind and complimentary about it and the Associated Press man asked for an autographed copy! The military government authorities are publishing it in a little book in German.

Joe Blumenfeld cabled me to call him and I did so on Friday. Of course it was politics and he wanted to know if I would be available. I agreed to write him a letter saying I had this job to finish first and that I would not get into a contest — but if the party wanted me I would run. That ends that — I know that McMahon and Golden and Co. do not want me and believe me when I tell you I do not care. However I do want to keep my hand in and my influence felt — this way it cannot be said that no one knew whether I was available or not and thus the onus is on the others. Joe is such a dear friend — he told me he had talked with you and that you know of his cable. I wished you were there to say a few words to me. But now my little one, it will not be long before I have you in my arms. I plan to get away from here

17. On August 31, 1945, the court allowed each defendant to make a statement. One of the things Göring said was, "The new allegation presented by Mr. Dodd in his final speech, that I had ordered Heydrich to kill the Jews, lacks every proof and is not true either."

just as soon as the trial is over with — that is, when the sentences are pronounced. I intend to sail home and as soon as I have my reservation I will let you know. I suppose I should be home soon after the first of October. It will depend on what ship I get — some take longer than others, as you know.

Do plan to meet me in New York and to spend a day or two or three there with me. Then I hope we can get away somewhere for even a longer time. What heaven it will be after these long months of separation and longing to see you and the children. You have been so brave and good about it all and thus you have made it possible for me to carry on over here. I send you my undying love and devotion and soon I will hold you in my arms and tell you all over again how much I love you.

Tom

Brussels, Belgium
September 5, 1946

Grace, my dearest one,

It is past midnight and I arrived here in Brussels only a short time ago. I left Nürnberg Tuesday morning and got to Frankfurt about 6 p.m. I had dinner with Joe and Margie Guimond and passed a pleasant evening with them.

I should tell you that I am traveling in a sixteen-cylinder Mercedes-Benz — it was Ribbentrop's car — and needless to say it has everything but a bath! It is a convertible and we have had the top down most of the time. A jeep and trailer are with us carrying the baggage. My bodyguard is also along — so we make up quite a caravan. We left Frankfurt yesterday morning and drove down the left bank of the Rhine for some distance — then we turned southwest and drove on to Luxembourg. It is a lovely little country — and the city is charming.

This morning I called on the American charge d'affairs—Mr. Waller. He is a very fine man and I enjoyed my visit. He has been in Luxembourg for fifteen years—and he clearly loves the place. I then called on the Minister of Justice—Victor Bodoson. We had a long talk about the Nazis. The poor Luxembourgers really suffered at the hands of the Germans—but that is another story which I will tell you some evening by our fire in Lebanon. We were driven around the city and after lunch I went to the U.S. military cemetery at Hamm—it is a beautifully kept place. But somehow no cemetery is ever really beautiful. And as I walked among the eight thousand graves my heart was heavy. I visited General Patton's grave and also the grave of General Betz—I knew him over here. He was the Judge Advocate. There were many people putting flowers on the graves—all Luxembourgers—thousands visit the cemetery every month, and it is comforting to see how interested these people are in our dead who liberated them. Luxembourg is almost normal—plenty of food, shops filled with things to buy, no black markets and no unemployed.

We left about three thirty and drove toward Brussels. Belgium is a lovely country. I saw a dog pulling a milk cart. Tell the children about it. We arrived in Namur at seven thirty and stopped for a nice steak dinner—which cost one dollar and fifty cents. In the restaurant was a magnificent French poodle—and he carries a pipe in his mouth! I shall never forget that dog. He has the most remarkable face. He sat up with this curved stem pipe in his mouth—and he looked better than some men I know.

Tomorrow I will visit here and in Antwerp and on Saturday I will drive to the Hague in Holland. It seems so good to be out of Germany and all its rubble and ruin and rottenness. I am going to Denmark from Holland and then to Norway and Sweden before returning to Nürnberg for the verdict.

Well, my dearest, in a few weeks I will be home with you. I cannot begin to tell you how I long for that day. Do take care of your precious self. I send you all of my love and devotion.

                                                            Tom

Wassenaar, Holland
September 9, 1946

Grace, my dearest one,

Brussels is positively "lush" — the shops are filled with all kinds of goods and the restaurants are loaded with food. One can buy anything if willing to pay the price. All of the low countries and the Scandinavian ones too are well off — or at least much better off than the rest of Europe. Belgium was not hurt very much by the war — it had no Nazi–civilian government and I believe the people collaborated considerably with the Germans. Of course now they all tell about the resistance — but I think they are too anxious to tell about it. Brussels is a very beautiful city. We had lunch at the Canterbury, and what a lunch! I felt ashamed thinking of other parts of the world with so little food.

Friday evening as we crossed into Holland we came on the dykes and canals. The windmills turn in the breeze. And I saw a few people wearing wooden shoes. The hay stacks are very carefully put up and on the tops of many of them the hay is made into a cross. We toured Rotterdam and saw the terrible damage done by the German air force in May of 1940. And we arrived at the Hague about noontime. A number of Americans are here — all handsome young men representing American oil companies. We met some of them and found them much alike — all pretty, all petty.

Saturday night the oil company young men entertained prospective Dutch customers here in the hotel. We sat around and watched. Yesterday, Sunday morning, I went to Mass nearby. It was a pretty church — but six — yes, dear — six collections were taken up. It went on all during the Mass, and it was most distracting.

Afterwards we toured the Hague and rode along the North Sea coast and saw all the great fortifications the Nazis built there. In the Hague the Nazis also built tremendous fortifications and from the suburbs they launched their V1s and V2s against London. Many fell in these parts and killed many people. But the worst damage to the Hague was the result of an English raid — a mistake raid. It destroyed much of the city.

Jackson wired that I could go to Connecticut if I thought I should. I will not do so. I really do not care what the delegates do. I am glad you will be there. Be sure to keep your eyes and ears open. For now, my dearest, adieu. I will write you from Nürnberg — all my love and devotion to you.

Tom

St. Gallen, Switzerland
September 14, 1946

Grace, my dearest one,

It was such a pleasure to talk with you last night. I felt that you would surely agree that I should not permit my name to be used for the Senate nomination. I must tell you how it all developed. First of all Joe wired me not to accept the Senate nomination and suggested that I refer all inquires to him. Thus I knew something was in the wind. Then came the wire from McMahon. It said, "Call me Hotel Taft collect soon as possible — urgent — immediately." So I called. He said. "A friend of yours, Leo Gaffney, is here with me. He came down to tell me you should be the candidate for governor. Tom, you cannot make the nomination for governor. I think you should run for the Senate. Baldwin will be tough to beat, but you know — life is uncertain. He had an operation last month. Get me?" I said, "Well, I am not keen about any nomination, etc. I will think it over and wire you." He said, "Leo says we are to get the damndest licking we ever got with Bowles — but there is a lot of background to this that I cannot explain now." I said, "Call Grace and get her reaction." He said, "Yes, I will." I said, "She doesn't care about having me in this business." [H]e said, "Please wire me, 'Yes.'" Then I called Joe and told him the story. He said, "Don't take it — all your friends say no." So I wired McMahon, as you know. Then I thought I should call you and let you know directly about it. I am glad about it all. I feel free — I do not want to run. Although I would have tried for the governorship.

Tom

Cannes, France
September 19, 1946

Grace, my dearest one,

Your cable came this morning and it was a relief to hear from you. Since Tuesday I have been trying to call. So it is Snow[18] and Tone — I assume Tone for the Senate. As you can imagine I am extremely curious about what happened. I do hope you write me all the details.

Cannes is a very, very lovely place. Everything you read about the brevity of the female bathing suits is true — and worse. They are all practically nude — really. I am more accustomed to it tonight — after two days on the beach — but the first session had all of us a bit uneasy. The girls are not, however, very attractive.

This afternoon we drove to Nice — the route runs along the sea and is most scenic. We reached Monaco and of course went to the casino at Monte Carlo. It was a fascinating experience. Such characters as one reads about in novels — old crones with pencil and paper, bearded gentlemen with the air of the gay nineties about them, flashy cosmopolites. Well, I bought three chips — just for souvenirs and that was all.

Tonight the movie world is having a big time here in Cannes — the city is all decorated, etc. I do not know what it is all about but we will watch the parade from the terrace — American, Russian, French, British, etc. movie people are here. I gather that it is called the battle of flowers or something of that sort.[19]

18. Wilbert Snow was elected governor of Connecticut in 1946.
19. At the Cannes festival that year, awards went to *The Lost Weekend, Brief Encounter,* and *The Great Turning Point* (a film from the USSR), among others.

Yes, the trial—or better, the verdict—has been put over for one week. Jackson arrives in Paris tomorrow morning. He had already started when the delay was announced. I am really quite disappointed about the delay—it has been so long. However, it cannot be much longer now.

Take good care of yourself and the children—I send again all of my love and devotion.

Tom

Nürnberg, Germany
September 26, 1946

Grace dearest,

This is probably the last full-dress letter that I will write to you from Germany. We know now that the verdict will come next Monday and Tuesday.

Justice Jackson was here when I got back [from Cannes]. We had a long chat and he told me how much he appreciated what I had done and he said he thought I was lucky not to be running this year. He told me that Jim Farley asked to be remembered to me and that Farley said I was wise not to run. Tuesday night I attended a dinner party given by Judge Parker. The Russians were there and dear old Judge Parker toasted them, wishing that the clouds would soon pass away. Last night I had dinner with Colonel and Mrs. Andrus and again the Russians were among the guests. I do like General Nikitchenko and Volckoff myself—and Colonel Smirnov and I are really good friends. They are very likeable personally.

Tonight Bill Jackson is having a dinner party and so we'll try to keep busy for these last few days, waiting for the end. There is nothing to do but wait now.

I received your letter telling me about the convention and it tickles me to think of you in a "smoke filled room" at the Bond [Hotel in

Hartford] with the politicians. You did just right, dear, and I am proud of you.

I sent you a wire today asking when we should meet in New York. It seemed to me that after this long time you should set the date — or a period of time — something like getting married, don't you think? I am so anxious to see you. I expect to leave here Tuesday, as soon as the sentences are given, and will drive to Frankfurt and spend the night with Margie and Joe. I will leave Frankfurt early the next day for Bremerhaven and sail within a few days — depending some on your answer to my wire. However, I will wire you when I leave and when I expect to arrive. I suggest that you drive down to New York and get us a nice room at the Biltmore or the Commodore. Don't make any dates with anyone. This is our second honeymoon and I don't want any third party along. When I get in I will call Lebanon and find out what hotel you are at. Of course it may be that you can meet the ship — that would be great. Anyway, dear, it is near at hand. I long to see you. I think I will just look at you for hours.

I will write a few lines before sailing but you know where my thoughts will be until I see you. Tell the children how anxious I am to see them, too. I love you Grace, dearest, with all my heart and soul.

Tom

EPILOGUE

WHITNEY R. HARRIS

As a navy lieutenant, Whitney R. Harris was a member of Robert H. Jackson's staff of prosecutors. He is the author of Tyranny on Trial, *an account of the Nuremberg trials.*

It was the afternoon of October 1, 1946, in courtroom 600 of the Palace of Justice, Nuremberg, Germany — the final day in the trial of the leaders of Nazi Germany who had been charged by the Allied powers with the commission of war crimes, crimes against humanity, and the waging of aggressive war in the course of World War II.

Every seat in the courtroom was occupied except the twenty-one chairs reserved for the accused. Defense counsel occupied the chairs before the prisoners' dock. Across the room the eight judges sat at the bench. To their left, the American, British, French, and Soviet prosecutors sat at the four prosecution tables. Behind them witnesses crowded the witness gallery.

United States Supreme Court Justice Robert H. Jackson, the U.S. chief of counsel, occupied the first seat of the American prosecution table. Across from him sat Thomas J. Dodd, his executive trial counsel. Behind him sat Colonel Robert G. Storey, his first executive trial counsel. Other American prosecutors at the table were Brigadier General Telford Taylor, Lieutenant Commander Whitney Harris, Lieutenant William Jackson, Lieutenant Colonel Jay Nimtz, Major Hartley Murray, and Captain Drexel Sprecher.

That afternoon, the court delivered their sentencing decisions, one prisoner at a time, based on the four counts of the indictment: I. conspiracy to wage aggressive war, II. crimes against peace, III. war crimes, and IV. crimes against humanity.

At ten minutes before three, the paneled door in the back of the prisoner dock slid silently open. The defendant Hermann Göring stepped out of the elevator which had brought him from the ground floor where other defendants waited. He stood at attention and quietly awaited the words of Lord Justice Lawrence that would decide his fate.

"Defendant Hermann Wilhelm Göring, on the counts of the indictment on which you have been convicted [all four], the International Military Tribunal sentences you to death by hanging."

The number-two Nazi turned on his heels and passed into the waiting elevator. The door closed and there was a hum of whispered voices in the courtroom as those present awaited the arrival of the next defendant, Hess. Rudolf Hess, who had flown his Messerschmitt to England in a futile effort to persuade the British to abandon the fight with Germany, having been found guilty on counts I and II, was sentenced to imprisonment for life. Other defendants (except for the missing Bormann) appeared in turn and received their sentences.

Martin Bormann: Guilty on counts III and IV, death by hanging
Karl Doenitz: Guilty on counts II and III, ten years' imprisonment
Hans Frank: Guilty on counts III and IV, death by hanging
Wilhelm Frick: Guilty on counts II, III, and IV, death by hanging
Hans Fritzsche: Not guilty
Walther Funk: Guilty of counts II, III, and IV, life imprisonment
Hermann Wilhelm Göring: Guilty on counts I, II, III, and IV, death
  by hanging
Rudolf Hess: Guilty on counts I and II, life imprisonment
Alfred Jodl: Guilty on counts I, II, III, and IV, death by hanging
Ernst Kaltenbrunner: Guilty on counts III and IV, death by hanging
Wilhelm Keitel: Guilty on counts I, II, III, and IV, death by hanging
Erich Raeder: Guilty on counts I, II, and III, life imprisonment
Alfred Rosenberg: Guilty on counts I, II, III, and IV, death by hanging
Fritz Sauckel: Guilty of counts III and IV, death by hanging

Hjalmar Schacht: Not guilty

Arthur Seyss-Inquart: Guilty on counts II, III, and IV, death by hanging

Albert Speer: Guilty on counts III and IV, twenty years' imprisonment

Julius Streicher: Guilty on count IV, death by hanging

Franz von Papen: Not guilty

Joachim von Ribbentrop: Guilty on counts I, II, III, and IV, death by hanging

Baldur von Schirach: Guilty on count IV, twenty years' imprisonment

The tribunal also declared as criminal organizations the Gestapo and SD, the Leadership Corps of the Nazi Party, and the SS.

Appeals were taken by all of the defendants to the Allied Control Council, except for Kaltenbrunner. The appeals were uniformly denied at a meeting of the Council on October 10. The executions were scheduled in the basement of the Palace of Justice for the overnight hours of October 15–16, 1946.

Shortly before midnight the electrifying word was released that Göring had cheated the hangman by taking poison while lying, ostensibly asleep, upon the bed in his cell. Death thus came to Göring by his own hand, as it had come to Hitler, Himmler, and Goebbels before him, even as the prison officer was walking to the cell block to give formal notice of the executions to take place that night.

At eleven minutes past one o'clock in the morning of October 16, the white-faced former foreign minister, Joachim von Ribbentrop, stepped through the door into the execution chamber and faced the gallows on which he and the others condemned by the tribunal were to be hanged. He died at 1:26 a.m. Each of the remaining defendants approached the gallows in turn and met the fate of common criminals.

After the executions the body of each man was placed in a simple wooden coffin. A tag bearing the name of the deceased was pinned to a coat, shirt, or sweater. With the hangman's noose still about his neck, each hanged man was photographed. The body of Hermann Göring was brought in and placed upon its box to be photographed with the others.

In the early-morning hours, two trucks carrying eleven caskets left the prison compound at the Palace of Justice bound for crematories at Dachau concentration camp near Munich, where the eleven corpses were burned to ashes. It was reported that in the evening the eleven urns containing the ashes were taken away to be emptied into the river Isar. The dust of the dead was carried along in the currents of the stream to the Danube — and thence to the sea.

The defendants who had received sentences of imprisonment were transferred to Spandau prison, which had been designed for some six hundred prisoners but was now reserved for the seven from Nuremberg. As the years passed, the defendants completed their terms and were released. The last prisoner was Rudolf Hess, who had been sentenced to life. On August 17, 1987, forty-one years after the final judgment of the tribunal, Hess managed somehow to commit suicide. With his death, Hitler's tyranny ended. Ended, too, was the contribution of Thomas J. Dodd to the proof of the crimes of the Hitler regime in the long hours which he devoted to this cause of humanity at Nuremberg, Germany — the greatest achievement of his life.

ACKNOWLEDGMENTS

I am grateful to the many friends, colleagues, and family members who embraced and enhanced this project. The support and advice of my siblings—Thomas Dodd, Carolyn Dodd, Jeremy Dodd, Martha Buonanno, and Nicholas Dodd—have proven crucial.

I want to pay a special thank you to my wife, Jackie Clegg Dodd. Jackie and I met long after my parents passed away, yet she brought a devotion, intensity, and passion to this effort as if she were one of their children. Jackie has spent countless hours with my father's letters, and even more hours with my siblings, in this undertaking. This project would not have happened without her.

I want to say a special word about Lary Bloom, my collaborator on this special project. I knew Lary by reputation, but not personally, when I approached him and asked him if he would read my father's letters from Nuremberg. As my father's son, I cherished these letters to my mother, but I felt too emotionally linked to the work to determine whether this first draft of history from *the* trial of the twentieth century had any real historical value. But for Lary's persuasion, this unique correspondence would have remained nothing more than a family heirloom. Lary's years of experience as an editor, writer, and interviewer were invaluable. I thank him but I suspect, more importantly, my father, Tom Dodd, thanks Lary Bloom for helping him publish his letters from Nuremberg.

In preparing this book, we had enormous help from the staff of the Thomas J. Dodd Research Center at the University of Connecticut. I owe a particular debt to Tom Wilsted, the director; Betsy Pittman, archivist and curator; and Linda Perrone of the University Libraries. Randy Sowell, archivist, and the staff of the Truman Presidential Museum & Library in Independence, Missouri, provided important documents. Jack Davis, who at the time was the publisher of *The Hartford Courant*, suggested the collaboration with my coauthor, and Claude Albert and Kathy McKula guided us through the newspaper's library of clippings from the Nuremberg era and my father's life in public service. John Barrett, law professor at St. John's University and biographer of Justice Robert H. Jackson, offered valuable perspective on international law, as did Joshua Tucker, associate professor of politics at New York University.

We benefited greatly from the advice of my literary agent, Esther Newberg of ICM. Esther has been a great friend for many years, and she personally knows my family. Sean Desmond, our supportive and skillful editor at Crown Publishing, provided innovative ideas that are evident throughout the narrative. My generous friends Elie Wiesel, Whitney R. Harris, and Walter Cronkite have been enthusiastic in making their significant contributions to the manuscript.

Others who provided us wise counsel and assistance included Patricia Walsh, Mindy Hanneman, Lori McGrogan, Janice O'Connell, Sheryl Cohen, Jennifer Goodman, Pat Hart, Amos Hochstein, Kathy Keup, Howard Brundage, Chuck Storey, Suzanne M. Levine, Ryan Drajewicz, Jess Maghan, Peter Walker, John Bennet, Rena Powell, Christina Mundschenk, Bayard Osborn, Jim Travis, Barbara S. Delaney, Cookie Segelstein, Jon Joslow, Suzanne Staubach, Roxanne Coady, Patsy Daly, Si Taubman, Carolyn Opper, Richard Calder, Amy Coleman, David Coleman, Rick Hornung, John and Tussi Kluge, Liener Temerlin, and Richard Freling.

INDEX

ABOUT THE AUTHORS

Christopher J. Dodd, son of the late Senator Thomas J. Dodd, is a U.S. senator from Connecticut. He is chairman of the Senate Banking, Housing, and Urban Affairs Committee and a senior member of the Senate Foreign Relations Committee and the Labor and Human Resources Committee. A former Peace Corps volunteer, Senator Dodd is a recipient of the Edmund S. Muskie Public Service Award and is also widely known for his work on children and family issues. He and his wife, Jackie Clegg Dodd, have two young daughters, Grace and Christina, and live in a converted schoolhouse in East Haddam, Connecticut.

Lary Bloom, author of *The Writer Within*, *Lary Bloom's Connecticut Notebook*, and other books, is a columnist for the *New York Times* and *Connecticut* magazine. He is also a playwright, lyricist, and memoir teacher and was the editor of the Sunday magazines of the *Miami Herald* and the *Hartford Courant*. He lives in Chester, Connecticut. His website is www.larybloom.net.

August 14, 1945
Nuremberg, Germany,

Grace, my dearest one;

Here I am in the dead city of Nuremberg.
I left Paris yesterday at 1.30 P.M. – stopped
in Frankfurt for a short while and arrived here
about six P.M. last night. Flying up we saw
many scars of the war – bridges down – buildings
in ruins – but when we entered Nuremberg
I saw for the first time in my life the
awful ruin that comes with war. This
city is devastated – the buildings, houses and
streets are a complete mess. Street cars
piled up, a mass of burned and twisted
steel. The rubble is everywhere. Soldiers
in helmets and armed on patrol. Nothing
but army vehicles on the roads & streets